THE COCAINE DIARIES

Paul Keany was born in Oxford, England, to Irish parents. In his late teens he joined the Royal Navy as an apprentice electrical engineer. After three years of dull toil on dry land he went AWOL and followed his parents to Dublin, where they had retired. He never left and has called it home for the past 30 years. In his last career he ran a one-man plumbing business till it hit the rocks in the recession. What he did to try to clear his debts can be found in the pages of this book. An aspiring novelist, he hopes it'll be the first book of many. He has two children – Katie and Daniel – from a previous marriage.

Jeff Farrell is an independent journalist. He spent three years working as a stringer in South America, reporting across the region for media including *The Guardian*, the *Daily Telegraph*, the *Miami Herald* and Irish national broadcaster RTÉ. He first interviewed Paul Keany in the notorious Los Teques prison, Venezuela – and Farrell is glad he got his story and made it out alive. For now he has returned to his home city of Dublin, where he craves a new adventure after months chained to his laptop writing Keany's story. He is a former staff journalist with Independent News and Media plc. He holds an MA in Journalism and is a member of the International Federation of Journalists. This is his first book. http://jefffarrelljournalism.com/

THE
COCAINE
DIARIES
A Venezuelan Prison Nightmare

PAUL KEANY WITH JEFF FARRELL

MAINSTREAM
PUBLISHING

EDINBURGH AND LONDON

This edition, 2013

First published in Great Britain in 2012 by
MAINSTREAM PUBLISHING COMPANY
(EDINBURGH) LTD
7 Albany Street
Edinburgh EH1 3UG

ISBN 9781780576077

Grateful acknowledgement is made to the band Aslan for kind
permission to reprint lyrics from 'Crazy World' (on p. 211)

A catalogue record for this book is available
from the British Library

Printed and bound by
CPI Group (UK) Ltd, Croydon, CR0 4YY

3 5 7 9 10 8 6 4 2

To my family, especially my children, Katie and Daniel, and friends. Thanks to you all for standing by me. Also to Father Pat and Viviana: I owe you my life. To anyone thinking of smuggling coke for 'easy' money – don't do it. You might end up dead.

Paul Keany

To the many great people I met during my travels in Venezuela: the horrors in this story show the tragic side of your country, not your strength in spirit and wonderful hospitality. *Que la verdad les haga libres.*

Jeff Farrell

ACKNOWLEDGEMENTS

I would like to thank Jeff Farrell for his hard work in putting this book together with me, and for quickly getting a publisher on board. Thanks to the Irish Council for Prisoners Overseas for their help. Big thanks also to all my friends for support with the 'escape fund': Barry Fitz, Dave Riley, Pat Keany, Kev Cummins and Big Frankie.

Paul Keany

I WOULD LIKE TO THANK FATHER PAT FOR HIS HELP IN CLINCHING the interview with Paul Keany inside Los Teques, a meeting that sowed the seeds for this book; to Rory Carroll of *The Guardian* for a roof over my head in Caracas, and endless journalistic advice – I owe you a big one; to Paul Keany for always being at my beck and call for interviews; to Dermot Deely for a place to write in Dublin; to my mother, Noeleen, for getting the manuscript to the publisher and always having positive words; to all my family – hopefully this time I have something to show for yet another epic adventure abroad – the 'real job' awaits!; to Donal Allman for feedback on an early draft; to my book editor Karyn Millar; to the universe for the 'coincidence' of myself and Keany being on the same flight home – without it this book wouldn't exist; and to everyone else there's no space to mention.

Jeff Farrell

CONTENTS

AUTHOR'S NOTE

BECAUSE OF THE SENSITIVE NATURE OF THE REVELATIONS AND ISSUES in this book, almost all names have been changed. Some of the inmates featured in the book, for example, are still in the Venezuelan prison system. Others involved in the welfare of prisoners want to be able to continue to visit inmates to give them support in any way they can. They have asked not to be named, fearing they would not be allowed to enter the jails again. The Venezuelan government is highly sensitive to criticisms of the deplorable and dangerous conditions in its prisons.

At times I have taken liberties with dialogue, putting quote marks around speech when it was recalled from Paul Keany's memory, so it therefore might not be totally accurate. That said, much of it is faithful and is taken from Keany's extensive diaries, which he kept on a daily basis to record his life and events inside Los Teques prison.

Jeff Farrell

PREFACE

THE PRISON COP SAT ON A CHAIR IN THE PASSAGEWAY, HIS EYES rising up from the floor to the gringo visitor walking towards him. 'Maxima,' I said. He stood up slowly, not bothering to answer, and took a truncheon from the holster on his navy uniform. He rapped it three times against a steel door to my right. A hatch slid back in the centre of the door and two eyeballs peeped out. A bolt slid back. The door eased open slowly. In front of me stood a teenager, no older than 18 or 19, dressed in white tracksuit bottoms. My eyes dropped down to the long metal object dangling from his hand. It was a shotgun. It didn't make sense. Why was this prison guard not in uniform?

'*Visita*,' I said. The gun-toting teenager stood aside. I stepped past him into a hallway in the Maxima wing. It was visit day and full of life. A tall, lean guy wearing jeans and a wine-coloured shirt walked up to me.

'*A quien buscas?*' ('Who are you looking for?') he asked. My eyes dropped down to his hand, which was casually holding a black revolver in front of his chest. Strange, I thought again. Another guard with no uniform. My eyes rose back up to his face.

'Paul,' I said. He nodded and walked off. After months of trying to get into Los Teques jail to interview a cocaine smuggler of Irish-British nationality, I was finally getting to talk to him. While I waited, I looked around. There were men, women and children sitting around on stools, chatting. Salsa music blared from a stereo in the corner, next to a

13

Christmas tree with twinkling lights. It was Sunday, and visit day was in full swing in the prison on the outskirts of Caracas.

The minutes passed and my thoughts went back to wondering why armed prison guards would wear street clothes. Minutes earlier I had been searched at the jail gate by soldiers brandishing machine guns and my passport ID was checked. All seemed normal in a prison. I then looked back at the teenager with the shotgun. He was dancing salsa steps along to the music from the stereo, his weapon swinging back and forth. No one batted an eyelid as to why a prison cop would act so casually. Then I finally accepted the obvious: he wasn't a cop – he was an inmate, and armed.

Paul Keany stepped into the passageway. Through round-rimmed glasses he gave me a questioning look that said, 'Who are you?' I told him I was a journalist, and that Father Patrick, a Caracas-based Irish priest who visited him, had told me how to get into the jail to talk to him and hear his story. I left out the word 'interview' so he wouldn't run off. 'Father Pat!' Keany said, smiling now.

We sat down on a bench and started to talk. Keany was forty-five and was in the early months of an eight-year sentence for cocaine smuggling. He was arrested in Maiquetía airport attempting to board a Dublin-bound flight with a stop-off in Paris. The cops had found almost six kilos of cocaine in his suitcase. His story, he told me, wasn't original. More than 200 other gringo drug mules locked up in Los Teques had the same tale to tell. 'Almost everybody gets caught.'

'But the prisoners here,' I said, changing the subject, 'they have guns?'

He laughed, explaining that inmate *jefes*, or bosses, and their foot soldiers ran the cell blocks. He had to pay them a *causa*, protection money, every week. 'Without them I'd be dead. There's inmates here who'd shoot me up just for being a gringo.'

It was all baffling. We continued to talk, and I wanted to

know more. Who had Keany bought the coke from? How much had he been paid? And so on. He was easy to chat with, explaining that he had been offered 10,000 euro by 'people' in Dublin to travel to Venezuela and carry drugs home. It would clear the debts he'd built up after his plumbing business went bust in the recession. Then he went on to the more fascinating side of the story: the jail.

Just a few nights before, he said, he had had to listen to a man being slowly knifed to death in a neighbouring wing, whimpering as his life bled away. Another day he had seen a woman's face shot off by her husband, an inmate off his head on crack. Keany shook his head as he told me this and went on to tell me how the whole prison was effectively in the hands of cell-block bosses. They were armed to the teeth with Uzis, revolvers, shotguns and even grenades. Shoot-outs and random killings were rife. Keany also said that visitors were often held up in the passageways by cell-block outcasts armed with knives. The whole prison was one big killing zone. 'I could end up coming out of here in a box,' said Keany. So could I, I thought. A few days earlier I had been robbed in Caracas with a gun held to my head. I was still shaken from it. This place was the last thing I needed. I handed Keany two bags of food I had brought for him, made my excuses and left.

It had taken months to chase down an interview with the *irlandés* in Los Teques. I knew there was a fellow Paddy locked up there from looking at statistics of Irish nationals locked up in the region. But as for who he was or his exact story, I had had no idea. First I followed the usual approach, which other foreign correspondents had told me about, and wrote to the Ministerio de Justicia requesting a formal press visit. I said I wanted to interview the irlandés and show the world how 'foolish' it was for gringos to smuggle cocaine through Venezuela. They didn't buy it and never replied, despite repeated emails, telephone calls and even doorstepping their press office in downtown Caracas.

I refused to give up. I started putting out calls to Irish priests I tracked down in Venezuela. They'd been there decades and were always helpful in lining up contacts and friends for stories I was researching. I got a hold of the details for one priest, Father Pat, and telephoned him. '*El padre no se encuentra*,' ('The Father isn't here') said his housemaid, adding that he was in Los Teques prison. My ears pricked up. There was my key to the story. I was sure he was in visiting the Irishman I knew was locked up there, and when I later got hold of Father Pat he confirmed that was where he had been. I told him of my frustration in trying to get into the prison through the authorities. 'Go as a visitor,' he said. 'Get there on Sunday morning, bring your passport and ask for Paul Keany.' I was sure the authorities wouldn't let a gringo past the front gate. Father Pat said they would, and they did.

But now, after the visit, I wondered how much of Keany's story was really true. Yes, I'd seen the inmates armed with guns through my own eyes – but random killings? A woman's face shot off by her husband? Inmates paying protection money to stay alive?

I made a call to the Venezuelan Prison Observatory, a prisoners' campaign group. They said *sí*, all the stories were real, and life in Los Teques was the same in all of the country's 30-odd jails. More than 400 people were killed every year in riots and random shootings, according to their statistics. The biggest body counts happened during prison riots when cell-block bosses fought it out, usually for the control of the supply and sale of coke, or over some other strife. Up to 20 and 30 were killed at a time. To prove it, the Observatory sent me pictures of the aftermath of a riot the year before in Santa Ana, a jail in the south-west of Venezuela, where a reported 19 were killed.

Later I opened the photos, which had been sent in email attachments. I nearly vomited over my laptop. The pictures didn't just show dead bodies shot up. One man hung from a goalpost in the prison yard, the rope tied under his arms and around his chest – his head had been cut off. Other bodies had their legs cut off and their insides ripped out. I was horrified that human beings could do this to each other. It didn't seem possible. But it was, and it happened a lot, the Observatory said. The government did little to tackle it.

So I had my 'big story'. I had the human-interest angle with Keany and independent comment to support his claims of a prison system run by the inmates themselves, lobbing grenades at each other when they fell out. I set about furiously pitching the story to the newsdesks of the Irish and British newspapers. One tabloid got back to me quickly; they wanted to run the story and needed a photo of Keany. I rang him in the jail on a mobile number for another inmate in his wing. 'No,' he said, 'no way.' He wouldn't go with a picture. The tabloid pulled out. Ditto for two other newspapers that wanted to run the piece. No photo, no story.

In the end I salvaged the report and filed a short audio story to Irish national broadcaster RTÉ, talking about Keany and the horrors inside Los Teques and prisons across Venezuela. The three-minute piece went out at about 8 a.m. on a Saturday. It came and passed without comment. No newsdesks beat their way to my door for more stories. No fanfare. Nothing.

I threw in the towel. Another 'scoop' had got away. I stayed on in Venezuela for a few more months, then left. I continued with my adventure across the region as a backpacker journalist, which lasted three years, with lengthy stays in Bolivia and Argentina.

On the last leg of my trip, in Colombia, I was burned out. It was time to go. I boarded a flight from Bogotá to Dublin in December 2010 to get home for Christmas. Later, in Dublin airport, I stood in the immigration line. I heard a familiar accent from a passenger in the queue next to me: broad English mixed with Dublin's northside. He was talking to an immigration official, getting grilled over why he had an emergency passport. 'It was robbed in Colombia.'

The man walked on, and I was still waiting in line. Then it sank in. That accent and that the guy's passport had been robbed. Seemed like a suspect story. A tale that an inmate on the run from Venezuela might use . . . It couldn't be. The seconds passed slowly. Finally I flashed my passport at the official and bolted through the airport. I spotted the same man at the baggage carousel and ran over.

'How ya doing?' I said. 'We met in Venezuela.' I was sure it was Keany now. The face was familiar but gaunt. I remembered him having fuller features. He studied me for a moment.

'You came in to see me in Los Teques.' He smiled. 'The reporter.'

I said I was. I then did the maths in my head. I had last seen him two years ago in jail and he had had at least another seven years of his sentence left then. 'We did a runner,' he said, 'got out on parole and bussed it to Colombia.' He introduced me to a man in his mid 20s standing next to him, who had also been locked up in Los Teques and had fled from Venezuela with him.

In later weeks, Keany and I met up as agreed. We both joked that it was mind-boggling we ended up on the same flight home from South America. What were the chances? Paul said he wanted to tell the world his story and asked if I would help him write it. You bet I would. Over the following months I spent countless hours hearing tales from a twisted world that swirled around in a cocktail of drugs, violence, death and squalor, all recalled with the aid of extensive diaries Keany had kept.

Of course I knew he was no angel. He was a convicted cocaine smuggler. But had I judged him I couldn't have written this story. So I put my journalist hat on and sat on the fence – a challenge at times. Still, Keany put his hands up from the word go and admitted he was guilty and what he did was wrong. And no matter what he'd done, he didn't deserve to be sexually assaulted by anti-drugs cops. No one deserves

PREFACE

that. And that act is proof that the line between criminals and law-enforcement officers in Venezuela is blurred at best.

In the following pages you will read about Keany's fight for survival in a dark and violent place. Yet there are light moments, where you will laugh out loud at some incredible and humorous tales. Above all, you will know the truth – the truth of what happens behind the bars in Venezuela's jails, as told by Keany with courage and honesty: his tale from a dark world where every day could have been his last. This is his story.

PROLOGUE

IT WON'T HAPPEN TO ME. THAT'S WHAT I THOUGHT WHEN I GOT ON THE plane to Venezuela. But it did – I got caught. It's funny, before I embarked on that ill-fated trip I used to watch the *Banged Up Abroad* series on the telly. Tales of Western drug mules locked up in fleapit prisons in the tropics. All had the same story – went on a 'holiday' to everywhere from Jamaica to Thailand to bring back a few kilos of coke or heroin in their suitcase or swallowed in capsules. A few thousand quid for their troubles. All 'easy' money. Then the cops nab them at the airport.

Looking back, I don't know why it didn't sink in that it could happen to me – it just didn't. I was forty-five with two teenage kids – I should have known better. For a payment of ten thousand euro I went to Venezuela to bring back to Dublin a suitcase packed with almost six kilos of cocaine. I didn't even know where the country was. I had to look it up on a map on the Internet before I left. The whole idea was stupid, but I needed the money. My plumbing business went bust at the beginning of the recession. I had a small bank loan and a new work van on finance and couldn't make the payments on either. My daughter was also living with me, and I wanted to keep her going too. The ten grand would have sorted me out.

In the end, I got to Caracas fine and picked up the 'goods'. On the way out at the airport, the cops moved in on me. I ended up in my own *Banged Up Abroad*. I was convicted for drug smuggling and sentenced to eight years in Los Teques jail.

I deserved it, you say. Drugs are bad, and anyone involved with them should be locked up and have to suffer. I accept that. I had no problem doing the time. But I was locked up in a cruel, violent world where I was abused, dehumanised, stabbed, had to dodge bullets and nearly lost my life. No one deserves that, I say.

And if the purpose of prison was to punish me for smuggling drugs and reform me, that didn't work either. I quickly went from a drug mule to a dealer inside Los Teques. It was the only way I could survive, the only way I could buy basics, such as a floor cushion to sleep on and a plate and mug to eat and drink with. Nothing was 'on the house'. I then went from dealing cocaine to becoming psychologically addicted to it. I needed a few lines to get through the day and night. All in all, I was sentenced for smuggling cocaine, then sent into a world where there was more coke than in all the streets of Ireland and Britain. No reform there.

Walking through the gates of Los Teques was like walking through a time warp. It was like going back 100 years into a Victorian jail. I had to sleep on the floor of a toilet for months and was later 'promoted' to a spot on the floor in the wing yard. Only after about a year did I get a bed – and only after paying about 150 euro to a cell-block inmate boss for the privilege. I had to share a toilet with up to 200 men and often ended up going in a bag when my bowels couldn't wait for the queues to end. The Venezuelans fought back at the authorities the only way they knew how – by kidnapping the visitors and hunger striking to have their demands for better conditions met. They rarely were, and the cycle went on. For some, the conditions and daily mental and physical torture became too much and they escaped – by cutting their own throats.

In Los Teques the cell-block bosses, or jefes, ran the show. They were inmates who ran their wings with their elected 'army councils'. They upheld the rule of law armed to the teeth with Uzis and grenades. They decided who lived or died and how much causa, or protection money, the prisoners in their wings had to pay them. Rows that erupted between rival cell blocks left scores dead and injured, and made headlines around the world.

The National Guard troops, who police the jails, had a hands-off approach to what went on inside the prison. Their job was to count heads and lock gates. They let the jefes run the show inside, while they sat back and profited from selling coke and arms to them – guns they would seize in 'random' searches and which miraculously ended up back in the hands of the inmate bosses. If I had been locked up for being a criminal, I often wondered which side of the bars I should be on. Even most of the lawyers and prison cops were bent – always on the take, offering to get us out for money. Yet few did. It was all one big rotten cesspit. An upside-down world. Surreal. I often expected the walls to open up and to see Steven Spielberg with a load of cameras.

From day one, my goal was to get out as quick as I could. I aimed for parole after 18 months inside and got it, thanks to a great lawyer. I was supposed to stay in Caracas for the next five years on parole. But after just a few days in the city I knew I had to get out of Venezuela altogether. I had a family to get back to. With my wits and some money, I fled across to neighbouring Colombia and then home.

I'm writing this story because I have to. It helps me deal with my demons. It is a tale of a stupid drug mule locked up in an evil world, and if it stops just one person from doing what I did, it will be worth it.

Chapter 1

GROUNDED

I HEAR A NAME CALLED OUT OVER THE AIRPORT'S PA SYSTEM: 'Passenger Keany, Paul.' Jesus, it can't be. I think I'm hearing things. 'Passenger Keany, Paul.' Again. No doubting it. My stomach knots. I hear it again, but this time among a dozen or so other passenger names. I begin to relax. Must be just some formality.

I'm leaning against a wall at a crowded boarding gate. I'm looking out at a twin-engine Airbus parked on the airport apron outside, its nose pointing towards the departures. I walk up to the Air France boarding gate. I join a queue with the other travellers called to step forward. I'm at the back. Two air stewardesses are checking passports. We step forwards one by one. I presume – or hope – we're being called to file onto the back of the plane. I know I'm seated there. The hostess glances at my passport and gives me a smile. 'Enjoy your flight, sir.' I nod and walk on. I'm a respectable businessman, of course, standing there in a suit – a sharp jacket, Ralph Lauren shirt and a tie, dark-blue slacks and black dress shoes.

Another stewardess ushers the group into the tunnel that leads to the aircraft – my lift home. A door suddenly opens to the left. A gust of hot air whooshes in. A male flight attendant waves us out the door. I step through and squint in the blinding midday sun. Below, I see two cops standing at the bottom of a concrete staircase. They're wearing bulletproof jackets. '*Policía*' is emblazoned across the front. Their hands hover near their pistols.

Oh my God. Alarm bells go off in my head. This looks like it's going wrong.

I follow the others. We file down the steps onto the tarmac below. The two policemen call us forward – a mixed bunch, mainly young backpacker types dressed in shorts and T-shirts. I hover at the back of the group and we walk under the terminal. The cops walk close behind me. They lead us over to an area into the bowels of the airport. Awaiting us are about 20 security personnel: airport police, cops and the Venezuelan National Guard. Then I see it: the '*Antidrogas*' emblem on one of the officer's uniforms.

My heart sinks. I panic. What have I done? What about my family at home? How will I tell them? My son and daughter, how will I break it to them? This was just supposed to be a free holiday in the sun. A few quid for carrying a suitcase home.

Two Guardia Nacional (National Guard) troops in olive-green uniforms each stand next to a suitcase. The passengers I see are all travelling alone – like me. The guards, armed with Kalashnikovs, call them over to their luggage. I also step forward. The cop beside me puts his arm out and stops me. '*Tú, no*,' ('Not you') he says.

It's over. I can feel it. I want to vomit.

The troops busy themselves opening the suitcases next to a machine that looks like an X-ray scanner. Cartons of cigarettes are pulled out. The boxes are ripped and thrown on the ground. There are also bottles of Venezuelan rum. The cops open them and sniff inside. 'No, no,' shout the French passengers. Their protests fall on deaf ears. The cops continue the search.

Now the check of their bags is over and they start to file off. One by one I watch them leave. I watch the last one walk away, wanting to run after him. I want to scream, 'It's him, it's him you're after.' But I don't.

Out of the corner of my eye I spot my suitcase, wrapped in the cellophane I thought would provide extra security. I paid about five euro in the departures halls for the shrink-wrap service.

All the guards and airport police are watching me now. I feel their eyes burning into me. I feel my life slipping away. The search of the other passengers was all just a decoy to get me – the big fish. I know it now. Keep your cool, I tell myself. It's not over yet.

I hear the footsteps of one cop behind me coming closer. He stops. More officials are everywhere now: customs, police, the drug squad, army, about 30 of them. The cop waves me forward. He babbles in Spanish something about a *maleta* (suitcase). I shrug; I haven't a clue what he's saying. But I know what's going on. I'm sweating now. I look around. Nowhere to run. One of the soldiers walks away. All the cops seem to be waiting for someone. Minutes tick away like hours.

Now an older officer in his 40s arrives and steps in front of me. 'This you case?' he says in English, interpreting for another cop. His face is stiff. No expression.

'It looks like mine, but I'm not 100 per cent,' I say, looking at my name scrawled in my handwriting on a tag hanging off the handle.

'*Sí,*' he tells the other guards, not bothering to interpret my false doubt. 'We have reason to believe you have *contrabanda* inside,' he says.

My eyes drop down and I see that the handle is sticking out, not sitting right. I want to puke. I can't believe it. Bollocks. This has got to be ten years minimum. Fuck. The boys back at the hotel must have got greedy and messed up packing the case. Fuckers – they should be here, not me.

The guard now cuts off the plastic wrapping around the case, like a metaphor for my life peeling away in front of me. Three tiny black darts are poking out of the side of the case, a technique they must use to find coke packed into luggage. Small white circles of powder have formed around the arrow tips.

The boys in green move in closer. A skinny guard opens my case and rummages through my belongings. He pulls out the fake designer clothes I was bringing home as presents for my son and daughter, and others in my family: a Hugo Boss T-shirt and Ralph Lauren shorts, a polo shirt. Now he pulls out plastic bags and scrunched-up newspapers packed in to fill out the case. The officers know the score. They easily spot the telltale signs of a mule's luggage. The troops and cops gather round, forming a circle. Their smiles widen. My tie feels tighter.

The guard leans over the black Wilson suitcase. He pulls out a small knife and rips the lining inside the case. At the bottom I can see a layer of black plastic, which is carbon paper meant to fool X-ray scanners. So much for that. He cuts the material again. The cops behind me move in closer. Others are standing on tables to get a better look. The guard cuts again. This time there's a layer of clear plastic, revealing white, densely packed powder. I slowly shake my head. This can't be happening. The circle of cops moves in closer again and starts to crowd me. I can see one guard, his hand resting on the barrel of his pistol. Others train their mobile-phone cameras on me.

Saturday, 11 October 2008. I was about to be a star.

* * *

Earlier, I'd stepped out of a taxi at the departures. The cab was a beat-up '70s sedan from the US. I flagged it in the centre of Caracas, where the cab inched through the city's grinding traffic jams while motorcycles whizzed in and out between the cars. Outside the urban sprawl of the city we reached a motorway. The traffic eased and fanned out across about six lanes. I watched the city pass by, soon leaving behind the hazy fog of fumes, the grim buildings of the urban centre giving way to the shantytowns of little red-bricked houses clinging to the hills around the valley walls looking down onto the motorway. The crudely built homes with tin roofs are where the poor live in Caracas, Venezuela's teeming capital city of some three million people.

I rolled down the window a bit. Hot air rushed in at me, but it was a fresh breeze blowing in north from the Caribbean. I ran through the events of the last couple of weeks in my head.

I followed orders, arrived in Caracas and checked into a hotel to wait for the call. 'There's been a delay. Get yourself a hooker or something to pass the time.'

That I didn't do. Instead I passed my days in a bar in Sabana Grande, a shopping area for cheap designer goods in Caracas. By night it was deserted – even the rats didn't seem to venture out amid the hundreds of bags of rubbish that clogged up the streets. I drank my time away in the pub, sipping beers while writing a crime book set in Dublin. Other than that I watched a bit of football, catching the odd Manchester United game. At night I had a meal, drank a bottle of rum and headed back to my cheap hotel.

Then the second call came.

'The bar on the corner. Five minutes.' A Dublin accent. Had to be him.

Damo sat in a booth. He was a tough-looking guy, stocky with a bald head. It was the first time we'd met. I slipped in beside him.

'Paul, sorry. You're getting on OK?' He seemed distant.

'OK.'

'There's been a change of plan,' he said, drumming his fingers on the neck of a bottle of beer. 'We need you to stay a bit longer. We haven't got the stuff yet. Can you change your flights and stay another week? We'll give you the money for it.'

'I don't know,' I said. I was thinking of my plumbing business back home and my teenage daughter, who was living with me, and the story I'd told everyone about going away for two weeks, not three.

'Look, I know you've a business back home and I understand if you have to go.' He was giving me a way out, which surprised me, for a drug smuggler. I thought for a minute. Another week, I can swing it.

'Yeah, it's all right, I can do it.' It was a decision I would regret for a long time.

The next day, on Damo's advice, I moved to Altamira, the banking district of Caracas. It was an upmarket area: lots of tall glass buildings; wide, leafy avenues lined with palm trees; four-by-four jeeps cruising into the drive-thrus of McDonald's and Wendy's. Little Miami. This was where the other half lived. It was the place to be, Damo said. 'The cops won't hassle you down there.' And they didn't. In Sabana Grande the police stopped me for a shakedown three times. I was pushed against a wall, spread-eagled and patted down. The sight of a gringo there was like waving a red flag to a bull. The cops knew what many were up to. But I never had anything on me.

* * *

I was in my hotel room, crashed out on the bed watching the TV. The only thing in English was the CNN news. The local stations in Spanish all seemed to show the same thing every evening: Venezuelan president Hugo Chávez dressed in a red shirt and beret and endlessly talking about a *revolución*.

Three dull thuds banged out on my hotel door. I sat up with a jolt. I stood up and slowly eased the door open. I saw Damo's baldy head.

'We're in the hotel in another room. Number 443. Come on up.'

A dark-skinned Venezuelan guy was in the room gathering up plastic bags on the floor. He looked up at me but didn't bother saying anything. 'It's all tidied up,' said Damo, on his knees leaning over a suitcase on the ground. 'Everything will be grand,' he said, now rolling up old newspapers to fill out the inside of it.

The room was clean and unused. Two single beds were still made up. Two bars of soap were propped on fluffed-up pillows. No other luggage. The lads weren't sticking around.

Damo stood up. 'There's the case, good luck,' he said, passing me the handle so I could wheel it. He looked relaxed. A normal day's work for him, I supposed. 'Be cool when you get to the airport. Nice and *tranquilo*. When you land in Dublin, call the lads. Somebody will meet you. Give them the case and you'll be sitting pretty, ten grand richer.'

I thought there should be more to explain. There wasn't.

* * *

The guard cuts into the plastic and takes out a sample of the white powder, balancing it on the knife blade. He puts it onto a piece of paper, opens the lid of a bottle and pours on a chemical. The National Guard and the airport cops are laughing now, jostling each other. My hands form fists. I know the test is a formality, but I want the gods to be on my side. Please let it be a bag of talcum powder.

The white powder fizzles orangey-red, then blue. '*Es positivo*,' he says. It's the real thing. Game over.

'*Muy bueno, gringo! Muy bueno*,' ('Very good') roar the soldiers and police standing around, laughing and cheering. I can't believe it all. Cameras flash. Snap. Bit early for the press, I think. The guard tilts the case up so they can get clear photos of the booty. With a further probe with his knife the cop rips the lining on the other side of the case and finds another stash of cocaine packed across the entire side. Now several of the soldiers take turns putting their arms around me and posing for pictures, like holiday snaps. Another gringo mule bites the dust. More cheers, louder this time. 'Heeeyyyy.' Hands clap. The soldiers step in for more photos with their catch. It must have been six months since they caught their last drug runner.

I wonder how many mantelpieces around Venezuela will be decorated with my mug shot.

'We're arresting you for the transportation of illegal drugs,' says the interpreter, cool as a cucumber. Just another day's work catching a mule. The guard standing behind me slips handcuffs on me that bite into my wrists. Two soldiers lead me away.

* * *

Simón Bolívar International Airport, Maiquetía: 30 minutes' drive north of Caracas, set amid gentle hills covered in lush vegetation that seem to spill into the sea below. A runway peppered with weeds poking out from worn tarmac. Jets take off and soar over the sea a few minutes north. Waves wash up on the Caribbean shoreline there that stretches west to Colombia and east towards the islands of Trinidad and Tobago, a short hop off the mainland.

Venezuela is a major route for smuggling cocaine from neighbouring Colombia, mostly to Europe. Some 200 tonnes of the drug pass through its borders every year, US anti-drug chiefs say. The Venezuelan government fires back by saying there wouldn't be this problem if gringos didn't want to shove it up their noses. The oil-rich country shares a frontier with Colombia – the world's biggest producer of cocaine after Peru – stretching more than 2,200 km along Venezuela's western border. Much of the frontier is porous, made up of mountains, jungles and even a desert to the north, making it impossible to entirely secure. The Venezuelan authorities have a mostly deserved reputation of being crooked, which doesn't help seal the borders to tonnes of cocaine in the multibillion-dollar global business. Much of it is smuggled out in freight containers or aboard private planes, mostly bound for rogue West African states, where it is processed and shipped to Spain and the rest of Europe. Smaller hauls of single-digit kilos also form part of the coke business, swallowed in condoms or hidden in suitcases on commercial airline flights. The people behind it are drug mules – people like me.

* * *

Earlier, I'd walked into the airport. It was no Heathrow – just a couple of badly lit poky halls with yellowed walls. The law was everywhere. Police busied about checking IDs. National Guard troops armed with machine guns roamed. I wasn't bothered; I was sure all would go well.

In the departures area I saw a worker in a red jumpsuit wrapping cases in cling film. I paid him a few euro to do mine; I liked the extra security. I walked over to the Air France check-in desk. The stewardess was a typical Venezuelan beauty with sallow skin and perfect sheen hair.

'*Inglés?*' I asked.

'Yes,' she said with a warm smile.

I handed over the black suitcase. She checked it in. No problem. I watched it disappear behind a plastic curtain. That was it. Down the chute. Home and dry. All was going to plan. I could already see my debts at home disappearing off my bank statement. And I felt OK; I was sure the case was packed well. Only a proper search would suss it out.

I went through a few formalities, queuing up to pay a departure tax. I fished out a few scrunched-up notes of the local currency – bolívares fuertes – from my pocket. I then passed through immigration and flashed my passport at an official. He curtly nodded, his eyes barely looking at me. Not a hitch. It was all plain sailing.

I had a couple of hours to go until my 2 p.m. flight to Charles de Gaulle. I walked around the duty-free shop. The usual cheap cigarettes and booze, mostly locally brewed rum and Scottish whisky, which upper-class Venezuelans are fond of. On the short walk down to the terminal I stopped at one of the bars. It was busy enough, but I saw there was room for one more at the bar and eased myself onto a stool. I ordered a steak sandwich and a local Polar beer. It was good and hit the nail on the head. I opened up the only book I'd found in English in a shop in Caracas: Snoop Dogg's autobiography.

* * *

The officers led me away from the baggage area. I was brought to the main building of the airport, where the drug squad had its office. I was seated at a table in a room with an antique-looking printer and a filing cabinet. It looked like a spare room rather than an interrogation room. I was left alone. The officers only popped their heads in now and again. Some security. A couple of cops appeared at the door along with the interpreter, who was around when anything important was happening. They were there to strip search me, he explained. First I had to empty all my belongings out on the table. I had a bunch of cash in my wallet in a mix of currencies: 500 euro, 200 dollars and 100 sterling. And of course my mobile phone. All in all, the tools of an international trader – or drug mule, in my case. I then whipped off my shirt and slacks and threw the tie on the ground. So much for my formal dress throwing the drug squad off the scent. I was told to lower my boxer shorts as well. I had to bend over and spread my cheeks.

'Have you swallowed any drugs?' said the interpreter.

'Don't you think there's enough in the case?'

He laughed.

I put my clothes back on but left the tie on the ground. No use for it now.

The other guard sorted through my belongings on the table and scribbled a report. I knew I'd never see the cash or the phone again – and I didn't.

'Can I make a call home?' I asked the interpreter. He gave me my mobile phone back, warning me I couldn't ring any drug-smuggler friends. 'Family,' I said.

'Two minutes only,' he said, still holding a poker face.

I scrolled through the contacts. Mick, my nephew's name, came up. I knew I could rely on him to break the news to the rest of the family without giving them a heart attack. At 19, he was young but had a good head on his shoulders. I dialled the number. After a few rings he answered. I was relieved. I knew it might be another ten years before I could talk to anyone from home again. It'd be a phone call neither of us would forget in a hurry. 'Mick, listen, this is your Uncle Paul.'

'Ah, Paul, where are you? Can I pick you up or anything?' said Mick, thinking I wanted a lift from the airport in Dublin. I kept in mind that I'd told everyone I was off sunning myself in Spain on a working holiday, helping a mate in his nightclub.

'No, Mick, just shut up and listen. Right, I've got two minutes to say what I have to say.'

'Why, what's wrong? What?'

'Mick, just shut up. You know the way I'm supposed to be in Spain on a working holiday?'

'Yeah, yeah.'

'Well, I'm not. I'm in a country in South America called Venezuela and I've just been arrested in the airport on drug-trafficking charges and I'm looking at about ten years in jail.'

'No, Paul, you're joking,' he said, but with a serious voice.

'Mick, I'm not joking. Now listen: I want you to tell all that I've said to your mother and of course Nana and Granddad.' I knew he could drop in to them because my mother and father lived just over the road.

'What the fuck am I going to say to them? Jesus Christ!' His voice started breaking up.

'Just tell the truth, it's the only way. And tell them I love them and I'm sorry.'

'OK, Paul, look . . .'

'I have to go, Mick. Goodbye.' The two minutes was almost gone. I had to hang up. I was close to tears, and I could tell Mick was too. I had a lump in my throat. All I could think of was my daughter, Katie, and my son, Daniel.

How would they take it? Those thoughts were tearing me apart.

The cop took the phone off me and put it down on the table. Forms were pulled out that I had to sign. I was prompted to stick my thumb in a sponge soaked with black ink and plant it beside my signature. One of the guards brought in a set of flat weighing scales to check the haul and prove to me they weren't cheating with the amount they were writing down. They plonked the two large bags of flat-packed cocaine in front of me.

'Six kilos,' said the interpreter. I shrugged. What did they think I was going to do – deny it and say I'd only three? Anyway, the sentence would have been the same, I'd learn.

I sat in that chair and watched the next few years rush past my eyes. This was a big seizure of contraband. The pricks who'd hired me had told me it was one or two kilos. Six fucking kilos . . . I knew I'd pay a heavy price for this: there'd be no three-year suspended sentence and a slap on the wrist. Not in South America. Ten to fifteen years I might get, and raped by the prison 'daddy'. I was 45; I might get out when I was 60. I felt as sick as a dog.

The two guards walked out of the room, one of them carrying the scales. Oddly, the cops left me alone with the bags of cocaine lying on the table in front of me. They had a street value of over 500,000 euro back in Ireland and the UK. A bit of this would be a nice currency in prison. Just before the guards had walked into the room with the scales, they had brought in some stuff for me: a spare shirt and a toiletry bag. Apart from a toothbrush, it contained a large bottle of talcum powder. The irony – someone must have been having a joke.

I realised the dire straits I was in, sitting here facing ten years locked up in a fleapit prison in the tropics. I decided to make the best of a bad situation with the coke sitting in front of me. I got on my feet and pulled off the top of the talc bottle on the floor. It came off easily, no simple feat given I was handcuffed, albeit at the front. I emptied the talc into a wastepaper bin. The cocaine on the table was mostly a fine powder, so I scooped it up into the talc bottle. It had spilled out of one of the thin, fragile plastic bags the guards had accidentally ripped when they roughly lifted it onto the scales. I brushed the cocaine into the talc bottle, filling it up. On the side it said the volume was 300 g – that would do. I put the top back on. I heard noises outside. Feet shuffling. Gotta hurry. I put the bottle back into the toiletry bag. I sat back down, sweating.

I waited for the guards to come back and do the next round of red tape with forms and the like. I noticed a dusty coat of fine coke powder on the table – probably from where I had spilt it filling up the talc bottle. Shit. I picked up a piece of paper off the floor and, using it like a credit card, I formed lines with the coke. I leaned over and sniffed up two, which was probably too much, because in no time I was out of my fucking mind. My mouth and head were numb. It was pure, unadulterated coke; the high purity was full throttle. I'm not big into coke, I never really liked it, but facing ten years banged up in a Latin American prison puts a different perspective on things.

The door opened. A drug-squad cop stepped in. I sat there buzzing. He lifted up the two wide bags. He saw a small bit of coke had come out on to the table, like a salt cellar had spilled over. I panicked. I was found out. But the guard just brushed it off the table with the palm of his hand, then walked away with the haul. I can only imagine what would have happened had I been caught.

I was left to sit there alone and stew a bit more. The door opened and another officer popped his head in and, with gestures, offered me food – the leftovers of a fast-food chicken meal in a box he held in his hand. I said no. Between the coke and a jail term hanging over me, I was too wound-up to have an appetite.

A new bunch of cops came in, more National Guard

troops. They weren't as lax as the guards who had been dealing with me so far – they were serious-looking guys with frowning faces. One of the guards slipped off my handcuffs and handed me over to them. It was time for me to go. I got an air that I was their catch – the trophy prisoner. I stood up and the three guards marched me upstairs and back into the airport, carrying the plastic bag with the toothbrush, the talcum-powder bottle of coke and the shirt. The airport was almost deserted – just a few cleaners pushing mops. No one paid me any attention. A gringo in handcuffs – no big deal.

We walked through the main entrance, a guard on either side of me. I was still off my head on the coke and didn't really care where we were going. My eyes darted back and forth. My body was numb. My mind was flying. I'd no idea what time it was; all I knew was that hours had passed since I'd arrived at the airport at about midday. It was dusk now.

The guards loaded me into the back of a white jeep with the 'Antidrogas' logo in black on the side. One of the troopers, a skinny guy in his late 20s, jumped into the back, while the other sat up front next to the driver. There were only a few cars around, a couple of taxis. The military vehicle sped off through the airport, past a billboard showing President Hugo Chávez in a red beret and smiling. I felt like he was laughing at me.

The jeep sped along the coast. I sat handcuffed in the back, looking out the window. The guards spoke rapid-fire Spanish. It blew over my head. I looked outside to the left at high-rise hotels. Dirty whitewashed walls next to houses with neat Spanish-colonial fronts, tin shacks and *pescadería* fish restaurants, every few minutes giving way to a gap through which I caught glimpses of a calm sea.

Chapter 2
INSIDE I'M CRYING

WE PULLED UP AT A SECURITY CHECKPOINT AT A DOCKYARD. MASSES of red, orange and yellow rusty containers were stacked two and three high. A sentry waved out of a security checkpoint and a barrier rose up. We passed through an open gate next to a yard ringed with a high fence. On the right, a wide road on a steep incline led to what looked like a car-ferry terminal above, where a few vehicles were parked. I thought we were going up the ramp, but the jeep then jerked left and came to a stop in the yard. I could make out from a sign on a wall that this was the drug squad's headquarters: *Comando Antidrogas* of the Guardia Nacional in Vargas state. Not that I cared where I was, really. I was still buzzing.

The guard escorted me out of the back of the jeep and marched me to a large hangar-style gate like a giant accordion. Inside, the guards spoke to other national troops dressed in the same olive-green military uniforms. I was led to a steel staircase and was sat down a few steps from the bottom. The guard cuffed my hands to a metal banister. I sat there taking in my surroundings as the guards busied about. I was seated on one of two steel staircases that rose up both sides of this tall, airy building. In front of me there was a guard at a table writing in a notebook. There were a few offices behind him and anti-drug troops passing back and forth.

The hours ticked away into the night, and I watched guards walk in and out with an array of weapons from one of the rooms, which was obviously an armoury. Kalashnikovs, rifles, pistols and shotguns – they signed them out with the officer at the table and disappeared outside, presumably going for shoot-outs with the small-time drug gangs that ruled over the *barrios* at night. In the yard outside I heard engines rev up.

Some of the guards spoke to me. I didn't understand much Spanish but could make out 'gringo', 'drogas' and '*ocho años*' ('eight years'). They walked away howling with laughter, knowing the typical sentence handed down to drug mules. Others just asked, '*Gringo, cuánta droga?*' ('How much of the drug?'). 'Six,' I answered, holding up the same number of fingers. Another walked up to me with a revolver and pushed out the chamber, showing me there were no bullets. He popped the chamber back in, pointed the barrel at my head and slowly started pulling the trigger. I buried my head into my forearms, which were cuffed to the banisters. My body tensed with fear. *Click*. More howls of laughter. All the guards did it to me at times, but the main culprit was a little guy with a moustache. I named him El Diablo, or the Devil. I could see there were no bullets in the chambers, but they didn't look like well-trained cops and I was afraid they could easily have left a round in by mistake and blown my head off. I shouted 'wankers' at them while they kept playing Venezuelan roulette with my head.

Shortly after the target-practice session with my skull, a guard emerged from the blue doors of a room where I think there was a small kitchen. The cop, an older guy, put a paper cup of water down next to me. He spoke in a friendly voice. The Spanish went over my head. He seemed like the only guard who was a decent human being, though, so I said, 'Bed, bed, sleep,' tilting my head onto my hand to get the message across. 'No,' he shrugged. I was exhausted now and was sure a cell awaited me with a bed – or even just a floor to sleep on. I was wrong.

My ass was grinding into the metal staircase, but I was thankful the guards had now uncuffed one of my hands from the banister. Whiling the hours away, my mind went off into dark thoughts. I was both paranoid and still buzzing from the coke, which didn't help. How could I have been so stupid to do this for ten grand? I wanted to be at home, having a pint down in the local pub with my mates. Then there was my family. What would they be thinking? Had Mick broken the news to my parents, that I had been caught drug smuggling? They were old, both my mother and father in their 70s. I wondered whether they would die while I spent years rotting in a cesspit prison in Latin America. And what would my son and daughter, Dano and Katie, think?

It was well into the night now, and I started to drift in and out of sleep, drowsy from the sticky air. The main body of troops had gone now. There was only the guard seated at the desk in front, a chubby guy with curly hair and a moustache. In what I thought was a mess room behind him I could hear other cops: the clink of glasses, their boisterous voices drifting out, getting rowdier as the night went on. Still, I dozed off.

A nudge woke me up from a groggy sleep. It was dark now, the only dim light from a bare bulb over one of the offices. The guard had stood up from the table and was in front of me. He was fatter than I'd thought, with a belly hanging out over his waistband. He had a cigarette dangling from his lip, red embers glowing. He spoke in whispers to another guard standing beside him. I didn't understand. The building was quiet now. I thought the whispers were to avoid waking the other cops, who I presumed were sleeping.

They uncuffed me from the banister. I stood up and the guard cuffed my hands behind my back. My legs and ass were sore and stiff. I was sure the staircase on the other side of the building led up to a network of prisons and cells. There I'd finally get a bed – or at least a floor to stretch out on.

But no – the two guards led me to a shower area in a room to the right. It was a tiny space with a toilet cubicle at one side and a pipe sticking out of the wall that served as a shower. More whispers. I then saw two other guards waiting inside the door – younger guys. What's going on here? I must be getting a wash – hosed and scrubbed down like you see in the prison movies. The guards started to laugh. More whispers. Giggles.

I was led forward and they made me face one of the walls. Two of the guards suddenly grabbed me at my waist. Fear jolted through me like a bolt of electricity. This was no wash. Jesus, what were they going to do to me?

I was pushed forward, my face shoved into the corner, touching the wall now. I heard the door close. The laughter grew louder.

Oh my God. What were they doing to me? If I screamed, would anyone come?

My upper body was pushed over so it was parallel with the floor. I started shouting, 'What's the story? What's the story?' My heart was racing. I knew this was bad. A hand reached around my waist. I was shifting back and forth, struggling against the strength of the three or four men who were now grabbing at my shoulders. I kicked back at them with my hard shoes on. A stick or some hard object lashed out against my legs. I felt short, sharp pains. I started to shout again, 'What's the story?' Hands grabbed my shoulders to still me. More laughter and giggles. A hand with some kind of material wrapped around it groped my face. I tried to bite the finger. A fist ploughed into the back of my neck. A rag was shoved into my mouth. I was breathing fast and heavily, gagging. My nostrils flared. I felt my belt open. My slacks dropped down. I instinctively knew what was going to happen, but I couldn't process it. It was like I was watching myself from a distance. An onlooker. Then I felt slimy shit like gel rubbed around my ass. Cold. Wet.

No. It can't be.

'Ha, ha, gringo,' one of them said.

One of them entered me from behind. The pain rushed through me. My breathing got faster. My nostrils flared again. My eyes bulged and felt like they'd pop out. My face was shoved back and forth into the wall. Hands were still on my shoulders, grabbing me. I saw my trousers around my ankles. Bang. Bang. Flesh plunged into me. Anger inside me boiled up. I wanted to reach out and destroy these people. Tear them apart.

It stopped. More laughter. Feet shuffling. Another of the guards entered me. Tears were welling in my eyes. Oh no. No. Flesh slapping against my ass. *Slap. Slap. Slap.* Then faster. My mind drifted off into another place. I wasn't there.

Suddenly the guard thrusting into me stopped. I heard the guards talking in a serious tone. I heard a voice from outside. I thought it was a woman's. I was still there in that position, doubled over. Face shoved into the wall. My breathing rapid. I feared I'd choke on the rag. My chest heaved up and down, lungs gasping for air for my nostrils being unable to suck in enough oxygen.

Somebody help.

The woman's voice drifted off. The hands lifted off my shoulders and I stood upright, still facing the wall. One of the guards turned on a tap and a few drops trickled from the pipe. The rag was pulled from my mouth. They turned me around. My eyes looked to the ground. 'Jesus, what's the story? What's the story?' I said, but lower this time, as if I knew it was useless. Their dirty deed was done. And now I felt like nothing. Humiliated. A human condom.

They stood to one side and let me wash myself with the trickles of water. I then picked up my shirt from the damp floor and dried myself. I got fully dressed with them watching – probably disappointed they didn't all get their way with me. Then they led me back to the stairs and I was cuffed to the banisters again. I wanted to shout, scream – but to who?

The bugger squad drifted off. The fat one with the moustache took up his post on the desk again. He looked over, grinning. Happy with his late-night fun. I couldn't look at him. I just sat there, filled only with hatred for these scum. Bastards.

When I got caught in the airport, I'd thought, 'Jesus, 15

years in jail and I'll get raped by the prison daddy.' I never thought it would be by the cops. I wondered whether getting raped was normal here. Maybe all the soldiers did this. I was afraid they'd kill me if I spoke out. And who would believe me – a drug mule? My word against four cops. I'd probably hear a rifle cocked and a bullet whizz my way. Who would come to save me? Thousands of miles from home in a strange, perverted country.

The anger soon left. In its place was shame. Emptiness. Pain – my rear end throbbing. I couldn't sit properly on the staircase. I had to shift left and right on my cheeks to find comfort. But it was useless. And I just felt horrible. I wanted to cry. Let the tears flow. But I wasn't going to show pain in front of the guard. I wouldn't give him that satisfaction. I only let myself cry inside. Let dry tears flow.

I started to doze again, my head resting on my forearms. I drifted off to the sound of buzzing around my shins. Now it was the mosquitoes' turn to penetrate me.

Chapter 3

STARVED AND CHARGED

THE NEXT MORNING I WOKE UP FROM AN UNCOMFORTABLE SLEEP and rubbed my eyes. My body ached from the discomfort of a whole day and night handcuffed to the banisters and sitting on the metal staircase. My ass was still grating on it. And now I was internally in pain, too, from the two guards who got their way with me the previous night. It was a horrible thought that I tried to push away, like it had been some nightmare.

My lower legs were covered in red bumps: mosquito bites. The itch was unbearable. I scratched at the red mounds – I counted 60 in all during the spare time I had sitting there doing nothing. I now wished I had the talcum powder I'd dumped in the airport to douse my legs.

My stomach groaned. The smell of food wafting out of one of the rooms didn't help. Cops were emerging from it carrying cups of coffee and what looked like sandwiches wrapped in paper. But nothing for the gringo. Still, the hole in my stomach wasn't getting much attention from my mind. I was more focused on how I might be locked up in this awful country for the next decade or so.

I sat there using my uncuffed hand to slap at my legs with the spare shirt I got along with the toiletry bag in the airport. It was my Irish rugby top, which I'd brought over from Dublin and that they'd let me keep at the airport. The horrible thoughts of the night before started seeping back again. And the physical pain was unbearable. I couldn't sit properly on the stairs. I felt a growth out of my ass, like my rectum had been pulled inside out. I could feel it, like there was a peach between my legs. I couldn't sit still. I had to keep shifting from cheek to cheek to avoid hitting that growth on the metal staircase.

My mind slowly woke up to this reality I was in. Locked up by life forms lower than animals. I wanted it to be a bad dream. I took in my surroundings. I knew I was in the drug squad's main building, but maybe it was a prison as well? It didn't make any sense. I couldn't ask anyone. None of the guards spoke English. I sat there looking around and wondering what would happen tonight – would the fuck squad be back? Ten, fifteen years of this . . . I started thinking about killing myself. The stairs I sat on led to a platform above, where a large blue drum full of water stood next to piles of rubbish and a locked door. There was a drop of about fifteen to twenty feet below. If I could somehow get out of the cuffs and get up there, I could use my trousers or something to hang myself. In that moment, death seemed better than this place.

* * *

'*Tú, tú mama huevo,*' ('You, you cocksucker') said one of the guards, walking up holding a newspaper. He tapped a finger at a short article. I'd made the papers, what looked like a local one. I didn't read Spanish, but I could make out '*aeropuerto*', '*cocaína*' and '*irlandés*'. There was no mention of my name or a photograph, thank God. I didn't want anyone back home other than my family to know I was locked up for smuggling drugs.

A few hours later, a stream of people came down from the opposite steep staircase. I was sure they were passengers from the car-ferry terminal above I'd seen the day before. That banished from my mind the thought that there was a proper prison up there. The passengers must have had to pass through the drug squad's area on their way out to the road outside. I counted about 40, probably workers coming over from nearby islands for jobs on the mainland.

Not an eyebrow was raised at the sight of a European man cuffed to stairs in a police building in the bowels of a ferry terminal. I'm not the palest of Paddies, but with my white skin and light-brown hair I stood out as a gringo. A few glanced over, but no one cared. They all seemed to know: another drug mule caught at the airport.

* * *

One of the office doors in front was open, so I looked in. I saw my black Wilson suitcase stuffed inside a large plastic bag. I couldn't believe it. My spirits were buoyed up, because I thought I could get a fresh T-shirt or jeans. What I was wearing was sticky and damp. 'Clothes, clothes,' I said to one guard, pointing at the case with my uncuffed hand. I started pulling at my blue shirt, which I'd been wearing for two days and was soaked with sweat in the humidity. I guessed Ralph Lauren shirts weren't made for drug smugglers handcuffed to stairs. A babble of Spanish came back from a shaking head. A 'no'. I thought it must have meant that the case was evidence and so off-limits.

However, a little later, the guards were parading around in the clothes from my suitcase. A lovely Brazilian football shirt I'd bought for my nephew. Nike shirts. All the gear I'd picked up for my family back home. 'Gracias, amigo. Gracias,' they said, sharing the clothes and walking around, laughing and grinning. A motley crew of morons. A fancy dress for freaks. Since they had taken my clothes, I imagined there wasn't any point in asking for the cash taken from me at the airport. Probably long ago shared out among the cops.

Later in the afternoon, a guard slipped the cuffs off. The metal clanked against the tubular banister. An escort of three guards led me out into the courtyard outside and into a dark-green military jeep. We sped west along the coastal road, and

I sat there taking in the sounds and sights after being cooped up on the stairs for the past day. I marvelled at small things we passed, like makeshift stalls selling rubber rings for kids, as well as snorkels and other stuff for a day at the beach. Others sold seafood snacks such as '*cocteles de camarones*', or prawn cocktails in plastic cups. I thought back to myself as a kid, running around the beach with a bucket and spade.

* * *

We were back in the airport. I couldn't believe it. It was quiet again. There were just a few passengers wheeling cases. I started having delusions that the cops had realised they'd made a mistake with me and I'd be escorted onto a flight home with a pat on the back. Maybe they just wanted the publicity of capturing a drug mule and were letting me leave. My imagination started running away with itself. Suddenly, we turned left and walked down a corridor into an office. So much for the plane home.

A man in a suit, shirt and tie stood there. Two guards stood on either side of me. 'Hallo sir, I am with Interpol,' the guy said.

'How ya doing,' I said. I looked around the office and felt I was back on the set of *Kojak*: chunky computer monitors, a brown carpet and an old, dusty desk.

'We must do fingerprints and photo,' said the Interpol official in accented English. I sat down and held out the palms of my hands. He ran a roller of ink across them and I planted them down on a sheet of paper, like a child's game in a crèche. I wasn't in much humour for conversation with any Venezuelans after last night and didn't talk to the guy at all. A guard shoved me over to stand against a white background, where the official clicked a handheld camera. *Snap*. I was officially an international drug smuggler. My name, prints and mug shot would probably pop up on Interpol searches across the world. But I realised the point of the whole thing was to see whether I was on the FBI's Ten Most Wanted list, that they were looking to see whether I was Carlos the Jackal and score kudos for capturing me. More like Paddy the Clown.

'You sign here,' the official said, thrusting a pen towards me. He then squeezed a blob of soap into my hands to wash off the ink and nodded towards another room. I was pushed through two swing doors, like in a western cantina. A pot gurgled on a two-ring stove. The waft of what smelled like a stew danced around my nostrils. Lovely jubbly, how long are we staying?

'I haven't had anything to eat for a day, what's the chance of a bit of stew?'

'It is not ready,' said the Interpol official curtly. The hunger went on.

I was now wondering when I'd get to see a lawyer or someone from the Irish embassy. But nothing.

* * *

Later that night, back at the drug-squad headquarters, the guards changed shift. I remembered one of them, a skinny soldier with a short haircut who looked about thirty. He was one of the guards who'd pinned me against the wall in the toilets while another two rammed their dicks into me. El Diablo was also knocking around, walking in and out of the armoury again, cocking guns and pointing them at my head. I didn't look at either of them, though, just kept my eyes towards the floor. I didn't even want to register them. Scum.

I later watched the other guards arm up as usual like they were gearing up for a stint in Afghanistan, taking on al-Qaeda with full-on assault gear: bulletproof vests, machine guns and an arsenal of weapons that would put the Delta Force to shame.

For the next two days I sat on the stairs cuffed to the banisters, getting hungrier and my backside still throbbing. The only time I got to move was when the guards brought me to the toilet once or twice a day. I hadn't eaten anything since my lunch at the airport and I was only being given one or two cups of water a day, so there wasn't much to pass. I could mostly ignore the physical discomfort; it was my mind that was the problem. I was confused about where I was being held. Was this the prison? If so, where was my cell? And would the guards let me starve to death? Why hadn't I been sentenced in a court? Even in a country like this, there must be judges. And on it went.

On the third morning, the guards went through their usual drill when taking me, their prisoner, out. Three of them escorted me to a military jeep parked in the yard. After about 20 minutes, we pulled up at a modern, state-of-the-art building where I could read '*justicia*'. I realised I was at a court. It was a fortified building right on the waterfront, with a wall at the back blocking the view of a sliver of a beach. It looked brand spanking new: one storey tall, and wide, with big glass doors. We pulled up at the side, where a sentry was posted at a security checkpoint. We drove through with a nod and pulled into a courtyard. I stepped out of the jeep and felt a lovely warm breeze blowing in gently from the Caribbean. I wanted to jump into the sea and freshen up in the water.

Inside the courthouse, I was led down to an underground level to cells that looked like they belonged in a Victorian dungeon: dirty, dark and damp smelling. The waft of urine and excrement drifted from a hole in the floor that was a toilet. Faded yellow light fell from bare bulbs. I heard a 'ya-ya-ya-hoohhh' cry before I saw what lay in the cells ahead. Seven to eight inmates sat around on L-shaped stone benches. A barred door squeaked open and I stepped through. The Venezuelan prisoners looked happy at the sight of the gringo. It would kill a bit of boredom. They started talking to me. All I could make out was 'gringo' and 'drogas'. They all knew I was a drug mule. I supposed any foreigner locked up in Venezuela was. They were a decent bunch and offered me sweets and smokes, and I enjoyed a bit of light banter with them. I sat back and watched as single cigarettes passed back and forth among the inmates through the bars of the adjacent cells.

One of the courthouse guards came and led me up the stairs again and then down a corridor. There I met an interpreter provided by the Venezuelan state – a fair-haired, fresh-faced man in his early 30s, with hazel eyes in stark contrast to his pale skin.

'I am Antonio,' he said.

'Paul, Paul Keany,' I said.

'Yes, Mr Keany, come with me, please.' He seemed to be new to the job. He kept backtracking after taking wrong turns as we walked around the building.

I was delighted by the chance to speak English. 'What's the story here? I've been sat cuffed to a staircase for four days with no food and been abused.' (I didn't say how, exactly, and wouldn't to any living soul in that country.)

'I know,' he shrugged. 'It's Venezuela.'

We stepped into a room – an informal court. The judge and lawyers, dressed in casual clothes, sat around tables for what was a preliminary hearing. The interpreter spoke to a big black woman who was introduced as my lawyer. I didn't understand her words, but through the interpreter she was dismissing my complaints about my treatment in the drug-squad HQ with a wave of her hand, as if to say, 'You committed a crime, tough.'

'Sorry for your troubles,' said the interpreter, his voice shaky. He seemed more nervous about the court case than I was and looked like he was going to start crying.

The preliminary hearing, which went on for about 15 minutes, was functional. I sat there and the interpreter spoke to me from time to time. I felt like a fly on the wall. I had to remind myself that it was me they were talking about – it felt like someone else. To pass the time, I watched the female judge. She was stunning, with luscious dark skin and sheen jet-black hair, and she was dressed in tight jeans. She looked like a Miss Venezuela and reminded me why the South American country has racked up the highest number of Miss World winners.

'If you plead guilty you will get eight years,' said the interpreter after the lawyer spoke with him. He had a look of shock on his face, as if he was going to do the time himself. He wasn't hardened to the ways of the Venezuelan justice system, I guessed. 'If you plead not guilty, you'll get eight years and maybe even up to fifteen,' he added.

I pleaded guilty. Eight years was a long time. Fifteen was worse. Here I was on the far side of the world, in a country where I didn't speak the language and which wasn't picking up any human rights medals for its treatment of prisoners.

* * *

Later, back at the drugs HQ, I was brought back to what had been home for the past four days: the staircase with the grated steel steps. My arm was cuffed back to the banister. There was still no food, only the odd cup of water brought by one or two cops who seemed more human than the others.

Hours passed and I looked up through a window high on the wall above the offices. It gave me a rectangular peephole out to the sky. I saw it was pitch black outside. All the activity with the guards had died down. There was just one cop seated at a desk in front of me, dozing, with his chin resting on his chest. My mind started going into escape mode. I took a bit of the coke from my stash with my free hand, tapping it from the talc bottle onto my knee and hoovering it up with my nose. I wanted to stay up all night and be alert for the best chance to break free. I asked the guard who'd been dozing at the desk on duty if I could use the toilet.

'Baño, baño,' ('Toilet, toilet') I said. It was just about the only Spanish word I'd learned. I'd use the little sliver of soap in my pocket I'd taken from a previous toilet visit. I took it out at the sink and lathered it on my wrist with some water, thinking

I could easily slither out of the cuffs later on. The plan didn't work. On the way out of the cubicle, the guard put the cuffs on tighter than ever. I felt my hands would turn blue because of the blood cut off. He led me back to the stairs and cuffed me to the banister again. I sat there throughout the night trying to ease my hands out, like a failed Harry Houdini. So much for my plan to flee, stowing away on a ship and drifting off into the Caribbean to the Atlantic and beyond and jumping ship in Cape Town or somewhere.

* * *

I woke up the next morning, wrecked. My wrists were covered in scrapes and marks from the cuffs. I was glad I had a long shirt on so the guards wouldn't see I'd been trying to get out and do a runner. One of them stood in front of me, talking. With a couple of movements of his arm I made out we were going somewhere. I knew it was time to go. The cuffs came off. I stood up and grabbed the plastic bag containing my only worldly possessions: the Irish rugby shirt, the toothbrush, the few toiletries, the prized 'talc' powder of 300-odd grams of coke. Where I was going I had no idea. But I wasn't sorry to leave. Anywhere was better than here.

* * *

In a coastal town we whizzed through narrow side streets, past run-down colonial buildings with peeled paint and broken plaster. I kept looking at buildings as we passed, thinking, 'Is this the prison? Is this the prison?' One had three floors with barred windows. I was sure it was the jail, but we drove right past it.

The jeep jerked to a sharp left and we pulled into a dusty courtyard. I stepped out with the young soldier. The yard was surrounded by little rooms with solid-looking doors painted in a dirty red, about 15 of them. They looked a bit like chalets in a holiday camp. I was sure this was to be my next home.

We walked past a group of youths dressed in shorts and T-shirts sitting on a path. They were handcuffed to each other. The guards lurched me forward into an office inside a building. An enormous fan whirred lazily above. It looked like the chopper blades of an antique helicopter turning in slow motion, stirring sticky air. A fat guard sat asleep in a chair, his head slumped forward; another sat at a desk shuffling papers.

One of the guards in charge spoke to me, pointing at the floor. I sat down on the concrete. After about half an hour, it was time to go through the red tape again. I held out my sweaty palms while one of the younger officers ran an ink roller back and forth over them. I planted my hands down on a sheet of white paper. I was getting good at this. The guard pushed a biro into my hand. I signed a squiggle at the bottom. A digital camera was hooked up to a computer with a chunky monitor (I was back on the set of *Kojak* again). *Snap*. The guards led me back outside. I had thought this was the prison. I was wrong again.

We soon sped through more side streets and came to a halt in another yard. We drove through big double doors. Inside, two guards stood behind a small counter: one a big woman who filled out her National Guard uniform; the other a huge fat fucker, a dark-skinned *moreno*.

The woman, who had a horrible grin, poked around my toiletry bag. She pulled out the bottle of talcum powder. My heart started racing. She popped off the lid and lifted it to her nose for a sniff. Satisfied it was only talc, she screwed the lid back on. Thank God.

The cop led me by the arm into a toilet to the right. We squeezed into a little cubicle. Oh no. Don't let it happen again. I tensed. My stomach tightened. I was sure now all the men in the olive-green uniforms were bugger boys. The guard slipped his fat hands into a pair of white surgical gloves. He then reached around for my belt and my trousers dropped around my ankles. Jesus. He pushed my upper body over and my head was hovering over the toilet bowl. I could feel my mind start to drift off to another place, to hide. I felt something slip into my rear end and poke about. What an invasion. But it was over quick. I heard the tight snap of the gloves coming off. The guard had only penetrated with his finger and was probably looking to see whether I had money hidden there. I'd later learn that was where the inmates stashed their cash, hidden up their ass in a condom. I stood back up straight. Fatso stood there giving my manhood a good look over. I pulled my trousers up, and he put his hands in my pockets and fished out a 50,000-bolo note (about ten euro), which I didn't even know was there. He stuffed it in his own pocket.

Back out at the counter after the anal exploration, the guards signed me over. *Señor irlandés. El gringo. Droga mula.* Property of Macuto jail.

Chapter 4

HOLIDAY IN THE SUN

I'D NEVER REALLY TAKEN DRUGS. JUST A BIT OF COKE HERE AND there at parties. Or off the back of a pub toilet with one of me mates. Only the odd weekend. I enjoyed the buzz of it. But I don't have an addictive personality, so I could walk away from coke and not look at it again for weeks.

In the early to mid-2000s in Dublin the place was awash with the stuff. The Irish economy was booming. The Celtic Tiger, they called it. Anyone with a half-decent job enjoyed a flash lifestyle. Short weekend hops around the world. Paris in spring, even Paddy's Day in New York. A holiday home or two in Spain, Turkey, Bulgaria or whichever country was on the up and where a 'bargain' home could be found. Sales of new cars soared. Mercs and Beemers rolled off car lots. Upmarket department stores like Brown Thomas on Dublin's Grafton Street heaved at the weekends. Shoppers nosed for big labels. Prada. Dolce & Gabbana. Take your pick. The pubs in Dublin city were teeming at night, too, revellers partying Monday to Sunday.

The excessive lifestyle didn't just mean goods and booze. It also meant coke. One newspaper story doing the rounds ran a yarn about a college study that found 100 per cent of banknotes in Ireland had traces of cocaine on them. The international press picked up on it. One paper had the witty headline 'Snow Me the Money'. Anti-drugs folk seized on the finding and said the cocaine problem in Ireland was an 'epidemic', pointing out just 65 per cent of dollar notes in the US had traces of cocaine. When hounded by the press for comment, one Irish minister came out and denied there was a problem. The funny thing, though, was that the Irish police, the Garda, said that convictions for cocaine-related crimes were up fourfold on previous years while seizures were up 20 per cent.

The demand for coke was fuelling gangland crime, too. The front pages of the daily tabloids regularly splashed with a story about one gang member blowing away a rival criminal in battles over turf to sell coke in working-class Dublin suburbs.

Overall, it was a time in Ireland when most had spare cash in their pockets and were enjoying the good life. For many that meant doing a few lines of coke at the weekend. It was dirt cheap because so many were buying it. One opposition politician in Dáil Éireann, the Irish parliament, lamenting about the epidemic in the country noted that a line of coke was cheaper than a pint.

Although I wasn't rich myself in the boom years, I was doing all right. I had started running my own plumbing business. There was loads of work. I was doing mostly small stuff, such as house extensions. I had work lined up months in advance. I was a one-man band – just myself and a little van. I was living back home with my folks in Coolock, a working-class area in Dublin's northside, sleeping in a box room. I had moved in to help my finances till I got the business properly moving. My expenses were low, so I had spare cash for a few lines of coke. When I did it it was mostly down in the local pub on a Friday night. Myself and a couple of other lads off the sites – brickies, sparks and so on – would chip in for a 'one-er'. That was a small bag of coke that cost 100 euro. We used to call a fellow we knew and he'd be down in minutes in his car to deliver it. Deals on Wheels, we'd call it. Dressed in scruffy overalls, we then took turns going into the jacks, the toilets, for a sniff, scooping the coke from the bag with a key or a coin. You'd hear fellows giggling away in the next cubicle. Everyone was at it.

I was in my early 40s and living a carefree lifestyle. I had no real worries or anyone to look after but myself. I had two children from a former marriage, both in their mid-teens – my son, Daniel, and my daughter, Katie. I was making payments to their mother, my ex-wife, for their upkeep, of course, but the fact that they didn't live with me meant I was a free man. I suppose many might see it as an immature lifestyle. Maybe it was. But I loved my children and they were very important to me. It wasn't just the case that I'd help moneywise with their schooling and clothes; they would stay with me a lot, too. They loved being around their nana and granddad in the house and hanging out with their cousins who lived across the road, where my sister Sharon lived with her kids.

Then one day I got a call from Katie that would change that.

'Da, can I go and live with you?'

'Of course you can, but did something happen?'

'I just want to move down to Dublin.'

I had divorced her mother many years ago. Katie had been living with her and her new husband in a house in the Midlands. I suspected from phone calls in the past that she wasn't getting much space at home. So, reading between the lines, that's why I thought she wanted to move out. She was a teenager and was pretty much saying she wanted a bit more freedom, which she said she wasn't getting there. Nights out at local discos and that, I supposed.

'Grand,' I said.

The only problem was I now had to go and rent an apartment. I found a two-bed flat down in Coolock not far from the Cadbury's chocolate factory. It cost me a grand a month. I had bills on top, too, and Katie's upkeep to take care of when she moved in. It was great living with her, watching her grow into a woman. Her whole life ahead of her. Her dreams of being a hairdresser. Anyway, the apartment and everything weren't a problem. The only other overheads I had were a personal loan of about 10,000 euro and 12,000 for a van I'd bought for the job. Work was flying, so it was all easy to cover.

Then the bubble burst. The economy plummeted. The headlines in the papers and on the telly were all about a property crash. It turned out the Irish hadn't been rich after all – it was all credit, banks throwing money at people for years. Everyone knew, but no one had wanted to believe it at the time. Now billionaire property developers were dropping like flies. Houses that had once been homes but were now commodities to trade and make a 'killing' on were badly hit. Houses that had been bought for, say, 400,000 euro had now dropped to about half that value in real terms. Negative equity was rife. The whole economy had revolved around the artificial price of a house. The banks stopped lending. When the dust started to settle, it turned out they were one of the biggest culprits. One bank chief, it turned out, had given himself over 100 million euro in personal loans at one point from account holders' money. It was all terrible.

Everyone started tightening their belts. House extensions, where I got most of my plumbing work, weren't at the top of anyone's list. My phone stopped ringing. Work dried up. My van sat in the parking space in my apartment block. 'Paul Keany – Plumber' it read on the side. Now it should have read 'Paul Keany – Needs Work'.

I still had money for a few pints on a Friday night. But sharing a bag of coke with the mates went out the window when I was worried about having enough money to pay my loans and keep myself and Katie going.

I was in the local pub one night, standing out in the smoking area having a cigarette. One of the usual dealers walked up to me.

'Paul, I have a one-er for you.'

'I'll pass. Too rich for my wallet.'

'Business bad for you too?'

'Nothing on the books.'

Silence hung in the air between the two of us. He was staring at me, like he was sizing me up for something. 'Paul, if you need a few quid I know lads who go for holidays in the sun and make good money to take home a little package.'

'How much?'

'About ten grand.'

'What would be in the package?'

'Ignorance is bliss.'

'Seems too good to be true,' I said, but it was obvious where this was going. 'To where?'

'Latin America, probably Mexico, but could be Spain.'

I stood there with my thoughts swishing around my head. It sounded like easy money. I was thinking it would clear the loan on the van and lessen my load a little. I was always up for adventure, and a risk, and wasn't too worried about the idea of getting caught, but I didn't commit there and then.

I threw my cigarette butt on the ground and stamped on it. 'OK, I'm interested, but I want to talk a bit more.'

'Easy, I'll organise a meeting with a fella for you.'

I'm no angel. I've had a few run-ins with the law. When I was 27 I got done for assaulting a copper in Dublin. I was on my stag night with about 15 mates. We walked into a pub on Abbey Street and the publican told us to leave. We didn't. Next minute, a motorbike copper arrived in his leathers and ordered us to get out. We did. Outside on the street, I went to walk into the next pub. I was in great spirits with my mates. Getting married and a baby boy on the way. I wanted to keep the party going.

The copper grabbed me by the shoulder. 'You can't go in there.'

'Get the fuck off me,' I said, pushing his arm away. Harder than I thought. He stumbled into his motorbike. Shit. All of a sudden the police were everywhere. I was bundled into a van and spent a few hours in Store Street Garda station. I got a £20 fine.

That was more than 15 years ago, and despite my brush

with the police I didn't have any criminal history involving drugs. Wasn't my game.

A few days later I was standing outside in the car park of a local pub in Coolock. A guy pulled up in a red Toyota. A short, stocky fellow got out, walked over and shook my hand. 'I believe you're interested in going on a holiday for us?'

'Something like that,' I laughed.

'Let's take a seat.' We sat down on the boot of his car, the pair of us dressed in dark-blue overalls. His name was Kevin and he was a brickie. No big player in the drug business, a part-timer, I'd heard. He and a few of his mates would chip in and buy a few kilos of coke abroad every couple of years. Sell it on. Make a few quid.

'It's simple. Holiday in the sun. Ten-grand pay. You get there and wait for a phone call. We give you a few thousand spending money for you to kill a bit of time. Just wait for the call. Somebody gives you a case with a package and you take it home.'

'That's it?'

'That's it.'

'Where to?'

'We don't know yet, we just need to know if you're in first.'

I sat there with my arms folded, looking at the ground. We didn't speak for a few moments. 'What if I get caught?'

'We'll sort you out, and if you come home with nothing we'll give you a few quid anyway. Win, lose or draw, you'll be taken care of.'

'All right, OK, that's cool,' I said. I knew the 'win, lose or draw' was bullshit, but I went along with it. I was sure I could pull off the run. 'I'm in.'

A couple of weeks passed and my mobile phone rang again. It was Kevin. 'Right, we have a destination: Venezuela.'

'Venezuela,' I said. A pause. I didn't want to sound like I'd never heard of it, but I hadn't and said nothing.

He gave me a date. 'Do you mind getting the tickets yourself? Go onto the Internet and get them on a credit card.

We'll sort you out after. It's just we don't want any trace leading back to us.'

'All right.' I went onto my computer at home to find out about Venezuela. Capital: Caracas. Weather: sunny. Language: Spanish. Sandy white beaches. Great nightlife. Other than the language, all sounded good to me.

The next day Kevin called around to my apartment. We sat in my office, which was a desk and a couple of chairs in the corner of my bedroom.

'You got the flight all right?'

'Yeah,' I said. 'A week from now.'

'Perfect. How much?'

'Eight hundred.'

He handed me a roll of euro notes from his pockets, all creased: fifties, twenties, hundreds, the whole lot. He counted out 800 on the bed and then handed me another bunch of cash.

'That's two grand in all for flights and spending money to keep you going. Just get there and check into a hotel in Caracas. Keep your phone on. Wait for the call.'

I needed a smokescreen for family and friends. I had a mate who had a couple of pubs in the south of Spain, which made it easy. I told everyone I was going for a holiday in the sun to help Vinnie out down in Marbella for two weeks. That's how long my trip to Venezuela was for. Katie was going on holiday to Spain for two weeks as well, a couple of days before I was due to leave, so the timing of my trip was perfect.

* * *

Dublin Airport. It was just after 8 a.m. I walked into the departures hall. In the corner of my eye I saw a bookshop. I walked in and picked up a Spanish phrase book. I had a flick through it. '*La cuenta* – the bill' said one phrase. That'll come in handy, I thought, and bought the book along with a crime novel. I checked my case in with Air France for the flight to

Caracas with a stop-off in Charles de Gaulle in Paris. I passed through security into departures, not giving much thought to the danger of the trip. I was actually excited about the whole thing. It was like being in a James Bond film or something: spies and drug dealers, murky dealings in foreign climes. At the time the *Banged Up Abroad* series on TV was all the rage, Western drug mules locked up in hellhole jails in the tropics – but that wouldn't happen to me.

Chapter 5
DODGING WESTERN UNION

A BLACK GUARD STOOD BESIDE THE SET OF STEEL GATES. 'HALLO, MY friend,' he said leeringly, putting on a nice-guy act with the little English he had. Probably buttering up the gringo in the hope of a few quid. I looked back at another cop behind the counter. He nodded towards the cells ahead and ran his finger across his neck in a slicing motion as if to say, 'You're for the chop.' The guard ushered me inside to the wing area.

Arms hung out of cell bars. Dark faces peered out, the whites of their eyes standing out from the gloom like torches shining out of a black hole. Sheets were tied to bars across the cells and stretched out as makeshift hammocks. The prison chant hollered out, ya-ya-ya-hoohhh, like animals howling. The whole place was like a zoo – a filthy one, reeking of piss.

We stepped through barred gates to the left and into a small rectangular yard. I was led into a wing. It was poky but clean and tidy, with TVs, a fridge and a small stove. It looked like it was where I'd be held, thank God, rather than the zoo. Standing there with the black slacks and dress shoes on, I probably looked like a coke kingpin the guards could bribe for cash: not the mule that I was. The cell was a two-room set-up with four single beds and a bunk. A guy walked up to me, a jovial fellow in his 40s with grey hair coiffed to the side. He spoke, but all I could make out from him was that his name was Fulvio and he was from 'Italia'. He picked up a scrap of paper and started scribbling on it. '*Aquí*' and '*allá*' ('here' and 'there') he said, drawing a picture of a courtroom and a building with bars he told me was Los Teques prison. I could make out he was fighting his conviction for being a drug mule, and the guards shipped him back and forth the short distance from this jail to the courtroom rather than the hour or so's hike to the main prison, Los Teques.

I caught a glimpse of a towering guy, about 6 ft 2 in., with a bald head in a room next to us. 'Jefe, boss,' said Fulvio.

The jefe was dressed in shorts and a vest and walked over to me. Another inmate, a slim guy with short, curly hair, stood beside him. 'Western Union, you phone home . . . you friend, you family,' he said in broken English. He spoke with a nasal, high-pitched voice, like he had a sock shoved up his nose. 'You pay 2,000 euro for stay here.'

I nearly choked. 'You must be fucking mad,' I said in rapid English.

'I . . . no . . . understand, very fast . . . Western Union, 2,000 euro,' he repeated. The boss looked down at me with a menacing glare. I knew what was going on – the boys were hounding the gringo for a big payout. It was game on straight away. A mobile phone was handed to me. I had to think and act fast. There was no one I could phone and ask for that sum of cash. Nor did I want to. If I'd had that kind of money I wouldn't be here in the first place. I whipped up a plan in my head. The two guys stood watching me; the jefe had his arms folded. I held the phone and tapped in the number of my Irish mobile phone, which had been seized by the cops at the airport.

'Hallo, this is Paul from BBL Plumbing. I'm not here at the moment to take your call, but if you would like to leave your name and number I will get back to you shortly.' That was my voicemail greeting. The pair leaned forward, listening in.

'Hi, this is Paul,' I said into my voicemail. In rapid English, with my strongest Dublin accent, I said, 'How-a-ya, Ma, Da, this is Paul. I need to organise 2,000 euro to be sent over to me.' The boss shoved a piece of paper in my hand. I read out the account details for a *banco* in Caracas. These guys were prepared. 'Make sure you get that to me as quick as you can,'

I added to the voicemail message I was leaving for myself, slowly this time. I stabbed at the call-end button and handed the phone back.

'I no understand,' said Nasal Voice. 'Very fast.' Great.

'I was just organising the money from my family,' I said.

Nasal Voice spoke to the wing boss, who looked at me. He seemed pleased and was probably spending the 2,000 euro in his head.

I walked around the narrow yard a bit to stretch my legs. I was exhausted from the day in the back of the jeep, driving here, there and everywhere. The hunger pains started gnawing at me again. My stomach started to contract and protest – probably wondering what the food strike was about. It was Tuesday evening. I worked out in my head it'd been five days since I'd eaten – my last meal was the steak sandwich at the airport the Friday before. Seemed like a distant memory now, both the food and getting caught with six kilos of cocaine.

In the wing, the boss and the lads started chopping meat and rattling pots and pans for dinner. I didn't have to wait long for mine. But rather than dining with the cellmates, the food came wrapped in tinfoil, shoved through the cell bars by one of the guards. I was delirious. I pulled back the wrapping. It was chicken mixed in with white rice. I sat down on the ground with Fulvio and started to eat. I gobbled up all the food. It tasted amazing, and I savoured the food in my mouth before swallowing, like I was eating the chicken for the first time in my life. Then I was sorry I'd eaten so quickly. I felt queasy. My stomach had obviously shrunk in the past five days without food.

Fulvio poured himself mango juice into a cup from a bottle the guards had put through the bars. He finished it in a couple of gulps and handed me the mug. I filled it up and downed some juice. My mouth felt like it was having a party with all the flavours after five days of a little water that tasted like it had been squeezed out of a sweaty towel.

Fulvio didn't speak English, but we chatted away and

developed a bond with gestures. It was good to connect with someone again. The two of us were just laughing all the time, and it was nice to be with someone outside the clique of the inmates in the wing. I could make out Fulvio was only a short-term inmate here.

Fulvio spoke away in Italian and Spanish, saying something about *policía* and making gestures towards the four lads who were cooking away on a two-hob stove in a small kitchenette. I could make out they were probably crooked cops or politicians or something. That was why they had the privilege of having their own food, which they stored in a fridge, and were locked up in a 'home-from-home' prison wing. The four of them ate together at a small table to the blare of televisions, one in each of the two main rooms and another in the corner. The boss and the others then connected a video game to the TV. They raced cars around a track while sitting on the lower bed of the bunks in one room. The cell boss, who Fulvio said was called Mario, waved at me to come over and join them. I was the flavour of the moment given that I'd bring in a windfall for him, he believed. Anyway, I waved him off – I hated computer games.

Fulvio gestured, asking why I was locked up here. '*Aeropuerto*,' I said to Fulvio, stretching out my arms like a plane. '*Drogas*.' But why I was locked up didn't need any further explanation. Fulvio knew the score. He said most gringos jailed in Venezuela were all in for the same thing: smuggling coke.

'*Todos*,' ('All') he said.

Afterwards, I took another stretch in the tiny yard. It was dark outside. I was ready to sleep. In the cell, Fulvio was pulling out a couple of thin mattresses and pillows that were kept in a large hole in the wall, doubled over. The four single beds, two in each room, were for the inmates higher up the pecking order. I rolled out the long, narrow mattress that was known as a *colchoneta*, which Fulvio had handed to me. I put it on the floor and lay down. Fulvio stretched out next to me.

There were four of us on the floor in all. I had my first proper sleep in days, my head propped up on a stained pillow that stank of sweat and piss.

* * *

'*Visita*,' a guard said to me, standing at the bars looking into the yard. '*Embajada*' ('Embassy'). Lovely jubbly; I'd been here a few days and now a diplomat had come to get me out of here. I allowed myself that giddy thought, knowing I wasn't going anywhere.

An old guy stood on the opposite side of the bars. He was in his late 60s, a small, tanned guy with a shock of white hair. 'Hello,' he said. 'My name is Richard McCabe. I'm the Irish consul. The Irish Embassy in Mexico, which deals with Venezuela, informed me you were here.' He spoke in an accent that wasn't Irish. More Yank than Paddy. Probably an Irish-American. 'I've been asked to drop in. How are they treating you, OK?' he said.

'I'm OK, yeah,' I said. 'I've had a bit of food here and I'm alive.' I didn't go into detail about being gang raped or cuffed to the stairs for days with no food in the drugs HQ. I knew our conversation wasn't private. A baboon-faced inmate with a machete tucked into his trousers stood next to me, the blade visibly poking out of his waistband, making both me and the consul nervous.

The visit was brief. He told me that there was nothing the Irish government could do for me, but that he would pass on legal papers and mail from my family. He would also call them and tell them how I was doing. So much for a lift home in the Irish government jet. The machete-wielding prisoner was on my side of the bars, but McCabe still seemed rattled. It looked to me like he was keen to leave.

I watched him rush off nervously from behind the bars. The consul didn't bring food, money, nothing – not that he had to. He stayed only a few minutes. The visit was a waste of time, really, but I didn't hold it against him for dashing off. I was grateful he would call my family. During our brief chat he also told me the Irish Department of Foreign Affairs in Dublin had been in touch with my family after being informed by Venezuelan officials I'd been arrested in Venezuela for drug smuggling.

* * *

Nasal Voice struck up a bit of a conversation in his poxy English. He was explaining that Macuto was a remand prison and the main jail where inmates were held was Los Teques, where he'd come from after spending years there. For what, I couldn't figure out. He made it clear the set-up here was a holiday camp compared to there. 'That big prison. I no like big prison. For me, very bad. I like here, Macuto.' I picked up he was at the end of his sentence and was on a day-release programme on which he studied English and other subjects in a nearby school.

The baboon-faced inmate walked in, sat down and spoke to the cell boss, looking over at me. He held a machete in his hand with a long, pointy blade. Fulvio later told me that was McKenzie. Why that was his name, I didn't know. I didn't imagine many Scots had set sail for the Caribbean shores of Venezuela. With his black skin, he certainly didn't look like his forefathers hailed from the rainy land where the sun came out less than in Ireland.

'Bad, bad man,' said Fulvio. McKenzie was the top-dog inmate in the prison cells in front I'd seen when I arrived, where the main body of inmates were held in decrepit conditions. At night you could hear screams and roars echoing around the wings. McKenzie was poking them with his trusted machete, I learned, spiking and stabbing at the inmates to keep them in check, and God only knows what else he did. I was off-limits, though; I could see the cell boss Mario talking and looking at me. I was the prize gringo prisoner, from whom he believed he'd get a big pay day down a Western Union cable. Later I'd learn that's why I'd been housed with this bunch, living in relative luxury compared to the rest of the jail. And McKenzie's reign over Macuto in the other two cell blocks, where about fifty prisoners were held, was infamous in the jail system.

* * *

Mario walked up to me, wagging his finger in my face. It was about a week after I'd arrived and, as I knew, not a red cent from me had hit his bank account. He looked pissed as he spoke. Nasal Voice gave me the rough translation. 'Money, no money come, Western Union.'

I shrugged. 'Mama, Papa, old,' I said, walking around the cell with an imaginary cane. 'Deaf, deaf,' I said loudly, pointing to my ear. I listened to Nasal Voice interpret and picked up the couple of words I knew. '*Padres . . . muy viejos,*' ('Parents . . . very old').

Mario handed me the mobile phone and I went through the motions again. I tapped out my Irish mobile phone number. My voicemail greeting started: 'Hallo, this is Paul from BBI. Plumbing . . .' I left myself another message. 'Look, Ma, Da, I really need this money – the 2,000 euro – please get it to me quickly.' Mario handed me the piece of paper with the banco details and I read them off again. I then said goodbye to my other self and hung up.

How long I'd get away with this act I didn't know, but I could see Mario was pissed off. McKenzie, who wandered in occasionally taking a break from his pastime of stabbing and cutting the mainstream inmates in the dungeon cells, sat there watching me. He was waving his machete in the air like a conductor in a symphony, pointing at me with the long blade.

'No,' said Mario, waving him off from chopping me into pieces. His hopes were still strong for the big pay day and getting 2,000 euro out of me. I had a plan: if my neck did ever end up on McKenzie's chopping block, I would offer Mario the coke I'd scooped up in the airport into the talcum-powder bottle. It was worth more than enough for a 'get-out-alive' card. In Ireland and the UK, some 300 g would fetch about 30,000 euro. Here, maybe a third of that, but still enough.

If that didn't work, I had Plan B: grabbing the machete off McKenzie if he went for me and stabbing him. I'd have to hurt him – and bad. So bad he'd have to be taken out of the jail and hospitalised. Otherwise, he'd come back gunning for me.

* * *

Myself and Fulvio hung around all day doing nothing much: sitting on the stone floor and talking, not really knowing what the other was saying. But his good humour kept me going when the prospect of eight years locked up in that country hung over me. He just sat there most of the time in howls of laughter. The evenings were similar. But on Saturdays the bosses played the video games incessantly for about 12 hours a day. They hooked the game console up to the TV and played in two teams in a baseball tournament, chalking up their points on a piece of paper with a marker. I'd roar out every few minutes, mimicking the English spoken in the game after one of them scored. 'Strike one' and 'home run' I'd shout out, to howls of laughter from Fulvio. They hadn't a clue what I was doing, glancing over at me with puzzled faces. After a while, Mario would make the shape of a gun with his hand, point it at me and go 'bang bang'.

* * *

I asked Nasal Voice for something to write on. 'Pen,' I said.

'Ah, yes, write, you write,' he said, soon getting me a pencil and a piece of paper. I sat on the floor scribbling furiously and started what would be the first entry in my diary. I wrote about getting caught at the airport and the first night at the drugs

HQ, and about what my family must have been thinking of me. What was I to them now? Drug-smuggler vermin? I also wanted to get something down for them in case anything happened to me and I never got home alive. The cell boyos looked over amazed as I scribbled away, absorbed in something as simple as a pencil and paper.

* * *

Mario stood in front of me again, with Nasal Voice in tow. It was my second week inside, and the wing boss wasn't pleased. Not a cent had landed in the Western Union account, obviously. He stood there saying, '*Otra llamada, otra llamada*' ('Another call, another call').

'No money, Western Union,' said Nasal Voice. 'You must pay for stay.'

'I'll do it again,' I said.

The boss shoved his mobile phone into my hand. I was ready to do my act in ringing my own mobile-phone number – but the boss had an ace up his sleeve. He handed me a piece of paper with another Irish number written on it. My eyes scanned left to right across '00 353', the Irish international code, then the '1' for Dublin. It couldn't be? I read on, and the other seven digits were the home phone number for my parents. I looked up at Mario. He was grinning. The gringo had been rumbled. There was nothing I could do but type in the phone number. My finger reluctantly prodded the rubber keypad. I didn't know what to think. I hadn't phoned my mother since I'd been caught. Although at 45 I was no kid, I knew both she and my father, in their 70s, would be sick with worry.

'My father, deaf, deaf, old,' I said to Nasal Voice, pointing at my ear in a valiant attempt to avoid making the call. Nasal Voice turned to Mario and I heard him say '*muy viejos*' ('very old'). It didn't matter, of course.

'Make call,' said Nasal Voice. I shrugged and rang the number.

'Hallo?' my father shouted, as he always did on the phone.

'Da, it's Paul,' I said, but sure enough he didn't hear me well.

'Who is it?'

'It's Paul, Da, it's Paul,' I shouted, while Mario and Nasal Voice stood there looking at each other as I roared into the phone.

'Ah, Paul, Paul,' he said. I heard him shouting for my mother. 'It's Paul. It's Paul.'

'Hallo,' my mother said.

'Hi, Ma, look, as you know I'm in jail in Venezuela. Sorry about this. Hopefully you can find it in your heart to forgive me.' God, what had I done to her?

'It doesn't matter. A mistake was made, a mistake was done,' she said in her typical forgiving way. 'Just as long as you're all right.' I could hear sadness in her voice, and it was hard. I felt a lump in my throat.

'Look, I'm going to have to read you out something,' I looked down at Mario's bank details. 'There's a couple of lads in here in the jail looking for money off me.' I read out the account number and address in Caracas, making sure to pepper my conversation with lots of 'Western Union' and '2,000 euro', the keywords the two clowns were listening out for. 'Just write that down, Ma.'

'What do you want me to do with this?' she said.

I replied in rapid English. 'Nothing, Ma, throw it away. I'm not paying these scum a penny.' I knew Mario and Nasal Voice wouldn't understand. I then hung up.

'I don't know. Very fast for me. I don't understand,' said Nasal Voice. My strategy seemed to have worked: Mario looked pleased, believing the money was coming down the line soon. My life was safe – for now.

I wondered how they had got my parents' Irish home phone number. It struck me that the only way could have been from the drug-squad officials in the airport from where I'd phoned my nephew. I had never written it down on any form. The airport officials must have colluded with the prison guards in Macuto for a slice of the gringo's dollars, along with the cell bosses. One big racket. The whole justice system seemed a joke.

* * *

Mario handed me his phone. '*Para ti, gringo*,' ('For you') he said. I thought this was odd. Who'd be calling me here?

'Yeah?' I answered.

'Paul, it's Paddy.' My brother, Jaysus.

'Where'd you get this number?'

'From Ma, they wrote it down after you phoned home. Listen, how are you?'

'I'm hanging in, grand.' There was no point in worrying anyone at home.

'I got a call from the British Embassy the other day. They phoned me to say, "We're sorry to inform you, but your brother Paul Keany has been arrested in Venezuela for the illegal importation of drugs."'

'No way.'

'Yeah, the other day.' Paddy lived in England, but how the British Embassy got his contact details I couldn't figure out. But great, I thought, I might be able to get the diplomatic clout of Mighty Blighty behind me; the Irish consul had made it clear that the Paddies had no power.

Mario was glaring at me. He was probably starting to wonder if I was playing him. I decided to hang up. 'Look, Paddy, I'd better go.'

'OK, Paul, stay as safe as you can.'

'I will.' It was great to talk to him but a hard reminder I was far from home.

* * *

Mario wasn't the only one trying to shake down the gringo

for money. I was called out for another *visita*. This time it was an *abogado*, or lawyer. I thought it odd; I hadn't asked for one. I lifted myself up off the stone floor in the wing where I was sitting with Fulvio, laughing at the wing boss racing his ice-cream truck again. We started to call him 'Super Mario' now, which, funnily, was the name of the video game.

Two funny-looking fat guys sat on the opposite side of the bars in the yard on a couple of plastic chairs the guards had put there for them. 'We come here today, myself and my brother, to offer you a proposition. For the modest sum of 10,000 euro, Ahmer and I can free you and you will be safely on your way home.' The pair came bearing gifts: a bag of food with some bread, cheese and ham. The man who had spoken pushed it through the bars, as well as soap and some toothpaste. I thought, ten grand, it's cheaper in a local supermarket. Anyway, I knew I'd get eight years in jail no matter what. 'We are already acting on behalf of another Irishman who is locked up in Los Teques prison.' I was dumbfounded. Another Paddy locked up in Venezuela? And a drug mule, no doubt.

The man explained he was an accountant and his brother was the lawyer but didn't speak English. The lawyer just sat there nodding his head, like a puppet on a string.

But I still knew these two were a pair of chancers; I could sniff it off them. 'Next,' I shouted out loud, so that the guard or whoever it was who was luring in the lawyers for the gringo gravy train in the hope of a commission could hear and not bother me again. I stood up while the pair looked at me in hope, waiting for an answer. I didn't reply. I stood up and walked away, making sure I took the gifts they brought to get me on board. I shared the food with Fulvio.

'*Muy bueno!*' ('Very good!') he said, nibbling away back in the wing.

Soon after, more lawyers came. All chancers. It was all the same story: 10,000 to 15,000 euro and I'd be on my way home. I told them all where to go. I just shouted 'next' out loud to the clown who was luring them in to me.

* * *

That night we had a few more bodies in the inn. I heard the door to the yard open and then voices. It was unusual for anyone to visit at this hour in the late evening. In stepped three fellas. One was a Mexican, the other was Venezuelan and the last was a guy from Costa Rica who spoke good English. 'Hi,' he said to me. He was chubby with a receding hairline, a jolly guy who I put down as about 40.

'How's it going?' I asked, and we chatted. He said he had been driving around with his car laden with coke after a pick-up along the coast when the cops swooped in.

'They were everywhere and came in shooting; someone must have tipped them off I had the drugs,' he said. His plans to board a flight to Holland later that night with some of the booty in his case had been thwarted.

Mario looked at myself and Costa Rica speaking English and had a brainstorm, seizing on the fact that there was another English speaker in the wing. Nearly two weeks had passed and he was still trying to squeeze me for cash, since not a cent had landed in his account. He spoke to Costa Rica, who interpreted for me.

'The boss says you are to call your family, he still hasn't got any money from you to Western Union. He says I make the call and give you the phone and I listen.'

'OK,' I shrugged, knowing there was nothing else I could do.

Mario handed Costa Rica his mobile phone. I watched him dial my parents' number, which was written on a piece of paper. 'Hallo, I am phoning from jail in Venezuela,' he said to whoever answered. I hoped it wasn't my mother, worried a gang of *asesinos* standing in a firing line were about to turn me into a watering can. 'I have Paul here and he is to talk to you,' said Costa Rica. Mario, Nasal Voice and all the newcomers leaned forward to listen in on the drama. Of course, none of them understood. Costa Rica handed me the phone.

'Hallo.' It was Mick, my nephew.

'Mick, it's Paul.'

'Alreet, Uncle Pauly, but what's going on?'

'Everything's OK, but just listen and write this down. These guys in jail are trying to get money out of me,' I said. Now, Costa Rica started reading off the bank account numbers from Mario's scrap of paper. I called them out.

'OK, Pauly, I have that.'

'Hold on a second, Mick.'

Costa Rica started talking to Mario, who started nodding what looked like approval. 'He says all OK.'

'Mick?' I spoke back into the phone.

'Yeah.'

'Don't bother sending it anyway.' I spoke in fast English, which I could see even Costa Rica didn't get. Anyway, he'd cottoned on quickly that the boss was trying to extort money from me. And I doubted he'd tell the boss my last flurry of words.

'What'll I do with the details?' said Mick.

'Throw them in the bin.'

'But will you be all right?'

'I'm a survivor. You know I am.' I could see I had to be in here.

* * *

The fat guard who'd poked his finger in my rear end stood at the cell door saying something to me about '*mañana*'.

'Tomorrow, my friend,' said Costa Rica, 'it looks like you go. To the big prison.' With Costa Rica interpreting, I got a bit of lowdown from Fulvio about Los Teques. That's where they said I was going. 'There are many Europeans speaking

English, Fulvio says. But it is very violent, a very strict and violent place.' Oh no, I thought. Fulvio took another sip of Coke and continued, Costa Rica interpreting his words. 'There is one special wing for the gringos. You can stay in this wing and get a job and be treated OK . . . and a woman director there is trying new things, mixing the Venezuelans with the gringos.'

I looked over at Nasal Voice. One of the guards was speaking to him and looking at me. Nasal Voice interpreted: 'He say tomorrow, go, to big prison. I tell you I no like big prison. Bad place. Bad people.' Mario looked up from racing his ice-cream truck and gave me a disapproving look. After three weeks he hadn't received a dime from me through Western Union. He must have known by now I'd played him with the calls. His face then softened into a smile. He spoke and started pointing at me. I guessed it was something like 'you have me', knowing it was game over with me in his bid to win the lottery.

The next morning it was confirmed. The fat guard walked into the poky cell where I was sitting on the stone floor chatting with Fulvio. 'Gringo, go, go.' I knew what he meant, so stood up and gathered my few bits and pieces. I shook hands with Fulvio. I wondered if I would see him again.

I pulled on my Irish rugby shirt with the logo of three small shamrocks on the breast. Maybe the 'luck o' the Irish' would work today? I picked up my sole possessions: a toiletry bag with a toothbrush and 'talc' powder. The guard handcuffed me and escorted me outside. I didn't know what to expect of the prison that awaited me. I presumed it'd be much like what I'd seen here. I'd be wrong.

A 'bus' was waiting in the yard: an army truck with rugged tyres and '*Militar*' written on the side. I stepped on. There were two guards cradling machine guns sat at the back.

'*Hola*,' said a girl, smiling, sitting handcuffed in one of the seats. I picked out that her name was Maria. She had a nice figure but a worn face, rough around the eyes with wrinkles like the grooves of a 7-inch record. Each one marking the hardships of her life, I imagined. There were also two male prisoners in separate seats. All spoke among themselves and with Maria. I sat there breathing in salt-tinged air, looking through the window as the truck roared through dusty side streets before heading out on the main coastal road.

After about two or three hours and a slow climb upwards for a few kilometres, the bus stopped on a ridge. Maria stood up from her seat, then bent over and gave me a kiss on the cheek, and to the others too. She'd bonded with us all on our journey into the next stage of our lives imprisoned in Venezuela. I watched her being escorted off the bus, walking with a sense of surrender – a woman who had given up whatever fight she'd had. I wondered how many guards would rape her, pounding into her, foreheads gleaming with sweat. Another groove notched up around Maria's eyes. More like an LP now than a 7-inch single.

Chapter 6

LOS TEQUES: AN EXPLOSIVE START

SOLDIERS STOOD IN WATCHTOWERS NEXT TO HEAVY MACHINE GUNS proppedup on tripods. A high wall stretched around the grey building topped with coils of barbed wire. A barrio of crudely built houses to the right. Tin roofs pinned down with bricks and old tyres.

This was the view from the military bus. It rumbled along a narrow road where piles of rubbish had gathered along the edge and plastic bags flapped on bushes. I was looking out the front, then swivelling my head around to catch glimpses through the dirty window at the back. Barbed wire. Soldiers. It had to be the jail, but I wasn't sure.

The bus braked to a halt. A line of traffic was held up behind. Horns beeped like a brass band warming up. The driver didn't care and took his time doing a three-point turn. Steel gates opened up at the entrance to the building and we took a sharp right into a narrow driveway. When we stopped I could see the prison a bit better. What struck me first was that it didn't look that big. It was a wide, squat building with two floors. The 'ya-ya-ya-hoohhh' wails echoed out. The prison cry I was now familiar with. I felt like McMurphy in *One Flew Over the Cuckoo's Nest*. But this place didn't look like any hospital behind bars. I didn't see myself doing time here in comfort, the only catch being I'd spend my days with loonies.

I looked up and saw barred windows stretched across a floor above. Arms and hands dangled out. Hundreds of faces were pressed up to the bars, eyes peering down at us. Whistling started, then piped up. The new fish had arrived. We were probably a welcome source of relief from their boredom.

A group of soldiers stood ahead in the driveway. National Guard troops. A guard barked orders. I followed Tubby and the other prisoner. We stepped down off the bus. The guard uncuffed us and we were shoved into an office in a little concrete hut with a dirty-green tin roof. The officer read names from a list. 'Pa-uwww-l Keany,' he pronounced my name.

'*Sí*,' I said, and he ticked a document on a clipboard in his hand.

The other two inmates were ordered one by one down into a narrow alleyway behind the office. I stood in the office, clutching my plastic bag. I had butterflies in my stomach. But I was more worried about the guard finding coke in the talc bottle than the prison.

It was my turn. I copied the others and stripped off, scattering my clothes into a loose pile next to me. I no longer cared about being naked in front of guards. The guard then ordered me down the alley. It was strewn with rubbish and stank of piss. Bend over. Legs apart. He gave me a good look over. No finger in the rear end, or worse. I then felt a shove and stood up. The guard gave me a quick nod back to my clothes. I put on my trousers. He then reached into my pocket, took a bundle of scrunched-up notes and put them in his own. Bastard.

A cop rattled keys. A barred gate opened. A cop escorted us through a dark passageway into the jail. Prisoners were walking around dressed in shorts and vests. Blank stares. Eyes glazed. All like zombies. Now I was really feeling like McMurphy. Where was Nurse Ratched?

In an office to the right there were about ten men – well turned out in pleated trousers and smart shirts. All seated at desks. Prison admin staff, I thought. I later found out they were inmates, but high up the prisoner pecking order, and mostly gay.

LOS TEQUES: AN EXPLOSIVE START

The three of us stood there – me, Tubby and the other, who said he was '*colombiano*'. A foreigner, like me, but he was closer to home. Another eight or nine inmates stood near the wall, some hunched down on the floor. It looked like they were being processed as well. One of them was a young guy on his hunkers, singing non-stop and whistling. It was like a bird call. He was blind, or at least visually impaired, his eyes half closed, eyelashes flickering. Everyone was cracking up laughing at him – the office workers, the whole lot. They acted like they knew him – he was probably a repeat offender. I couldn't make out if he was mad or just didn't care about going to jail.

The other inmates filed out after being processed. Fingerprinted and photographed. Now it was our turn. I stepped forward with the other two. One of the admin boys yapped away in Spanish. I shrugged. Tubby and the Colombian were probably giggling to themselves at the gringo – facing up to eight years in jail in a country where he didn't speak the lingo. They'd be right to. I picked out that the wing we'd be jailed in was 'Maxima'. Tubby's face dropped. Jesus, why? 'Maxima' must be some sort of maximum-security wing for hardened criminals and Pablo Escobar-style drug lords. Good God, what horrors lay ahead?

We stayed in the office for hours and hours, waiting – for what I didn't know. Later, a worker gave us a packet of plain crackers and a *cafecito* – a small plastic cup of sweet black coffee. I thought this place mightn't be so bad after all. I was wrong.

After a while a European inmate walked into the office. His name was Peter, a German in his 40s. 'Hi,' he said, shaking my hand. 'I was told to come down and be your interpreter.' He had a couple of days' stubble, wore glasses and had a balding head of grey hair, like a horseshoe shape marked onto the top of his head.

'None of these fucks speak English,' I said.

'I know, I've been told to help.' The admin guy started

talking to Peter. 'What colour are your eyes?' said Peter.

'Blue,' I said.

Peter translated, '*Azul.*' And then the usual questions I was used to: 'What's your name?' It was more like getting signed up for a dating site than enrolling for eight years in jail. 'What about your weight, what is it?' A lot less than it was three weeks ago, but I decided not to say that.

'Thirteen stone,' I said.

'Height?' said Peter. He seemed to be enjoying the diversion in his day.

There was nothing to measure or weigh me, it was all a joke.

'How old are you?'

'Forty-five,' I said. And so on. I was then fingerprinted and photographed. Then the guy firing off questions spoke to Peter. It looked like he was telling him to push off.

When we stepped into the passageway, one of the prison guards, who were all dressed in navy-blue uniforms, spoke to him. He nodded at my dark-blue slacks. They hadn't been quite pressed and clean since the day I'd walked into Simón Bolívar airport more than three weeks ago. Now they were scruffy with dust marks and crumpled. 'Hey, man, he says you have to give up your trousers later. They're too like what the cops wear,' said Peter.

'What?' I said. I thought he was joking.

'You can't wear dark clothes,' he said. 'They're afraid one of us might escape dressed in them at night.' Great, I thought, I'm only in the door and the guards have lifted my cash and my trousers. 'I'll see you around,' he then said, and left. He looked sad to go. And although I was dying to know more about the jail, I wasn't in the mood for chit chat.

Myself and the two other new fish were led back into the dark passageway outside. More lost, tortured souls wandered around: inmates with vacant eyes, probably off their heads on drugs. We stopped and waited for a tall barred gate to open. A guard stood up, a truncheon hanging from his belt. Keys rattled in the lock. A passageway lay ahead. I could smell dampness. We walked through. There were three doors close together at the end of the corridor. Eyeballs peered out of spyholes and followed me, like you see in paintings in haunted-house movies. On the right at the end of the passageway, the guard banged out against the door with his baton. Three hollow knocks. An eyeball peeped out at us through a spyhole; then another at the bottom of the door. I heard a bolt sliding back. The door opened, and we stepped into a wing.

The guard left. The door shut behind us.

No turning back.

It looked like I was in some kind of recreation area in a narrow hall about 20 ft long. A high, bare concrete ceiling. A battered fridge in one corner. Guys sat around on wooden benches and stools watching a blaring telly. Daylight streamed in from a door at the other end of the hall. There were laughs and jokes at us, the new arrivals. One inmate ran up, grabbed the plastic bag from my hand and ran off. I didn't take the bait and chase him, even though I was conscious I had a talc bottle full of coke that I could deal out for a few quid. Anyway, my cool-headedness might be a life-saver in here. Minutes later the thug came and gave it back to me, looking half sorry.

The prisoners were all dressed casually: jeans, T-shirts, vests, runners and flip-flops. They were talking excitedly among themselves, probably about the newbies. I hadn't a clue what they were saying. One of them pointed to an area to the left at the front of the hall. '*Por allá, por allá,*' ('In there, in there') he said. We walked down a short passageway. It was dark. No daylight – just a couple of bulbs giving out weak light. We stepped into a cell, which was bare but for a couple of beds and a toilet at the back. I could see it was just a hole in the floor, and there was a pipe sticking out of the wall for a shower.

A 'reception party' awaited us: a big black guy and another couple of prisoners in shorts and vests. One was a tall black man, bald. He was dressed in a nice shirt, Levi's jeans and Nike runners. He stood in the background and didn't speak, but he had an air of authority. The giggles and chatter among the prisoners stopped. The mood was sombre and heavy. I had been pretty cool, but now I was getting worried.

The boss started reading out the rules. Their rules, not the prison's. The tall black guy held an automatic weapon in his hand. Another had what looked like a .38 revolver, waving it around and pointing it at us. Staring at us, he was a slimy little fucker, grinning ear to ear. He opened the chamber to show us it had a full round of bullets, then pushed it back in and started pointing the barrel at us again. I couldn't believe what I was seeing. How could prisoners have guns? Fulvio never warned me about this.

After the boss finished his spiel, the Colombian and Tubby walked off. The gun-toting prisoners gestured for me to stay. Then into the cell stepped another black guy.

'I'm Mike, now listen up, dude,' he said in perfect English with a New Yawk accent. 'These guys are the bosses. They tell you what you can do and can't do in here.'

I nodded.

'If there's a curtain pulled over the toilet you can't enter,' started Mike. 'You have to pay an entrance fee of 1,000,000 bolos [about 200 euro] to stay here and after that 20,000 [about 4 euro] a month. That's for the causa, the cause, the money we use to protect you from other prisoners who'll want to kill you, and keep the wing going in good shape, painting and cleaning.'

Kill me? Jesus. After that, Mike's words were all going over my head. My eyes just darted back and forth to the revolver waving at me, the slimy fuck still spinning the chamber and pointing the silver barrel at me. What the fuck was going on here? What were they doing with guns? It didn't make sense.

'You do roll call twice a day,' continued Mike, explaining that the guards would enter the wing twice a day to do a headcount, 'and you have to call out your number . . . Cook your own food if you have any; if not, there's a shop. You don't go out into other wings alone without protection from us or you'll be killed by the prisoners there. And don't ever look at a woman who comes in for a visit.' If I wasn't sure what would happen if I broke the rules, Mike put me straight. 'You'll learn fast in this place or you're dead.'

* * *

I walked out into the yard. Some of the inmates lazed about, sitting on 'buckets': empty Castrol oil cans and paint tins. Others paced back and forth taking exercise in the yard. It was basically an oblong area about 20 ft by 80 ft, which they called the patio. It was surrounded by high walls, beyond which neighbouring wings were housed. Half the open roof area was covered with a grey tarpaulin held up by a mish-mash of wires drilled into the wall. There was an area sectioned off with corrugated iron to the right, which was a makeshift kitchen with a two-ring stove where a guy was cooking; another man was standing nude, showering with water from a pipe sticking out of the wall.

A guy walked over to me. He was pale, dark-haired and slim and a bit smaller than me. 'Hey, where are you from?' he said, making conversation, since I stood wearing my green Irish rugby shirt with shamrocks.

'Ireland,' I said. 'I'm a new arrival.'

'I'm Edward, or Eddy they call me,' he said, 'from Manchester. What you in for?'

'Carrying cocaine. Caught at the airport.'

'Just like me,' smiled Eddy. 'I didn't even make it to the check-in desk.' I looked at him: his head was a bit like a pincushion, with piercings on his nose, ears and lower lip. He also had tattoos: two dragons breathing flames on the back of his hands and his name tattooed letter by letter on the knuckles on each hand. I imagined him walking through customs carrying his suitcase, sending off warning signals to the cops.

A few of the Venezuelan inmates came up to me, knowing straight away what the gringo was banged up for. I understood them from the few words I'd learned. '*Maleta . . . cuántos kilos?*' ('Suitcase . . . how many kilos?') asked one.

'Six,' I said, holding up that number of fingers.

'Don't mind those Veno lags. Morons,' said Eddy. 'Now,' he continued, 'here's how it works here. You get money, and you get money quick. To pay your rent so the bosses will protect you. That's how you'll survive.' He said I'd have to get someone from back home to wire the 200-euro payment to the bosses through Western Union. It was a bargain compared to the 2,000 euro the crooked cops wanted from me in Macuto. 'And get yourself a bucket – it's where you store your valuables, clothes and toiletries – everything. Nobody will steal your stuff or they get a beating from the bosses. You'll also need it to sit down on.'

'The bosses?'

'The guys you just met in the cell. Fidel, the jefe, he's a cunt. Then there's Carlos, the tall baldy guy, and the *luceros*.' He nodded to the prisoners walking around with knives. 'Those scum,' he said. 'They're the eyes of the bosses when the jefes are inside in the cells bagging coke or beating up some poor bastard. They'll try to wind you up, run away with food or take your cigarettes. Don't react. They're not allowed to touch you, but they'll squeal you out to the bosses and they'll give you a beating.'

An explosion suddenly boomed inside the jail. God, what was that? The sound was muffled, absorbed by the walls in the prison by the time it hit the yard where we stood. Inmates huddled together. Worried faces. The prisoner bosses ran about, their guns drawn: revolvers, automatic weapons and shotguns. They closed the main door to the yard. Mobile phones started ringing. Bosses shouted into them. I stood there, shocked. The explosion didn't sound like there was construction work going on or something; it was more like a bomb. But it couldn't be, surely?

'Could be a grenade,' said Eddy, who didn't seem bothered by the commotion. 'The bosses here, they've more weapons than the army outside. Enough for a small war.' Calm started to settle over the yard. Eddy interpreted the flurry of Spanish between the prisoners in the yard. 'Looks like some guy blew himself up with a grenade,' he laughed, 'by accident.' This place was getting worse.

Minutes later, shouts of 'Wendy, Wendy' volleyed back and forth.

'That means it's dinner time,' said Eddy.

'Why?'

'Wendy's, the fast-food chain. They think the word means food in English.'

There was a mad clatter of cups, bowls, plates and cutlery. It was early evening now. 'It's time to chow down,' said Eddy. He said twice a day we'd eat in the *rancho grande*, or the big canteen. 'You'll have to eat out of the trays they give you. You've only got five minutes in there. Get yourself something to eat out of for the next time so you can bring the food back to the yard.'

I followed the others out into the passageway. There was a concrete stairwell on the left, bits of rubble scattered about. I saw a pool of dark blood on the floor and red splashes on the wall. I walked past a room on the right that looked like an infirmary, with a plinth inside. There was no sign of a body covered with a sheet. Whatever had happened to the guy who blew himself up, he wasn't getting medical attention. He was probably in a bucket now. I didn't care; I was starving and wanted to eat. So did the other inmates. One by one we stepped over pieces of bone, sinew and spongy stuff that was probably brain matter – all the leftovers of a rushed clean-up job.

The rancho grande was a massive hall with long stone benches and stone seats. Nothing that could be picked up. Bits of rice and other food were scattered around the floor in the canteen. I stood in the queue. In front of me I met a guy called Ricardo, from Holland. He was a giant of a guy, about 6 ft 4 in. and muscular, with tight, curly hair. He said his mother was Colombian and his father Dutch. He filled me in about Wendy. 'Get yourself a plate and cutlery so you can take food back to the wing and eat in peace – otherwise you have to eat here and they'll rush you out quickly.'

At the top of the line I was given a steel tray, with the shapes of a bowl and plate carved into it. Two dollops of food: rice and sardines. A kitchen worker handed the tray back to me across a counter. I walked over and stood beside one of the benches, put my feet on one of the stone seats and ate. I picked the food up with my fingers, shovelling it into me. It didn't taste like much, but I was starving. I watched others eat with their improvised tools: plastic Coke bottles cut in half to scoop up the food.

Minutes later the luceros walked into the rancho, yelling. It was time to go. Everyone moved swiftly. No one dared argue with them.

In the wing, all the talk among the lags out in the yard was about the explosion. 'He blew himself up with the grenade, it's definite they say,' said Eddy, speaking excitedly. He seemed to be enjoying the explosive antics in the jail.

Another guy came over and stood next to Eddy. He was Silvio, an Italian. He had sallow skin and brown eyes and looked to be in his early 30s. 'One of the prisoners,' he said in good English, 'he was on his way up to the roof. Put it in his pocket and the pin popped out by accident.' Silvio was a nervous-looking character, and gave me a warning. 'My friend, Paul, be aware and be on your guard all the time. This is a crazy place.'

'I can see that.'

'Paul, you can get coke here,' he said. 'It'll help you through your time.'

'I don't do coke.'

'What do you mean you don't do coke? What were you getting on the plane for if you don't do coke?' he said, laughing and looking at Eddy.

'For the money.'

'OK,' he shrugged, 'whatever you want.'

All of a sudden a lanky fellow started walking around barking orders, shouting, 'Colchoneta, colchoneta.' I didn't understand but had enough cop-on to know it was something to do with bedding. We were standing there in the yard under a dark sky.

The wing burst into a hive of activity. I was standing in the yard looking inside. I hadn't had a detailed tour of Maxima yet but could make out that it was made up of three cells. From the yard I could see down into cell two, where inmates were climbing up on a storage area, which was a ledge sticking out from the wall. They were pulling cushions and firing them onto the floor and at whoever walked by.

The tall fellow, who was about 6 ft 3 in. and thin as a rake, was shouting 'colchoneta'. He walked towards me. I was standing next to the Colombian guy who had been on the bus with me. The tall guy babbled in Spanish. It was all double-Dutch to me. I stood there shrugging my shoulders and holding my arms out, smiling. I didn't know what else to do. I looked around, but there was no sign of Eddy or Silvio to help me interpret. Everyone was toing and froing with the cushions and knew exactly what to do – except for me and this Colombian. At least he spoke the lingo. The tall guy gave up on me when he realised he might as well be talking to a chair and turned and spoke to the Colombian, but he glanced at me too when he spoke. At least I think he did: his head and right eyeball were animated and moving as he spoke, but his left eye was rigid, the pupil staring straight ahead towards the wall. It was obviously a glass eye; it looked like a marble had been shoved into his eye socket and held in with glue.

'That's Canario, he'll sort you out,' Eddy shouted over, a cushion under his arm. The tall fellow in front of me was named after his homeland, like many of the others. He was from the Canary Islands.

The Spaniard shoved a 'mattress' at the Colombian and

nodded at me. It was a long, thin, dirty-orange cushion, about an inch thick and just wide enough for one. I followed the Colombian through the hallway leading into the wing. As I walked by the cells I snatched glances inside. The beds were a mixture of bunks and singles. There must not have been enough: fellows were putting their colchonetas on the floor.

In the hallway, the Colombian put the colchoneta on the ground next to the wall on which a giant flatscreen TV was blaring. A few others did too, bedding down next to us. Colombiano then got down on the floor, stretched out on the colchoneta and pulled a large scarf or sheet around him, which he used like a shawl. The 'mattress' was only big enough for one. How was this going to work? I thought. He turned on his side and pointed to the other half of the cushion. That was my bed. I slipped out off my dress shoes and lay down next to him on the giant sponge, pulling a small towel I'd taken from Macuto around me. The 'mattress' smelled like cat's piss. Four or five others were squeezed onto a colchoneta next to us. There'd be no rolling over onto the other side. If I ever found the moggie that was pissing on the cushions I wouldn't get to swing it very far.

I was exhausted. I'd been on the go from about five in the morning, bussed halfway across the coast of Venezuela and then dumped here in the 'big prison', Los Teques. I hadn't even been here a full day, but I'd had a revolver waved at me and walked through flesh and bone in the corridor after a lag blew himself up with a grenade. I didn't know what to think of the place. But I certainly had time to do so.

Sleep was far away. The TV was on over my head, and there were noises from a few prisoners sitting on a bench behind us, snorting and laughing. My thoughts were going through the usual cycle about the botched drug run. Forty-five years of age – what was I thinking? And for ten grand? What would Katie do when she found out her da was locked up for drug smuggling in South America? And my parents, in their 70s, would I see them again? Right then, I decided I would do everything I could to get out of this place. I was looking at eight years. I'd be 53 or 54 if I did my full time. But I remembered the lawyer in the court saying it was possible to get parole after a couple of years. I vowed I would. I couldn't spend eight years of my life here. I'd rather die.

Hours later I dozed off to the chorus of a fellow shouting, '*Pantry solo, todo bien*' ('Hallway clear, all good'). A few hours later a different prisoner started the same chant. They seemed to be taking turns on sentry duty at the wing door, peering out through bars into the corridor outside. What they were watching for I didn't know. I soon would.

Chapter 7

BEHIND THE CURTAIN

I WOKE UP TO THE ROARS OF THE WING HENCHMEN SHOUTING AT THE inmates to wake them. I sat up. My body ached from a night on the hard floor on a thin cushion, but I was getting used to sleeping like this. Soft light poured in at the opposite end of the hallway, replacing the grey gloom that was there the night before. I was exhausted. It was like I'd only just put my head down. That's because I barely had. It was only dawn. I stood up and stretched. All the other inmates were busying about rolling up their colchonetas and tying them up with string. The Colombian did the same with the one we had slept on. The 'mattresses' were then all stored on the high ledge in cell two.

I walked into the yard. Some inmates were queuing up for the toilet and washroom at the far wall on the right. Showers were the manual sort: two drums of water stood in the corner and a plastic bowl floated on top. You dipped the bowl into what was once an oil barrel, threw the water over your head and let it roll over your body. There were a good few in the queue, wearing shorts and flip-flops, carrying towels, T-shirts and whatever else to dry themselves with. I didn't bother with the wait. I just walked over to a rusty tap sticking out of the wall, turned it on and splashed water on my face. There was no sign of a mirror so I had no idea what I looked like. I could feel the bristles on my face, though; I hadn't shaved for a couple of days.

I saw Eddy in the yard, drying his hair with a T-shirt. 'Sleep well?' he smiled.

'Like a baby, yeah,' I laughed.

'Don't worry, you get used to the floor.' It felt great again to have a native English speaker to talk to, and Eddy seemed like a good guy.

Soon after, there was a scramble for the wing door. I followed Silvio, Eddy and Ricardo out into the passageway. The blood splatters on the wall and the pool of blood from the night before were gone. In their place was the smell of disinfectant. We passed by the Number 7 wing door on the left. Arms hung out, dirty hands holding cups, rattling against bars. They were like monkeys in a zoo. For security reasons only one wing went to the rancho at a time. Just as well.

'If we all went at the same time there'd be war,' said Eddy. 'A bloodbath.'

I kept my distance, standing well clear of their cell door. Two prison cops sat slumped in chairs, cigarettes dangling from their lips. A couple of the luceros from Maxima stood in the corridor, knife handles sticking out of their waistbands. They were our real protection, I could see, our hired muscle paid for with the causa money.

In the rancho, breakfast was being dished out by the kitchen workers – prisoners from other wings. I stood in the queue. An *arepa*, like a small pancake made from cornflour, was plonked onto one of the plastic trays and handed to me. Another worker was pouring coffee into cups he was placing on a tin counter, and I picked one up. Silvio and Ricardo and most of the others had their own cups and plates. They headed back to the wing with their food. I stood by a stone bench and peeped inside one of the arepas. It was filled with sardines, or at least I presumed that's what it was – flat slivers of grey flesh that smelled of fish. It looked awful, but I was starving. I gobbled it down with gulps of milky, sweet coffee.

* * *

In the yard, I could see others weren't bothered with the rancho. One prisoner was eating fried eggs.

'That's Roberto,' said Silvio, seeing me looking at him dining in style.

'Sí, Paul, my name Roberto,' he said. Roberto had a trimmed moustache and eyebrows that grew together slightly in the middle. He was Italian, like Silvio. 'I speaking English,' he added. Everyone laughed.

'He likes prison life in style,' said Silvio. 'Pays people to do his cooking.' It seemed that if you had money you could live better here – even if you were still locked up.

* * *

The wing after breakfast was in spring-clean mode. Cups and plates were washed and stored away. Bottles of bleach were poured over the yard. Buckets were filled with water and whooshed over the area. Floors were swept and scrubbed. Rubbish was gathered up in the cells and tidied away. It was a big clean-up. The *tobos*, or buckets, the used paint tins where the inmates kept their possessions, were all picked up and stored down at a back wall in a corner next to the toilet; some were shoved under a stone ledge where there was a little two-hob stove with a jumble of electric wires trailing from the back of it. The whole sight reminded me of a painter's yard.

The cleaning didn't stop there. The lags were also giving themselves a good spruce-up. Shorts and vests were ditched in favour of jeans or slacks and long-sleeved shirts. I also watched one fella putting gel into his hair, using a broken piece of jagged glass as a mirror.

Silvio walked by carrying his tobo.

'What's the story here?' I said.

'Visit day. Wednesdays, Saturdays and Sundays.'

'Who's going to visit me here?' I laughed.

'Like me, nobody. Our place is over there.' He nodded over to the corner. There was a guy taking down a plastic washing line that hung from one side of the yard to the other. There were clothes hanging on it yesterday – now it had another purpose. The guy lifted one side of the line down off a hook on the wall and started threading it through the hoops of a plastic curtain. He hung it back up and it stretched across a small area in the yard. A floral pattern in full bloom on a white background.

'*Verde. Verde*,' shouted a lookout man at the wing door, peeping through a spyhole into the passageway outside.

'That's the troops,' said Eddy. 'Time for the "*número*".' The *verde* (green) was the nickname they gave the National Guard soldiers in their olive-green uniforms. The prisoners then scurried about taking a seat around the entire perimeter of the yard wall, sitting down on any free tobo they could get. A little black and white dog was also scampering around, a mongrel of a sheepdog that seemed to belong to one of the inmates. By the time I copped on to what to do there weren't any buckets left to sit on. I quickly walked over to Eddy and sat down on my hunkers next to him.

Five National Guard troops marched in through the wing door. They fanned out across the yard, cradling pump-action shotguns. The barrels pointed toward the ground but not so low that they couldn't be lifted in an instant to blast out a few rounds.

I looked at the other inmates. Some were half sleeping, slouched over, dozing; a few looked like they'd topple over. It was only about 6 a.m. I looked over at the wing boss and his henchmen. There were none of the inmates' guns in sight, probably hidden now.

But the troops were on guard, edgy. Eyes darted back and forth at us. Two of them faced the wall where myself and Eddy sat; the other two faced the other wall on the other side of the yard, keeping guard on the inmates there. All angles covered. I was starting to get the idea of who was afraid of who around here.

'They're going to call our numbers,' Eddy said to me. 'If you fuck up the number, they'll fuck you up.' I knew the score from Macuto and from the headcount the evening before but still couldn't say my number.

'I don't speak Spanish.'

Eddy came to the rescue. 'I'll shout you. Piece of piss.'

'What'll I do?'

'Nothing. As I said, keep quiet and leave it to me.'

A prison cop started the headcount. He didn't waste a second, beginning at one end of the line of inmates, pointing his finger at the first prisoner.

'*Uno,*' said the first prisoner. A National Guard, an old guy, ticked off a sheet attached to a clipboard he held.

'*Dos,*' said the second inmate. And so on down the line. The cop was getting closer to me. I was getting edgy. '*Treinta-cinco,*' ('35') said Eddy. He then put his hand on my head and said to the guard '*treinta-seis*' ('36'). It went around the yard till the last man. I didn't understand the numbers, but it looked like there were easily more than a hundred inmates in the count. I wondered where they'd all come from. There hadn't seemed to be more than about 50 the night before. The wing didn't look like it could hold more than that.

With the headcount over the troops then pulled out, walking backwards nervously towards the wing door, shotgun barrels dangling in mid-air.

The door slammed. '*Luz, luz,*' shouted one of the luceros, swinging around a knife tied to his wrist.

'That means a "light",' said Silvio. 'Stand still, face the back wall and don't move. I'll tell you about it all later.'

I stood there along with all the other inmates, staring down at the back wall of the yard. A door behind us leading into the cells slammed shut. Silence fell over the yard. A second ago it was full of life: people joking and laughing. Now everyone was still, like when you freeze-frame a video and see the characters stop moving. I could hear other sounds more clearly now: bongos being drummed in a wing above the yard, over our hallway area – *doom-da-da-doom* – along with a hypnotic chant the prisoners there were singing. It sounded like a prayer, followed by loud applause. I felt like I was in a gospel church in Harlem. The sounds from that wing were quickly drowned out. A stereo in our wing started up. Salsa music kicked off. Trumpets and other brass instruments tooting away. It was deafening. The whole thing was weird. I felt like I'd walked into the Copacabana in full swing, only to have a doorman walk up to me with a knife and tell me to 'shut up and stand still'.

'Normal,' shouted a lucero after about 15 minutes, hollering over the din of the music. Everyone was at ease after playing statues. I turned around and the luceros stood there with knives. The highlites were the second in command to the boss and were standing alongside him, all tooled up for a small war. Revolvers. Shotguns. Automatic weapons. Pistols and DIY guns that looked like they were made out of pipes. They were all done up to the nines, too, in trousers, nice shirts and polished shoes.

Silvio must have read the puzzled look on my face. 'The luz, it means light in Spanish. It means something has come to light, to the bosses' attention. And that means we have to go to the yard, stand still or sit down and face the back wall.'

'For what?'

'So they can get their guns and ammo out of their hiding places. Holes in the ground, all over the place.'

Plastic chairs that had been stacked three or four high were then taken down and spread out across the yard area, a row each against the two longer walls in the rectangular yard; two rows were also set up in the middle. All in all there were enough chairs to seat about 40 or 50. I could now see why some of them called the yard the 'patio'.

'Let's go, behind the curtain,' said Silvio. 'That's our place for the day.'

I walked in and sat down on a paint bucket. Eddy and Silvio sat next to me, and Ricardo a couple of buckets down next to a few Venezuelans. Grown men forced to sit on paint buckets behind a flowery curtain. It was mad. 'Nice day for a sit-in,' I laughed.

'Yes, and all day to do it, Paul,' said Silvio.

'How long does it last for?'

'Seven, seven and a half hours. Till about 3.30.'

I guessed it was about 10 am. 'How do we fill the time?'

'Sit and stare into space,' laughed Eddy. 'If you've no visitors you're not allowed out to the yard. Not unless someone with a visit invites you, and then you have to be dressed right. Jeans or trousers, no shorts, and a long-sleeved top.'

'It's the *familia*, Paul,' said Silvio. 'The family, it is sacred in Venezuela. It is held in the utmost respect. That's why the prisoners dress up and clean up the wing.'

Ricardo was sitting on a paint tin, flexing his muscles. He seemed to keep to himself.

'And don't ever stare at anyone's bird, mate. Don't even make eye contact,' said Eddy. 'Do and you're dead.' He made a gun sign with two fingers pointed at his head.

'What?'

'It's considered a lack of respect. Men have been shot for doing it.' I made a mental note not to eye anyone's bird. 'At the very least you'll get a luz. You'll get called into the boss's cell for a beating.'

I changed the subject. I was full of questions. Nothing here made sense to me. 'The guns, I don't get it. How do they have guns?'

'Most are courtesy of the National Guard,' said Silvio. 'Most of the home-made ones are called pipe guns and made by Vampy, one of the prisoners. He's a dab hand with a metal file and a solder.' Los Teques was getting more bizarre by the moment.

'Without them and their guns it'd be worse,' said Eddy. 'Other wings would storm in and shoot us up. Some of them hate gringos. Here in Maxima they don't care what you are as long as you pay the causa. Gays. Paedos. Rapists. They're all here, mate, take your pick.'

'And the causa?'

'The causa, cash so they can tool themselves up. They smuggle in coke and sell it to us at extortionate prices.' He laughed. 'They even use the money to buy paint and give the walls a makeover.'

Behind the curtain I could hear the shuffle of chairs and the smell of food wafting in, like chicken and what I thought was beef stew, that the visitors had brought in. I craved good food. I hadn't eaten a proper bite since the boyos in Macuto had fed me well, hoping to win the lottery off me down a Western Union cable.

The music was still blaring. I wanted to know why. 'That's to drown out the wails of them all shagging in the cells,' said Eddy.

'You're joking me?'

'No. In the cells. They hang sheets up around the beds. Bit of privacy. You bring your girl in and wey-hey. They take turns with the beds. The *chicas* can scream away in orgasmic excitement. No one can hear.' This place was getting more off the wall.

My thoughts suddenly darkened and I went quiet. The memories of that night in the drug-police building flowed back. The bugger squad. Would it be the same here?

I returned to staring at the wall, shifting left to right on the paint bucket when one side of my arse went numb. Other than that the only relief from the boredom was a trip to the toilet to our right. I heard some of the Venezuelan lads in there, snorting and giggling. Others sat snoring on their buckets, blankets over their heads. Exhausted from no sleep, like me. As usual I started wondering how I was going to stick this place for eight years, and the madness of it – inmates walking around with guns and orgies in the cells with their girlfriends and wives. Lunacy. A circus behind bars.

* * *

The boys in green marched into the yard for the evening

headcount, looking more vigilant this time – probably worried one of the inmates had sneaked out the gate with the missus. There was a woman with them. A bottle blonde. She had long, wavy hair, tied up and with yellow curls dangling around her forehead. She wore tight jeans and had a pair of high black boots up to her knees. To me, she looked more like a bird out on the pull than a prison director.

'Who's that?' I whispered to Eddy.

'Director, mate. Top dog.'

The cop started the count. At my turn, Eddy clapped me on the shoulder and shouted out my number, which changed depending on where I was sitting in the row of inmates. Nelson Mandela may have been prisoner number 46664 in all his years in jail, but in Los Teques your number was one higher than the lag on your left. Prison order Venezuelan-style.

* * *

The next morning it was time for Spanish classes. I didn't have to go, but it was a chance to get out of the wing. And I knew knowing more than *hola* and *cerveza* would be useful. Not that I cared to talk with Venezuelans. I hated them, for what the bugger squad had done to me. I hadn't really met a good Venezuelan yet. But I knew the lingo would come in handy.

The classroom was on the second floor. It was my first time anywhere outside Maxima and the canteen. Most of the administration offices were here. Prison workers such as secretaries were typing away, hunched over keyboards. Silvio had told us we had to scrub up a bit for this part of the jail. He usually looked like a tramp himself in a vest and shorts, but he had now smartened up into a shirt, jacket and shoes. Roberto, the other Italian, wore pressed trousers and a shirt – and I even got a whiff of cologne. Who he was trying to impress I didn't know. I reckoned he was getting good money in from the outside, a couple of Western Unions a month. I was still wearing my shoes that I'd worn when I was caught at the airport, as well as the blue Ralph Lauren shirt and a pair of jeans.

I sat down at one of the little hard chairs with an arm rest and a little ledge to put a copybook on. It was like the desks I used in school when I was a kid. Forty-five years of age and I was back in them.

The class were a mixed bunch, including a Canadian, two Yanks and a German.

'Hey, Irish. Hey, Eye-Ar-Ay. How's it going?' said one Yank to me.

'I'm not in the IRA.' I shrugged.

'Don't let them know that. They all think you're a terrorist.' We both laughed.

There were about a dozen others in the classroom: Italians such as Roberto and gringos like me learning Spanish and Venezuelans learning English – all taught by Silvio. This should be fun. Silvio was a master of many tongues. His father was Italian and his mother French. He lived in London, where he worked as a cinema-screen projectionist.

Silvio took up his post at the front of the classroom. The first lesson wasn't about learning a new lingo – it was about how to escape Venezuela. He stood next to a giant map of South America on the wall and pointed at Caracas, just in from Venezuela's northern Caribbean coast. The capital was about halfway between the Colombian border to the west and Venezuela's eastern coast.

'Here is Caracas here,' said Silvio, pointing at the capital on the map. He was all serious, as if he was teaching us Spanish grammar. 'And here is San Cristóbal here,' he said, pointing at a provincial city way down south, close to Venezuela's western border with Colombia. He nodded back at Caracas. 'You can get a coach from here to San Cristóbal, which takes about 18 hours. Lots of army checkpoints. And from San Cristóbal you can get across the border, which is only a few kilometres away. When there, you are free.' We all sat there giggling. In a way it was a language lesson, because he went around the class explaining it in Spanish, Italian and English.

But how would we get out of Los Teques to get there, I wondered. Silvio explained that after 18 months you were eligible for parole: to get a job on the outside approved by the prison. All you had to do was pass a psychological assessment in Spanish, have work lined up and go to live with a family, and have it all approved by a judge. So when you got parole you boarded a long-distance bus in Caracas and disappeared into the wilderness, then emerged later in Colombia, all going well.

'Yes, is good plan,' said Roberto. Yeah, sounded good to me too, but at this stage I thought learning Spanish would be a bigger challenge.

Going to the Spanish classes helped speed up getting parole and was looked upon favourably by the prison chiefs. Silvio explained that the language classes took place twice a week, were scheduled to last three hours, from 9 a.m. to midday, and counted as a full day of your sentence. He said more than a year of two classes a week would be equivalent to about a hundred days off our sentence. I could see myself going to a lot of Spanish lessons.

* * *

Most gringo inmates had been through the same rigmarole as me after they were caught at the airport: they were processed and held in remand in Macuto before being moved to Los Teques. McKenzie's reputation there was infamous in most of the jails.

'That bastard,' said Hanz, a thin guy from Switzerland with shaggy dark hair and a beard. 'He robbed me of everything: cash, clothes – even my sandals. I had nothing. Kept threatening me with this bloody machete. "*Te mato, gringo,"* ["I kill you"] he kept shouting. I had pains in my ribs for weeks after that place. He kept jabbing me.'

'I'd believe it,' I said, 'I was told about him, but he never bothered me.'

'Never bothered you?' he said, louder than before. 'He make everybody's life hell.'

'I stayed in the nice wing with ex-cops,' I laughed. 'Good food and treatment.'

'That is unbelievable,' he said, 'I know that place, but it is only for the dirty police. How'd you get to stay there?'

'I arrived in a suit and fancy shoes. Think they thought I'd money. Tried to get me to pay a 2,000-euro bribe to them through Western Union from home.'

'And you paid?' His eyebrows lifted up and seemed to knot together.

'No way. Gave them the runaround.' Looking at Hanz, I could see why the ex-cops didn't want him in the wing. He was skinny as a rake. Looked like a typical backpacker tramp. He'd been travelling around Colombia for about a year before getting to Venezuela, where he ran out of cash. Taking a case back to Switzerland seemed like 'easy money' on his way home. Instead he ended up in this dump.

* * *

About five weeks had passed since I got caught. I hadn't spoken to my family since the quick phone call to my ma from Macuto. I also hadn't heard another word from the consul since his brief visit to me there. Now that I was in Los Teques, which in theory would be home for up to eight years, I genuinely needed a Western Union transfer this time. I wanted to phone home and get a money wire sent over. The jefe wanted his weekly causa money, and the 200-euro 'entry fee' to stay in the wing. I also needed cash on top of that sum to live here. I had nothing – no cup, no saucer, no knife and fork, no colchoneta. Nothing was 'on the house'.

New Yawk Mike was my middleman for dealing with the jefe, since I had no Spanish. We were standing in the yard and I went over to him. 'Mike, what's the story with making a call home?'

'Hey man, don't worry, I'll get you a phone. All cool.' He was a chilled-out 'dude'. Minutes later he was back with a mobile phone. I hadn't thought it'd be that easy. I rang the number for my sister, which I had in my head. It was about 5 p.m. in Los Teques and about 10 p.m. in Dublin.

The phone started ringing. I got a bit anxious. The usual thoughts went through my head. What had I done to my family? Would they think I was drug vermin?

'Hallo.' It was my sister's voice.

'Hi, Sharon, it's Paul,' I said.

'Ah, how are ya?' she said, sounding excited to hear from me.

'I'm OK, Gal,' I said, using the name I'd called her since we were kids.

'It's great to hear from you,' she said in a sad voice. Then she put on her big-sister hat. 'How's your health? How's your weight? Are you eating OK?' You'd know she was a nurse; she always asked about my well-being.

'I'm doing OK,' I said. Everything she asked I just said, 'Sound, not a bother, all good.' I didn't want anyone at home to worry any more than they already were.

'Look, I need a few quid sent over. It's to pay to get into this place.'

'What?'

'It's crazy here, you have to pay to stay.' I asked her for 350 euro.

'No problem,' she replied quickly, 'I'll send that tomorrow after work.' I gave her the name and address for a girl in Colombia, which Mike had given me. I told Sharon 200 of the 350 euro would be gone on the 'entry fee'. The other 150 euro was to get me going with bedding, a plate and bowl, and a few other basics. If that sounded odd, she didn't say.

'Where are you?'

'I'm in the big prison in Los Teques, outside Caracas.'

'What's it like?'

'Grand.' I doubted she believed me. I just didn't see the point in telling the truth.

'OK.'

I'd mentioned to my mother in the phone call from Macuto that I could get sprung from jail for 20 grand. That was what one of the hocus-pocus lawyers said. I had told the family that and it stuck in their heads. Sharon said she'd spoken to one of my mates, Ryan, who ran a construction company and had made a good few quid in the boom years. 'He says he'll get you the 20 grand, or we'll get someone to put the money up. And we've been talking to solicitors.' They had it in their heads I could pay off someone and sail out the front door.

'No one sends a penny unless it's 100 per cent sure,' I said. 'And tell no one to come over. I don't want anyone visiting me. The place is a death-trap – all of Caracas.'

I didn't know it when I called, but Katie was there too and she got on the phone.

'Da,' said Katie. A lump swelled in my throat. 'How are ya?'

'I'm all right, darling, I'm all right.' Katie, I'm so sorry, I thought.

'You'll be home in no time,' she said through tears. 'We'll sort it.'

'Look, Katie, I've been caught here. I'll be here for a few years, darling. Nothing can be done.' What had I done to her, leaving her in the lurch like that?

She had moved in with my sister after the rent ran out on the apartment where we lived. I remembered I had a couple of grand in a bank account at home. It was a slush fund to pay bills and the rent on the apartment. I wanted her to have it. 'You know my bank account number – empty it. You have the pin number,' I said, shouting into the phone. I was standing in the yard with one finger in my ear to block out the noise of chatter, laughter and music.

I stood there, taking in my thoughts while speaking to my sister and Katie. It was very hard. But I had to prepare myself mentally for this place. If I was thinking, 'When will I get out? When will I get out?' I'd drive myself mad. That's why I didn't want to hear any illusions from my family that I could grease a few palms and walk out the prison gate. Or get out any way other than serving my time. As I gathered my thoughts, I took in my surroundings. There were fellas walking around off their heads on crack, like zombies – extras off the set of *Dawn of the Dead*.

I spoke to Katie for a few minutes more, just chatting about her hairdressing apprenticeship, but it was heartbreaking talking to her. I knew I'd let her down. We agreed to talk another day; it was too noisy anyway.

'Bye, Da,' said Katie. I didn't know it then, but it would be the last time she would speak to me.

Chapter 8

TOOLS OF THE TRADE

MUFFLED SCREAMS FILTERED INTO THE YARD. THE SHRIEKS OF A MAN who knew his life would be over in minutes. We could hear him trying to flee *banditos* armed with crudely made knives – cell bars broken off and filed down to deadly weapons. The scurrying of feet. Then it stopped and we knew they'd caught him. He must have known he couldn't escape their blades inside the walls of the cramped wing. But a rat cornered will do what it can to save its skin. More screams. They had him. He was now yelping like a dog.

A hush had fallen over the yard as we listened. I was sitting on a bucket next to Silvio. '*Cuchillo,*' ('Knife') said inmates in the yard. 'Somebody's having their last day,' said Silvio. Moments before there had been the usual joking and laughing in the yard and horsing around. Not then. The only talk was in hushed tones as we sat there looking at each other or just staring at the ground. Helpless. The man's life delivered up to the demons of Los Teques, coming to an end in this concrete circus. His shrieks then gave way to a slow, steady whimpering as his life ebbed away. It all went on for about 20 minutes. Then silence.

This wasn't in the Maxima wing, however, thank God. It was in the Number 7 cell block next door. The cries had been wafting in through the vents in the wall that separated our yard from that wing, the narrow slats bringing air into their windowless dungeon and sending us back the sounds of this man as he was gasping in his last breaths. His shrieks rattled me. Even though the cries were coming from the next wing

111

and I couldn't see the man, the sounds were amplified in my head, as if I were in there watching the knives sink into his flesh. Hearing those horrific, inescapable sounds strengthened my goal: to get parole after 18 months and get out of here. I sat there and told myself that Los Teques would not claim my life. I planned to keep my head down and my nose clean, to do my time and get out. I wasn't going to get sidetracked with drugs or other crap.

I looked around the yard. The luceros, the henchmen, stood there swinging their knives, chewing gum. Just another day. The salsa music had been turned down so they could listen to the cries. Like they enjoyed it, getting a kick out of hearing a man die.

The next day, word came down explaining what was behind the killing. I was sitting with Eddy, Silvio and Ricardo chatting in the yard. We sat on a wooden bench like a church pew, shaded from the sun by jeans hanging from a plastic cord above that served as a washing line. 'He had been robbing off the other prisoners,' said Eddy. 'So the others ran after him and stabbed him.'

'Robbing what?' I said

'Who knows?' shrugged Eddy. 'Money. A bar of soap from someone's bucket.'

'They'd knife him to death just for that?' I said. I was horrified.

'Your bucket is all you have, mate. Another man's things are sacred here.'

Silvio and Eddy gave me an overview of Los Teques. There were seven proper wings in all, each cell block called a *pabellón*, or pavilion, by the Veno inmates, and named by their numbers. Wing 1 and Wing 2 were just that, but some had nicknames according to the English-speaking lags I spoke to. Wing 3 was La Iglesia, or the Church, and was run by Bible-bashing evangelicals: no drugs, sex, no vices at all were allowed there. Wing 4 was called the Special; Wing 5, where I was held, was known as Maxima, or 'maximum', while

Wing 6 was Mostrico. None of those names had any meaning that I could see. Wing 7, which was next door to us and where most of the worst crackheads and murderers seemed to be held, we called the Bandito wing. Few got out alive, I'd heard. It was a bit like Hotel California – you can check in, but you can never check out.

Then there were the overspill areas, which housed outcast inmates or were turned into wings because of overcrowding. There was the *enfermería,* or clinic, which was an annexe next to a medical office. It was supposed to be for sick inmates to recover in, but about 50 prisoners had been moved in and now called it home. Then there was the Fresa, or Strawberry, wing, a small area under the stairs in the passageway where about 30 gays had holed up. It was also known as the Pink wing. In most cell blocks they weren't accepted and would be beaten and thrown into the passageways, so they had to make their own home. Maxima was the exception – it took in all the prison's outcasts: ex-cops, kiddy fiddlers, rapists, the whole lot. Their causa money was good in Maxima, I supposed. Fidel, the jefe, was said to be a rapist, so I supposed his moral standards weren't high.

Los Teques held between 1,000 and 1,200 inmates, depending on who you spoke to, all crammed into a jail built for about 350. About 200 prisoners were foreigners – all drug mules, of course, just like me.

Each cell block had its own army-style council that ruled over their wing. At the top was the jefe, or boss, and below him two underbosses we called 'highlites', who were like lieutenants. Beneath them were a handful of subordinates, like sergeants. They were all armed: revolvers, shotguns, pistols, homemade pipe guns and even grenades. At the very bottom of the pecking order were the luceros, or foot soldiers. Armed only with knives, they were the eyes and ears of the bosses. They watched over us plebs out in the yard or wherever we were while the jefe and his underlings went about the important business of bagging coke, hiding guns and the like.

All inmates paid a causa to the boss of their cell block and his 'soldiers'. Anyone who didn't would be beaten and thrown into the passageway, where the outcasts who slept there would cut them up with knives. The jefes were powerful and held the rule of law over each cell block. Inside the jail they ran the show. There was a handful of prison cops, but they were mostly powerless, armed with batons and antique-looking pistols. They were no match for the firepower of the jefes and they knew it. 'They run for cover when the jefes start shooting,' laughed Eddy.

The National Guard were in charge of the jail perimeter. Their job was to count heads, lock gates and make sure no one escaped. They had a hands-off approach to what went on inside the prison. Their turf was the jail boundaries – who and what came in and out of the jail – and they also carried out cell-block searches.

The wing bosses lived cushy lives: or, at least, as good as it could get in jail. Inmates cooked their food and washed their clothes; they probably made a personal fortune from the causa, feathering their nests for when they got out; and they sat around all day watching TV and calling the shots as to what us common inmates did all day, be it cleaning or playing statues in the yard.

The jefes were bitter rivals, but by and large they respected each other. Nobody wanted a war. Not the jefes, not the general inmates, no one. That's why the wings were carefully segregated. Cell blocks would only go to the canteen one wing at a time to avoid a possible shoot-out.

When a blow-up did happen the consequences were grave: scores riddled with bullets and ripped apart by knives. Silvio told me about a battle the previous Easter that left a reported 12 dead. 'Up there, on the roof,' he said, nodding up from the yard to a high ledge about 20 ft above. 'They blasted away at each other for hours. Two wings. Grenades went off. The roof was destroyed. Nobody's been allowed up since. They're still trying to repair it.' God, get me out of here.

The good news, if it could be called that, was that random killings didn't usually happen in most wings, including Maxima. That was why we paid the causa. As much as I detested the luceros who walked around the yard swinging knives, and the highlites and jefes who carried guns, it all made some sort of sick sense. It created order. Nobody laid a finger on you in the wing. Only the padrino and the 'made men' could, but even this seemed to be rare. A beating was reserved for inmates who stepped out of line. 'Fuck around,' said Eddy, 'and they'll fuck with you, my friend.'

The reasons for getting your number called for a beating ranged from the trivial, in my eyes, to the bizarre. Some things were sacred, as Eddy said. You never opened up another prisoner's bucket, where you kept your few worldly possessions – a few toiletries and probably a small bit of cash and, for the Venos, a nice shirt and runners for visit day. Anybody could pop off a lid and rifle through another inmate's things. But they didn't. There was respect. It might be respect motivated by fear – but it worked. In Maxima, there was order.

Beatings were also doled out to kiddy fiddlers. When they arrived in the wing they were beaten to a pulp and carried into the yard. They had their own spot in the corner where flies buzzed around the bins. There was no stigma attached to rapists in Maxima, though. It seemed as though Fidel deemed them a better class of prisoner.

His second in command was Carlos. He was about 6 ft 2 in., bald and ripped with muscle. The lags said he was a bank robber. They also said he was the real wing boss and called the shots but preferred to keep a low profile. He was knocking off one of the female cops who worked up in the offices. Everyone knew. She'd walk into Maxima and a luz would be called. Whoever was in the hallway watching TV would have to clear off into the patio. She'd disappear into Cell 1, where all the bosses slept, and into Carlos's 'buggy' behind the black curtains drawn around his bed. A buggy was a bed cordoned off with curtains to allow privacy for inmates and their wives on conjugal visits. He probably had the best bed to get on, a big double. His buggy was kitted out with a big TV and free weights, which he pumped to keep his body toned and fit.

But Carlos stayed in the background. He was outside of Maxima a lot, walking around with the handle of his silver Colt sticking out of his belt. Nobody touched him. According to the inmates, most days at lunchtime he spent up in the computer room. The chica cop would arrive, then they'd lock the door and only giggles would be heard. There were no secrets in Los Teques. Not even behind closed doors.

Down the chain again was the Chief, a native Indian guy who ran a little shop next to the hallway. He was from the Amazon jungle in the south-west of Venezuela. He was barrel-chested with long wild hair and flared nostrils. He looked like a Maori: you could picture him on a rugby pitch with the Kiwis doing the All Blacks' war dance.

Most of the guns were smuggled into the wing, but the jefes couldn't rely on smuggled weapons alone to keep their little platoons armed. They had their own in-house toolmakers putting together DIY guns and knives. In Maxima the toolmaker was El Perro, or the Dogman. He made knives and guns for the bosses and luceros. The material came from the hardware in the cell block. Perro would use a rectangle of metal he'd cut out of a toilet door to make knives. He'd use a strip about two inches wide and eight inches long. He'd then spend the next two days sitting on a chair he had made for himself especially, where he sat filing the steel. It was high with a small desk attached, like a classroom table. He would sit up there in the yard looking down at us like an umpire at a tennis match. After two days the rectangular strip of metal would be filed down to a nice point at one end and have a comfortable handle at the other. He was meticulous with his work. He would even attach a nice embroidered cloth around the handle for comfort and a long strip of material so the luceros could tie the knife around their wrists. I doubt anyone stabbed by such a knife appreciated the quality of the Dogman's work.

He also turned his hand to making improvised pipe guns. He would cut down the tubular bars on the cell doors for that. They were cylindrical and empty inside and were perfect for gun barrels. With other pieces of metal he ripped off doors, he would make an intricate chamber where a bullet could be popped in. This rectangular section would then be connected to the barrel made from the hollow cell bars. In the bullet section a shotgun shell would be loaded in and would sit neatly against a spring. In the hands of the bosses it became a deadly weapon. They would pull back a big elastic band like a bungee cord at the rear end of the gun, as if they were pulling back a catapult, release it, and the bullet would shoot out – in this case a shotgun shell zipping through the inside of a cell bar. The force was enough to rip through a man's body at close range.

All in all, El Perro was responsible for arming the Maxima henchmen, and because of that he was popular with the boss and given his own bed in a cell. There were only about thirty-five beds, a mixture of singles and bunks, in the three cells in the wing, reserved for the bosses and their sidekicks. The other 70 to 80 of us squeezed onto the floor at night. So El Perro was doing well. The jefe didn't really like him, nobody did, but he was useful. The Dogman earned his name from crawling around the wing on his hands and knees howling like a lunatic when he was on the crack cocaine.

He was forever asking me for my false front teeth, which I took out sometimes to clean. El Perro had barely a tooth in his head, just a couple of molars in his upper gums, which was why he had the other nickname of Vampy. 'Para mí, para mí,' ('For me, for me') he would say, pointing at my plastic teeth any time I took them out for a good rinse.

'Piss off,' was my answer.

He also gave the prison guards a headache, I'd say. They were in and out of the wing regularly replacing toilet and cell doors after he'd stripped them down to metal skeletons.

The danger in Los Teques was mostly outside the wing in the corridors where the crackhead cell-block outcasts lived, sleeping on the floor and pissing and shitting in a corner. No one wanted them in any cell block or pavilion. They had no money, no families who visited them, nothing. They survived by holding up inmates in the passageways with crude knives, two or three at a time shaking down a prisoner for a few bolos or a cigarette.

* * *

It was a Sunday and the visits were on again. The director started to open up the rancho as a place for us PWVs (Prisoners Without Visitors), mainly the foreigners, to go. For people who had no one to shag down in the cells was what she really meant. At about 11 a.m., as the visitors started flowing into Maxima, I decided to get out from behind the curtain, walk to the rancho to stretch my legs and have a smoke. I went with another inmate, an Italian from Sicily we called Vito. He was a thin, tall guy with grey hair and reminded me of jailed mafia boss John Gotti. In the passageway we stopped at the barred gate and waited for the cop to open it up. We could see the visitors coming in, women and children, waiting for another barred gate ahead to open so they could enter the passageways. I could make out two women at the front of the queue, a younger woman and an older lady. But I couldn't really see their faces. You weren't allowed to look at visitors, especially women. So myself and Vito just chatted away with our eyes to the ground, taking peeps through the bars.

Suddenly, out of the corner of my eye I could make out one inmate coming down the stairs to the left from one of the wings upstairs. At the bottom step he suddenly charged to the gates. The two women were standing on the opposite side. He pulled something from his belt. I instinctively looked up.

He had a revolver in his hand. He pointed it at the younger woman's head. *Boom-boom-boom*. Three piercing shots rang out, echoing through the bare stone passageways. The woman's head exploded, like a tomato shot by an arrow. Bits of it splattered on the older lady's face. The woman slumped down on her knees and then collapsed, her body twitching like a fish on the end of a hook. The older lady went down on her knees too, wailing and screeching, 'Wah, wah.' Her hands were cradling what was left of the woman's head. Blood was everywhere. The cops jumped up and grabbed the guy. Myself and Vito looked at the sight, then at each other. 'What the fuck was that?' I said to him. Two troops ran in. The cop at the gate where we were standing started shouting at us to go back: '*Regresa, regresa*' ('Go back, go back').

In Maxima, we went back behind the curtain and told the others, Roberto and Silvio. 'The woman, the guy just ran at her, pulled out a gun and shot her,' I said. I couldn't believe it. I was rattled. It was one of those moments in Los Teques I wanted to believe wasn't real. 'What the fuck was all that?' I said. 'This place is crazy.'

'Another day in Los Teques,' said Eddy.

'You need to be careful all the time,' said Silvio. 'Especially in the passageways. Those crackhead trash will stab you for the price of a stone.'

What made it worse was that it was a visitor who was killed, and a woman. In Venezuela, the familia was supposed to be sacred. Anyone who started trouble on visit day would be shot. That was the rule.

But Eddy was right – an hour later the visits were back on. The rancho was shut down, but mothers, nieces, daughters and so on continued filing into Maxima with bags of food, whiling away the afternoon eating and shagging their partners in the cells. The whole prison was one sick, sadistic place. Life was nothing.

We later heard the women were a mother and daughter.

'It was his wife, that's whose head he blew off,' said Silvio.

'I'd hate to see what he does to his enemies,' said Eddy.

'They say he was off his head on crack,' said Silvio. 'That his wife missed the last visit day and in his drugged-out mind he believed she was with another man.'

'Not unusual in these waters,' said Eddy.

'No, they said she missed the day because she was sick.'

After that I was on edge. I'd heard one killing and gunfire for months, but this was the first time I'd seen someone murdered right in front of my eyes. I realised how easy it was to get killed in here. You just piss off the wrong person who happens to be on crack and has a gun and you're dead. I could only make sure it wasn't me. I wasn't going to die here. I had a family to get home to some day.

Chapter 9

MESSENGER FROM GOD

'*IRLANDÉS, VISITA,*' SAID ONE OF THE LUCEROS TO ME, POINTING OUT to the passageway. I was sure it was the Irish consul, the old guy. I hadn't seen him since my first few days in Macuto, which was over two months ago. That seemed like a lifetime ago now. So I walked out into the corridor and up to the barred gate where one of the *aguas* – the cops, so called because they were dressed in navy-blue uniforms – was on sentry, sitting on a chair. There was no sign of the consul. Up ahead I saw a small man, about my height, with narrow shoulders. His hair was brushed to the side and he wore glasses. The cop stood up and opened the gate, and I walked through. 'I'm Father Pat,' said my visitor, holding out a hand.

'How ya doing,' I said. He was dressed smartly in civvies: shirt, jacket and trousers. No dog collar. I put him down as being in his late 60s.

'The consul told me you were here,' he said. He spoke in a slow drawl. 'I visit the Irish who come for a stay,' he laughed. 'Billy, the other lad, he'll be down in about an hour. Did you meet him?'

I was amazed. Another Paddy in this hellhole and an Irish priest who visits prisoners from the old country. 'Never met him,' I answered. 'A couple of dodgy lawyers in Macuto jail told me there was someone else, but I've never seen him. I was starting to think it was just some story.'

'Billy's young,' said Father Pat. 'Mid-20s. Has been in about a year. And those lawyers, they're doing good work to get him out.'

'Pair of chancers – said for 10,000 euro they could get me free and home. Didn't believe a word.'

'Ah, yes, but they do good work.'

I doubted it. I told him how I got caught in the airport after trying to do a run for a drug gang back home.

'I see,' he said, his face showing no emotions. He wasn't one for judging. He was a fan of Irish sports, the GAA, and filled me in about a couple of the football games back in Ireland. The sliding economy back home got a mention too. 'It's getting worse, I hear.'

'I'd still rather that than be here,' I said, and Father Pat laughed.

I told Father Pat about the beatings, stabbings and murders I'd seen and heard about. 'I know, it's crazy,' he said, shaking his head, a trace of sorrow in his voice. 'That's the way it is in the jails, Paul, and all over Venezuela. I'd like to tell you otherwise.' I didn't tell him what the cops did to me in the National Guard's antidrogas headquarters. That night was now filed away in the dark corners of my mind.

Father Pat went on to give me some background on the government. President Hugo Chávez was the chief and he had been in power since 1999. He was elected in a landslide victory on a ticket to take the country's oil wealth out of the hands of Venezuela's wealthy minority and spread it out to the majority poor who lived in the slums. It was a revolución, Chávez called it. He also won praise for improving human rights, such as getting better access to education for the poor.

'To some he's a god,' said Father Pat. 'They believe that. They'd die for him.'

'The state of this place,' I said, 'no sign of angels in here.' We both laughed.

All the while the crackhead cell-block outcasts in the passageways were walking up to Father Pat with tall stories for money. 'Padre, I am sick and need to call my mama.' He passed no comment and just fished note after note from his pockets to give to them: small sums of 2,000 bolos (about 40 cents).

'You know what they're going to do with that?' I said. 'They'll put that towards buying part of a stone. You know, crack cocaine.' But he made no comment. I stood there clenching my teeth. I wanted to punch the cell-block outcast scum and send them packing.

Father Pat, who said he had been a priest stationed in Venezuela for more than 35 years, gave me his take on the revolution. He was no fan. The poor were less hungry all right, but Chávez was currying favour with the underclass. 'Breadcrumbs for a vote.' Piece by piece, Chávez was turning Venezuela into a Cuban-style country, a communist government masquerading as a socialist revolution. It was my first real insight into Venezuelan politics. You were either for or against Chávez. 'They want to either kill him or take a bullet for him,' said Father Pat, 'there's nothing in the middle.'

Some good news for me was that Father Pat said he could get me some money from an NGO back home in Dublin. The Irish Council for Prisoners Overseas sent over cash to inmates such as myself locked up abroad to make life a bit better in hellhole prisons like Los Teques. 'I'll bring it in for you,' he said. 'I did it for Billy. They send it to me.' It was a one-off payment of 500 euro. I was delighted. Every penny would be needed inside. I didn't even have a cup or a plate, or my own cushion to sleep on.

'I'm not planning on staying here for eight years,' I said, telling Father Pat about my plan to apply for early parole after eighteen months – and get it.

'It's possible,' he said cautiously, 'but you'd have to get your Spanish together.' Father Pat knew about the psychological test you had to pass to qualify for parole – which you had to do in the local tongue.

All of a sudden he pulled a small Bible out of a shoulder bag he was carrying. 'I'm just going to say a few words,' he said. He read a couple of Gospels and catechisms, phrases such as 'love thy brother' echoing throughout the passageway where a few days before I'd seen a man shoot his wife's head off. I was no Mass-goer, but I remembered the prayers off by heart from my days as an altar boy when I was a nipper. The words flowed back to me and then we ended it. 'Amen,' said Father Pat.

'Amen.'

'God be with you.'

'God be with you.' I wasn't a religious man, but I was open to any solace from this place I was in. If it was a priest with a Bible, so be it.

Father Pat then took hold of a little silver box swinging off the end of a medallion he wore. It was where he kept the host for the Communion. He popped open the lid, took out one of the wafers and placed in my hand.

'Amen,' said Father Pat, blessing himself.

'Amen.' I felt my spirits lift.

* * *

I needed to make money – and fast. I wanted to sort myself out with a few basics, such as a tobo to store my few toiletries and clothes, like my Irish rugby jersey. I also needed kitchen basics, such as a fork. I was getting tired of scooping up the food with my fingers in the rancho. I still had the coke from the haul the cops seized in the airport. I wasn't sure what to do with it. I knew flogging it in the wing might mean a beating from the bosses – or maybe a bullet. Selling drugs was their trade. Making money was ultimately why they were jefes – and in this case they made a killing off their captive customers in the wing. But I needed cash to tide me over till my sister's Western Union came through. The 350 euro I'd asked for might take a while. It was going to Mike's contact in Colombia. How long it would take to arrive in Caracas I had no idea.

I had the coke in the talc bottle hidden in my wash bag. But it had been a few months since I'd got caught in Simón Bolívar airport. Did coke go off? I didn't know, but I thought it wise to try it out before thinking of selling it. I didn't want to snort it myself. My head wasn't in a good place, and the last thing I needed was a load of paranoia from the coke. I was good mates with Eddy and thought he would make a good guinea pig. The idea twigged in my head when one evening everyone was talking about it being his birthday the next day. I had the perfect gift for him.

'I have a surprise for you tomorrow.'

'What?' said Eddy, picking his nose.

'A few grams.'

'Where'd you get it from?' he said quickly. We were standing out in the yard and he looked around to see if anyone was listening, then turned back to me.

'I swallowed a couple of balloons. If I shit it out in the morning I'll give you a bit.' That was the story that I gave. I wanted him to think I'd swallowed the coke in condoms and that's how I had got it into the jail. That's how many did. They'd carry it for weeks like that, passing it out when they went to the toilet, then washing it (or not) and swallowing it again. I didn't want Eddy to know I had a talc bottle full of about 300 g of coke in a wash bag sitting on the ground in the yard. I trusted him, but it was best he didn't know. At the time, a gram inside cost twenty-five thousand bolos, or about five euro. So I had a stash of some five million bolos, or one thousand euro – massive money in the prison. So much that a crackhead would slit your throat to get it.

* * *

It was a bit after 9 p.m. and the usual time to go to sleep. I'd been moved from my spot on the floor in the hallway where I spent my first night and had been given a 'lovely' space in the toilet. That night myself and two others went through our nightly routine preparing the floor where the three of us would squash into the small area.

After the last of the prisoners bathed, by ladling water over their heads from an oil drum in the corner, myself, Ricardo and a Veno went into our 'bedroom'. We first ran a couple of rags over the floor to dry up the water. Then, armed with pieces of cardboard, we stood over the small area next to the squat toilet and spent about ten minutes fanning the floor to dry it as best we could. The pieces of cardboard then became our under sheets. We put down a piece each and rolled our colchonetas over them. The Veno tucked himself up against one of the walls and Ricardo against the other. A gap of just a few feet in the middle was my space. It was awful. I could only sleep on my side. And the whack of BO off the Veno was terrible. He worked in the kitchen and stank of stale sweat and whatever slop they'd cooked that day.

None of us was comfortable. Over a few nights we tried to bed down in different ways to see which worked best. In the beginning we'd agreed to sleep with our heads at opposite ends. 'Irishman, you are smaller than me,' said Ricardo, 'it is better this way.'

'We'll try it out,' I said. My head was now close to the door to the toilet, with my feet stretching out nestling between Ricardo's head and the Veno's. It didn't work – for me, anyway. Inmates wandering in to use the toilet in the middle of the night were stepping on my face. It went on till the next morning. 'Aggghh, fucking bastard,' I shouted every few minutes after my forehead or the side of my face got stood on.

On my first morning after a night in the toilet I woke up to the usual cries from the lucero shouting 'levántate' ('get up'). I wanted to punch him in the face. I hadn't got a wink all night. I stood up and stretched, my knees cracking, feeling as if my bones had been put through a grinder. The ground was covered in sticky piss. I lifted up my colchoneta and as usual the cardboard was soggy around the edges and the cushion damp. I felt like a caged animal lying in piss – and not even my own.

Vampy wasn't impressed in the morning, as I'd been

waking up most of the 70-odd bodies squashed on the floor in the cell next to us with my roars. '*Tú, mama huevo,*' ('You, cocksucker') he said with a scowl over my roars at night from the toilet. 'Fucking, fucking bastard.' I waved him off. I was wrecked and not in the mood for him. And what was he complaining about? He had his own bed – a privilege for arming the bosses with his DIY weapons.

* * *

I was standing out in the yard chatting to Silvio. One of the inmates started shouting at me and pointing up. '*Irlandés, compañero,* your country.' I raised my eyes to a ledge about 20 ft above, to the Church wing. The Church wing was where inmates went to dry out. A nuthouse run by evangelicals. Good for rehab, I was told. No drugs, no sex with visits, nothing. There was a guy with a mop of mousey-brown hair and pale skin.

'Father Pat told me about you,' he said. 'You're the Irish guy?' It was Billy, the other Paddy. So he really did exist.

'Yeah, that's me. Are you coming down?' I shouted up.

'I dunno, I might do. I'll talk to the jefe.' He needed permission first.

That was the chat over. Short and sweet. It was too hard to talk to him at a height, shouting over the noise of everyone else chatting.

* * *

Most of the afternoons I passed sitting out in the yard. Many of the others were out on jobs they'd been assigned by the prison: lugging out rubbish, working in the kitchen or sweeping floors. That's why Maxima was known as the workers' wing: most had some job keeping the jail going. Those of us who stayed in the cell block were mostly the gringos who didn't have good enough Spanish to work in the prison. There wasn't much to do other than sit in the hallway and watch DVDs. They were on around the clock, action flicks such as *Rambo* or Steven Seagal movies. Mostly stupid stuff with blood and guts. For the Venos, right up their street.

Myself and another gringo, Macedonia, took to playing chess in the afternoons to pass the time, a game I had learned as a kid. He had a job in the mornings out in the driveway area inside the main gate, lugging bags of rubbish and sweeping and cleaning. One afternoon as usual we sat down on two buckets and laid out a chessboard on another. 'Play, Paul,' he said, laughing. 'I show how we always win in my country.'

'Easy for you Russky commies,' I laughed. 'You were brought up on the game.' It was his board. He didn't smoke or do drugs and had paid the jefe to have the chessboard smuggled in for him. His English wasn't great, but I enjoyed the chat with him. He was one of the few inmates older than me. I put him down as about 50. He was a tall fellow, well built with a hard, chiselled face and a short haircut. The lags said he had been a sergeant back home.

About half an hour into the game (Macedonia was winning again, damn) one of the Venos came over, standing over the game. He laughed and made silly gestures, as if the game was stupid. More like he was. A scrawny little moron. All of a sudden he lashed out at the board and it went flying, the chess pieces scattering on the ground.

Macedonia jumped to his feet and grabbed the Veno by the throat. The blood drained out of the Veno's face. It was a knee-jerk reaction from Macedonia, not thinking about what the bosses might do. The Veno ran off, shocked, looking like his pride was hurt. Macedonia just shrugged and set up the board and pieces again for a new game.

'Let's get this moving,' I said. 'Forget about that clown.'

'Yes, the game,' said Macedonia. 'Stupid man stop us. I kill him.'

Minutes later, Fidel ran out. His acne-scarred face was

raging with anger. Myself and Macedonia looked at each other and knew we were in trouble. The Veno he pushed wasn't a 'made' man or even a lucero, but he cooked food for Fidel and his henchmen. Oh shit, I thought, we're in for it. Macedonia stood up. He had decent Spanish and told Fidel that the Veno had ruined our *juego* (game), tumbling the board over to show him.

'*Está bien,*' ('OK') said Fidel. He calmed down and walked away.

We thought that was that. Shortly afterwards we set up the pieces and had the game going. Two luceros then appeared at the door into the yard, carrying the Veno. One had him by the feet and the other had him by his hands, carrying him like a sack of potatoes. He was writhing and groaning. They dropped him on a spot on the ground. His arms were all blotchy and bruised, like old bananas. He lay there whimpering.

Myself and Macedonia were shocked. We couldn't believe it. The boss must have called a luz, giving the luceros the order to beat up our villain. I can't say we weren't satisfied, but I did feel a bit sorry for him. What surprised me was that Fidel took our side; a gringo laying a finger on a Veno was a no-no. They didn't like us, but we paid the causa and the boss knew our money was good. I learned that day that not only could you not hit another prisoner, you couldn't even get in their face.

* * *

I was walking through the passageway to the wing after the morning Spanish class. Up ahead I saw Costa Rica from Macuto jail.

'Paul, hallo,' he said, smiling. We shook hands.

'Great, good to see you.' I noticed he was carrying a Bible. 'Where's your Papa?' I said, joking. Papa was an old Mexican guy Costa Rica had taken under his wing in Macuto.

'Upstairs in another cell block. About five Mexicans taking care of him. His brothers.' I could tell he didn't want much chitchat and we parted. He hadn't mentioned he was in the Church wing, but it was obvious that he was from carrying the Palabra de Dios, the Bible. I could tell he was a relaxed, spiritual guy and genuinely wanted to do his time as quietly as possible. No drugs or violence. And the Church seemed to be the place for it. So they said.

* * *

The prisoner seemed to be having a row on the payphone. He stood in the passageway shouting into it. '*Sí*' and '*hijo de puta*' ('son of a bitch') was all I understood. In the same hand as the phone he held a gun, the barrel pointing near his head. I was with Silvio going towards the canteen. Suddenly the gun went off. A loud crack echoed out. Red mist sprayed out over the payphone. I stopped in my tracks and just stared. I watched half his head exploding. Brain and bone. What was left of his head tilted backwards and he keeled over. I wanted to puke at the sight.

'Oh my God, Paul, my God,' said Silvio, 'this place is terrible.' I just stood there shaking my head, my eyes not believing what they saw.

A couple of cops ran out from their office. I was ushered back to Maxima. '*Regresa, ahora*' ('Go back, now'). Back in the yard I stood there shaking my head again. What I saw didn't make sense. A man in a prison talking on the phone with a gun, then shooting his head off. An upside-down world.

I was later told that the Venos thought holding the gun and the phone in the same hand was cool. I'd say he was cool now all right, his body freezing in the morgue.

* * *

Billy arrived in the wing. 'How's it going? I'm Billy,' he said. He had mousey-brown hair, a crooked nose and eyes spaced a bit too wide apart. He was thin but had a bit of a pot belly. He had a sports bag slung over his shoulder and was carrying a tobo and a thin colchoneta rolled up under his arm.

We shook hands. 'You look like you're sticking around?' I said.

'Yeah,' he said, 'for good.' He blurted out his words rather than speaking them.

'How long you here?'

'About 14 months.'

'Caught at the airport?'

'Yep, barely out of the taxi. Walked in the front door and the cops pulled me over. Did a search and I was done. Three kilos. Got eight years.' He told the story in a matter-of-fact way, as if he was recalling going to the shop to buy a pint of milk. He was an easy-going guy with a cheesy grin and had a bit of a blank look to him. The world did its thing and Billy did his thing. He didn't seem bothered about what came his way. Even doing eight years in Los Teques. He was 26 and got caught at 25. He was wasting the best years of his life behind bars.

He had taken a bit of coke in his first months in the jail, like most, but then it became an all-day habit, which didn't do anyone any good. That set him up for a six-month rehab spell in La Iglesia, or the Church wing. No drugs, no drink, nothing.

'How'd it go up there?'

'My head was in bits with the charlie. Cleaned me up. Just had to say a few prayers and carry a Bible and they left me alone.' He wasn't a religious type, but carrying the book of God around the jail was like a badge of protection. Nobody touched you, Billy explained; the Church wing was under the rule of Wing 1. The jefe there was one of the biggest drug runners and outlaws in Venezuela. He was the most feared inmate in the jail. In the Church wing they had no guns or knives to protect themselves, but the inmates paid their causa to him. In return the evangelicals who ran La Iglesia enjoyed his protection. The Bible they carried was their badge: mess with me and fear the wrath of God, or, in this case, the Wing 1 padrino.

Although they were evangelicals, Billy explained, they were the usual mix of inmates: rapists, murderers, kiddy fiddlers and all-round sickos. One was even a genuine ex-pastor. He stood up in the wing and gave sermons every evening, banishing devils and damning sinners to hell. We heard he was locked up because of swindling his flock to the tune of thousands in a fraud scam.

Later that day Billy sat down beside me on the ground in the yard for the headcount. The usual band of troops filed in.

'Can you call out my number?' I asked. 'I can't speak this poxy language.'

'No bother.' He spoke decent Spanish and knew all the local slang, which made the Venos laugh.

The cop started his count from the row of inmates lined up around the yard. '*Uno. Dos. Tres* . . .' He came to Billy, who I worked out was about number thirty-something in the headcount, and pointed his index finger at him. '*Treinta-seis.*' ('Thirty-six.') The finger pointed at me. Billy put his hand on my shoulder and called out '*treinta-siete*' ('thirty-seven'). As well as having an amigo from the homeland I now had another body to fall back on for the headcount.

Later on Vampy came over, babbling 'número, número' and pointing at me, his lips rising at times, showing his baby gums and two molars poking out. A tall, skinny Dracula, a Venezuelan phantom. 'He says you should be calling out your own number,' said Billy, interpreting. 'If I can do it, you can.'

'Wankers,' I said to Billy, looking into Vampy's face. 'All wankers.' Vampy walked away with a grunt.

'Ha ha, boy, you're right there,' said Billy.

Silvio and a few other Italians came over, including Vito and Roberto. 'Welcome to Maxima, mate,' said Eddy, extending his hand. Billy took it, looking down at his name, 'Eddy', tattooed on his knuckles. 'How was the Church? You a Bible basher?'

'No, but I got clean,' said Billy. He wouldn't be for long.

* * *

It was December, and with Christmas on the way I decided I was going to make some home brew, for no reason other than that I wanted to have a drink to mark the festive season. I also saw it as a way to make a bit of cash. I told Billy I wanted to ask the jefe for permission first. You never did anything out of the ordinary without getting the nod. 'Let's go,' said Billy boy. We walked into Fidel's cell, where he was stretched out on his bed watching his little portable TV. Some stupid *novela* soap opera with a girl crying over losing her boyfriend. The jefes were addicted to that crap. Some hard men. Carlos was standing by his big double bed curling weights, his biceps rising up and down like two babies' heads trying to pop out of his arms.

'I want to make some booze, some wine. Billy, tell him.' He stood next to me, and interpreted.

'*Sí, no problema.*'

I'd got the OK from the Godfather; all was good. Now all I needed were the tools and the ingredients. I'd been making home brew for years back in Ireland, so I already had the knowledge. I needed a vat to make the brew: an empty ten-litre water bottle came in handy for that. I also needed rice and sugar: I got that off the lags in the kitchens for a few bolos. The big problem was the yeast. No one seemed to have it. Billy had a brainwave. 'We'll ask Father Pat on the next visit!' he said, grinning.

'Father Pat, yeah, that might work.' But I couldn't see a priest being party to my plans to get merrily on high over the festive season. I'd have to think about that one.

Chapter 10

STORM TROOPERS

THE BOYS IN GREEN MARCHED INTO THE YARD. ABOUT HALF A DOZEN armed with the usual pump-action shotguns. Fingers resting close to the trigger. Just another número. It was morning, and we all sat around the yard on our buckets waiting for the headcount to start. I sat perched on a paint tin beside Silvio so he could shout my number. '*Uno, dos, tres* . . .' The cop stood in front of me for my turn. He pointed his finger at me, like he was staring down the barrel of a gun. Silvio called my number and I watched the cop go round the yard with the headcount while a National Guard ticked off his roll sheet on a clipboard.

At the last number, one of the verdes lifted up the barrel of his shotgun and fired into the air. *Boom-boom*. '*Búsqueda*,' ('Search') shouted another verde. We all jumped to our feet. The soldier cocked his rifle and fired again. *Click-click, boom*. '*Al sotea*,' ('To the roof') the soldier barked in Spanish again. There was a mad scramble to the door into the cells. A soldier aimed his rifle and shot at our backs as we ran. Men cried out, screaming and shouting. I couldn't believe this was happening.

Inside in the cells the guards shouted orders. '*Correte, gringo, correte*,' ('Run, gringo, run') one shouted at me. I ran toward the narrow door into the passageway. There was a bottleneck of bodies, like a stampede of elephants trying to run through the eye of a needle, pushing and shoving. Other soldiers stood there, their swords drawn, lashing out at us with the flats of the blades as we ran out the door. I scrambled out and felt the blade

135

slap at me, a sharp flick like a bite. But it was on my ass, softening the blow.

Eddy and Silvio were up ahead, running. Other troops stood next to the stairs. '*Arriba, arriba,*' ('Up, up') they shouted, pointing to the stairs on the left that led up towards the roof. I ran on. I copied the others and put my hands on top of my head. The troops kicked out at us with heavy-duty military boots as we passed. I stood at the top of the stairs. My heart raced. I could feel it pounding in my ears like a bass drum.

None of the English speakers were nearby, so I couldn't find out what was going on. The inmates were filing into a line on the second floor, heading up to the roof. Calm had settled in now. The panic was gone. Troops barked orders. Prisoners pulled their clothes off at the top of the stairs. Guards shoved inmates out onto the roof. Now it was my turn. The soldier shouted a flurry of Spanish. 'Gringo' was all I picked up, but I knew what to do. I quickly pulled off my jeans and T-shirt. One guard with surgical gloves grabbed my groin and groped around. He pushed my back and I bent over, standing there while the cop looked at my ass. '*Vete,*' ('Go') he barked.

I quickly grabbed my bundle of clothes off the floor, pulled them on and ran out onto the roof. There was already another wing of inmates up there, more than 200 men lying on the ground with their hands behind their heads, foreheads pressed into the ground. The troops, armed with shotguns, marched around the perimeter of the wall keeping watch. I could see others in a watchtower above, aiming machine guns our way. I ran over, joined a line and lay down on the roof. Face touching the ground. Some of the inmates were shouting among themselves. Hundreds more inmates were now pouring out of the door to the roof. The whole prison was obviously being searched. All lay on the ground, hands behind heads.

The army started a headcount. A soldier went up and

down the lines of men stretched out on the ground – legs apart like giant starfish washed up on a beach. I heard the soldier come closer as he passed each prisoner, each calling his own number. I panicked. I couldn't see Silvio or Eddy to help me. The numbers came closer. The squeak of boots nearer. What would they do to me if I messed up the number? '*No español*,' ('No Spanish'), I said. The soldier called out my number and moved on. Lucky.

Now the fear and panic started to go. I relaxed a bit. There was obviously a big search of the wings going on. Now, with the fear fizzling out, I remembered I had been in a toilet queue in the wing, bursting to go when the troops marched in. I'd forgotten with the shock of the soldiers rounding us up. Now it was coming back. My stomach groaned with cramps. I had to go, but I couldn't. I convinced myself I could hold it. Then time went on. About an hour passed and we still lay there, faces on the concrete. Boots marching back and forth.

My stomach groaned again. More cramps. I squeezed my abdomen and tried to stop them. My face grimaced. Hold it, Paul, hold it. Suddenly my rear end exploded in my jeans. I lay there thinking I hadn't gone to the toilet in my trousers since I was a kid and had just done it next to more than 1,000 grown men. The smell was bad, but I didn't think anyone noticed. I knew one of the lags behind me, Maleta. So I started to make light of it and blamed him. 'Maleta, Maleta,' I shouted, 'smell, smell.' Some of the Venos understood and started laughing. I doubted they believed it was him, but it got a laugh and I felt a bit better.

Another hour passed. Then another, and still I was lying there in trousers soiled by my own excrement. I was glad there was a bit of a breeze.

Finally, after about three hours, the army called another headcount and we were all then marched down to the cells. I walked along the passageway towards Maxima, feeling the sludge in my trousers. I got through the door and made a beeline to the toilet to finish my business.

I stepped back out and took a survey of the cell block. The wing was in bits. The boys in green had turned the place upside down. Mattresses had been ripped apart. Garbage bags had been upturned. The buckets had all been emptied out and the whole yard was a sea of the prisoners' belongings. Clothes, toothbrushes, runners, flip-flops, everything was strewn over every inch of ground in the yard. Prisoners went crawling down on their hands and knees, looking for their possessions and gathering them together. One man wept when he looked in his bucket and saw one of the troops had taken a dump in it. Other troops had pissed in them. Some inmates found their clothes seeped in urine and sludge next to a manhole. The soldiers had obviously used them to search the sewers, lying on the clothes to keep themselves clean.

It was all a sickening and sorry sight. These were men who had almost nothing, and the little they did have had been destroyed. It was senseless vandalism. The National Guards, to me, weren't soldiers, men of combat who defended their people and got respect. In my book they were just thugs and bandits – no better than the murderers and rapists they were guarding. Maybe worse. They were in a position of authority and they abused it.

Some of the lads had gashes on the backs of their legs and across their arms from the troops smashing down on us with swords. One inmate had a nasty cut on his upper arm. '*Verdes, hijos de putas,*' ('Verdes, sons of bitches') shouted a Veno. '*Verdes, mama huevo*' ('Verde, cocksuckers').

Ricardo showed me his upper arm. 'Look, Paul, look. They got me, bastards.' He'd been hit with the bullets the troops shot at us as we ran scurrying from the yard. His arm was covered in little dents the size of peanuts. 'This is the second time they've done this to me, these wounds. They did the same in a search before.' The bullets the troops fired weren't meant to kill, just hurt: like buckshot that hunters use to fire at birds, the bullets spraying out in a scattergun way to increase the number of targets but not strong enough to pierce a man's skin a few metres away.

The bosses walked around taking in the damage. They were hit hardest, as they had luxuries such as TVs. Three of the portable ones they kept beside their beds were on the ground, smashed. One boss looked like he was close to tears after inspecting his stereo. It didn't work when he tried to power it up. The guards had pissed on it and left a puddle of urine on the floor. I saw another of the bosses pulling at the plaster that was now hanging off the walls in the cells. It was where the jefe and his 'troops' hid guns and ammo in the walls.

I started to look around the yard for my own belongings. I saw my talc bottle on the ground. I grabbed it and popped off the lid. I couldn't believe it. The coke was all still there and intact. My stash had survived yet another búsqueda.

We started to clean up and put the wing in order. With the anger starting to fizzle out, the standing joke was all about how I'd dirtied my jeans up on the roof. The bosses were jeering me, saying I had *miedo* (fear) of the troops in the search. The Venos started calling me 'Kaká, Kaká' and laughing. I thought this was great, smiling that they were calling me after the nickname of the famous Brazilian footballer Ricardo Izecson dos Santos Leite. 'No, *caca* – it's Spanish for having a shit,' said Eddy. That wiped the grin off my face.

That evening it was time for the wing's weekly meeting. It was always held on Monday, which was, conveniently, the day the wing was torn apart. The air was tense. We prisoners took our place sitting on our buckets in the yard. The jefe and his henchmen stood by the cell-block door, looking bare without their arsenal of heavy weapons. I could see they'd been badly hit by the raid, but they still had pistols and revolvers the army couldn't find. The luceros still had their knives, too, swinging on their wrists.

The weekly meetings were supposed to be a chance for

inmates to voice any gripes or suggest how to improve the running of Maxima, but if anyone did speak up they were always laughed at or shouted down by the bosses, so few bothered. We all knew the meeting was a farce: mob rule pretending to be a democracy, and the bosses making out they were actually earning their causa by doing stuff for us. It was usually banal things raised at the meeting, such as the bosses telling us the price of detergent had gone up so they had to raise two million bolos, or four hundred euro, for cleaning products for the wing for a month. No one believed them – that was about twice the salary of a cop or nurse in Venezuela. If you spoke out, though, you might get called in for a meeting with a baseball bat.

Everyone was edgy. The wing had been pulled apart, and the bosses in particular needed to recoup their losses of TVs, stereos, mobile phones, cash and guns. Fidel wasn't pleased with the loss, stomping back and forth next to his army council, giving a sermon. All I could really make out was *plata* (money) and other words such as *armas* (guns). Worried faces. Furrowed brows. Sighs. I knew this meant something bad for us but not exactly what. I got up off the bucket where I sat and went up to Eddy.

'I don't get it. What's going on, all the talk about money?'

'It's not good, that's what it is,' he said. 'There's a special causa. It's 100,000 bolos [or 20 euro] to get new guns and ammo. And we pay for it.'

'And everyone accepts it?'

Hanz walked over, scratching his beard, and joined in. 'Yes, you pay,' he shrugged. 'You think they'll make cardboard boxes so we can put in voting papers?'

'It's bullshit,' said Eddy. 'Bunch of bastards, mate, all bastards.'

'We can pay it OK,' said Hanz, putting things into perspective. 'Most of us get money from our embassies or back home. Twenty euro is not much, but the Venezuelans, for them it's a lot.' True enough, 20 euro wasn't much out of the 350 that were on their way to me, but it was a big jump for the Venos. The usual causa was 5,000 bolos (about a euro) a week. The 100,000-bolo causa, about 20 euro, was a big hike. Most inmates knew they'd have problems getting it.

But the irony was that the bosses would restock their guns and other contraband from the same source that robbed them of it: the National Guard. Nothing got in or out of the jail without them knowing about it. The verdes might not police the wings but they controlled who and what came in and out of Los Teques. I was getting a picture of another cycle in the prison's life: the army would storm the wings and seize weapons, then later the same arms would end up back in the hands of the bosses. You could get what you wanted into the prison – TVs, phones, guns – but at twice the street price. It was one big racket.

'As well as to rearm themselves, they want the cash for Crimbo,' said Eddy. 'A tree and decorations, food and entertainment for all their families.' He buckled over laughing. You had to; it was too much to take seriously. I was wondering whether I was in Neverland Ranch rather than Los Teques. I kept waiting for Michael Jackson to moonwalk and sing out a chorus of 'Beat It'.

* * *

My Western Union from my sister still hadn't come through. Eddy, though, loved the coke sample I'd given him on his birthday a few weeks before, and he started selling it for me. He was bringing in cash for a few sales. I earned about fifty or sixty thousand bolos and went 'shopping': I finally bought my own tobo. It was an old cooking-oil drum one of the lads sold me from the kitchen. I also bought myself a bowl, spoon, plate, knife and fork and a mug. Now I was able to go to the rancho and get the slop in my own bowl and take it back to the yard and sit down and eat. And not with my fingers.

But my business plan wasn't quite working out with Eddy.

I was sure much of the coke was disappearing up his nose. I'd given him about six or seven grams to sell at thirty thousand bolos a pop. It was five thousand above the odds, but it was more potent than the stuff the jefes were selling. So I'd given Eddy about seven grams, but he'd only given me the money for two sales. My blood was boiling.

I knew what was going on. Eddy was into the crack and was a loose cannon. In the yard in the evening I'd watch him sit down with the other zombies, smoking crack out of crudely made pipes. They were little glass vials with a hole punched in the side and an empty biro shoved in. The stone was put in the vial and lit, with the crackhead sucking on the end of the biro. They were zonked afterwards, walking around spaced. Eddy would often run about looking for a white mouse. 'Did you see him? Did you see him?' he'd say, smiling. No one ever answered him, and he'd run off into a cell or a toilet looking for the elusive rodent. I was livid with him, though. I'd given him more than 200,000 bolos' worth of coke and he'd earned only about 60,000 bolos, snorting the rest. He was wasting my time.

I pulled him up in the yard after the headcount one day before the luceros started their evening shift selling coke and crack. 'Eddy, this isn't working. I'm trying to make a few quid here. You're not selling the coke, you're snorting it. You just wanna get wasted.'

'I know,' he said, his eyes studying the ground, 'I'm sorry.' He was a nice guy and I couldn't get annoyed with him for long, but I needed another salesman. And Eddy, in fairness to him, didn't tell anyone about the stash. I noticed he'd sold a couple of lines to Silvio and Roberto. I trusted Silvio and went to him when he stepped out from the cells.

'Silvio, I'm trying to run a little business.'

'A business?'

'Selling coke.' He raised his eyebrows. 'That stuff you bought off Eddy the other day is mine.'

'That was yours? Where'd you get it? It's dynamite.'

'I swallowed it in a few johnnies. Look, it's not working out with Eddy; he's selling most of it to buy crack for himself. I need someone else.'

'I could have told you that; you should have come to me first.'

'I wasn't sure who to go to first, so I just gave it to him.'

'How much are you selling it for?'

'It's thirty thousand across the board for a gram. I don't care if they want one gram or twenty grams – that's my price. I won't take any less.'

Silvio had a good network of potential customers among the Italians. His countrymen wouldn't snort and tell, he assured me. The jail was full of them. I was starting to think drug smuggling was a national pastime in Italy. We agreed he would sell it to his buddies in the Special wing. He had a mate who ran the shop there who could flog it to the load of Italians in the wing. So we put our plan into motion. Silvio put out the feelers to the shopkeeper and he put in an order for ten grams. Brilliant, I thought. We even had a great spot to divvy out the coke: the classroom. I brought my talc bottle to the next Spanish lesson. After the others left we put on our drug-dealer hats. On a table next to the map of South America, I popped open the talc-bottle lid and tapped out the ten-gram deal onto a sheet of paper, guessing the weight.

Silvio's eyes nearly popped out of his head. 'Where you get all this?' he said.

'Swallowed a few balloons.' I was sticking to my story.

Silvio later went up to the Special to do the sale. I was sure I could trust him and rely on him. He liked his bit of coke, but he wasn't an addict. He didn't go around strung out on the stuff. I agreed to give him a nice kickback of a gram or so per ten-gram sale, and he was happy with that.

The Italians gave my 'merchandise' the thumbs up. 'Paul,' said Silvio, as we sat in the yard, 'this guy, he says he's never seen a grade this good. He wants another ten grams.'

That's 300,000 bolos, I thought, nice little earner. 'Done

deal.' I knew I'd need money in here; nothing was free. The list of weekly expenses was adding up: the causa, and cash I would need in the future, as I was looking at up to eight years in here. I also had my eye on a bed. I wanted to get off the floor some day. Getting your hands on a bed wasn't just about money, you had to wait for someone to go free or die. Let's see.

* * *

After Spanish class on Thursday morning, we divvied up another round of coke, then myself and Silvio left the classroom and went down to the cantina. It was about 1 p.m.: time for the kitchen and admin workers, including Silvio, and a few of the cops to eat. I followed him in on the off chance I might get a bit of rice and beans – or even chicken, which the workers got. The chicken was skin and bones by the time the dish of the day had worked its way down the pecking order from prison staff to inmate workers and then to common prisoners like me; sardines was about it every day. Silvio sat down on one of the stone benches next to a cop with a gap-toothed grin. I was bursting to use the toilet. I walked past the cookers at the back wall and went towards the toilet there.

'*Baño, ocupado? Ocupado?*' ('Toilet, busy? Busy?') I gave a rap on the door with my knuckles. There was no lock on the steel door and you had to knock. No answer. I stepped in and started taking a leak. I heard a shuffle of feet behind me. I swivelled my neck around to look back at the door. Two of the cell-block outcasts who lived in the passageway stood there: one was black with an afro mop, while the other had fine, straight hair and odd-looking eyes spaced closely together.

I quickly pulled up my zip. This was trouble.

My eyes glanced down at their hands; they were both tooled up. One held a long, thin DIY knife that looked like a kebab skewer; the other's weapon looked like a piece of a pipe filed to a sharp point.

The adrenalin started pumping. My hands tensed. I instinctively felt for the pen I had in my pocket; it might the only thing to use as a weapon.

'*Tú, ropa, ahora,*' ('You, clothes, now') said the guy with the afro, gesturing for me to let him search me. The other stood at the door keeping watch.

'No,' I said, turning around and waving him off. I wasn't letting these two shits shake me down. My eyes darted down to their knives. I thought of shouting for help, but there was no point. It was the jungle and you had to defend yourself.

The guy with the afro lunged forward. I put my hands out to defend myself, slamming into his chest and pushing him away. He stumbled back, but his right arm swung around in a fast arc. I felt a thump just below my left armpit. I instinctively went for the pen. I pulled it out, and before he could regain his balance I plunged it towards his right eye, bringing the pen down from a height over my head. I missed, but the tip sunk into the space between his eye and the upper bridge of his nose. 'Aggh, aggh,' he started grunting and groaning like an animal, flailing around grabbing at his eyes, his hands trembling. The other outcast ran off, knowing the cries of his accomplice might bring the workers running in.

I had to get out of there. If the prison staff or the kitchen workers came in I knew I'd be in trouble. Didn't matter if I was only defending myself. The Afro boy was still groaning, falling against the wall and slumping down on his knees.

I stepped out and walked quickly into the canteen. Silvio looked up at me.

'I'm going back to Maxima. I'm after getting into a fight.'

His eyes looked like they'd seen something frightening. He stood up. 'I saw the two going in; I meant to warn you.'

'I better get back to the wing.'

'Go.'

I walked out to the gates to the passageway that led down

to Maxima. A cop was on guard. The gates were only opened at certain times and I knew they'd open up in the next few minutes at this time of day. I stood there looking casual. I felt a warm wetness below my left armpit. I was wearing a dark T-shirt but looked down and saw a damp mark. I folded my arms, feeling moistness on my fingers, worried the cop seated at the gates would see the blood and haul me off for an interrogation.

Minutes passed like hours. Waves of pain started to kick in under my arm with the rush of adrenalin wearing off. I gritted my teeth. I was panicking, expecting one of the cell-block outcasts to come back; they wouldn't fight in front of the cop, but I didn't want to take the chance.

After about five minutes, the cop stood up and opened the gate. Thank God. His keys rattled in the rusty lock. I walked as quick as I could down the passageway. I banged on the wing door. The eyeball of the lag on lookout peered out of the spyhole.

'Maxima,' I said. The door swung back and I stepped in. I saw Eddy. 'I just stabbed someone in the face with a pen.'

'You wha'?' he said, his eyebrows rising up like two birds taking flight.

'And I've been stabbed, here under my arm.'

'Who did it? Who did it?' he said quickly, excited.

'Couple of the scumbags in the passageway. Followed me into the pisser in the canteen. One of them lunged at me with a knife and got me.'

'Let's go to Fidel, see what he says.'

Fidel was sitting on his bed in Cell 1. Eddy told him in Spanish what had happened. Any run-ins with prisoners in other cell blocks had to be reported in case they grew into something bigger.

I just nodded at Fidel. '*Cuchillo grande*' ('Big knife').

'What'd he look like?' said Eddy.

'Afro hairstyle. Early 40s.'

'He says not to go out on your own again. He says if it's

who he thinks it is he'll be gunning for revenge.'

'Right, I wanna get this sorted out,' I said, nodding to my arms, which were still folded. Eddy led me over to another lag, who pulled down a DIY first-aid kit in a cardboard box from a ledge. There were bandages, a few pills and cotton buds.

I lifted up my T-shirt, gritting my teeth as I stretched up my left arm to get it off. There was a red puncture hole in my skin and messy blotches of blood.

'*Nada, nada,*' laughed the inmate.

'Nothing, he says, only a scratch,' said Eddy.

'Good, tell him to do something.' The DIY doctor wiped the wound with some homemade disinfectant made out of vinegar and put on a bandage.

That was that. I'd survived my first attack in Los Teques, but now I had to be on the lookout for a revenge stabbing.

Chapter 11

CANCER WISH

I'D BEEN COOPED UP FOR THE LAST FEW MONTHS IN THE MAXIMA wing, the cantina and the classroom. That was it. That's how narrow my life had become. Thank God for the yard and the view out into the sky. I don't know what I would have done locked up in a dark dungeon like the Number 7 wing where there wasn't even a window and natural light.

There was a roof area above, next door to the Maxima yard. Silvio had been telling me it had been open to inmates in the whole prison in the past. There was a big recreation area for sports and you could hang out all day and lie in the sun. It was hard to believe.

But access had been shut down the Easter before after a gun battle between cell blocks broke out on the roof. Silvio said the riot left about half a dozen dead. The warring inmates battled with automatic weapons and even grenades, leaving much of the roof damaged. I'd heard construction work going on for months, drills whirring and the hollow crack of hammers.

The director was keen to reopen the roof, seeing it as another way of improving the lot of the inmates in Los Teques. She believed that if she opened up the jail and gave the prisoners the run of it we would all end up one happy family. Rows between cell blocks would then be resolved by the jefes with a gentleman's handshake. I liked her thinking, but brotherly love seemed in short supply in Venezuela . . . let alone inside a jail filled with inmates armed to the teeth.

The plan was to open up the roof on different days for

149

selected wings. It would be open to us in Maxima on Mondays and Thursdays from early afternoon till headcount in the evening. When the first Monday came I was all excited about the trip up. We all were; we were looking forward to a bit of space.

In the afternoon it was our turn. I walked up the stairs in the passageway and emerged onto the roof. There was a basketball court, all marked out professionally and with new hoops; a small football pitch drawn out with white-painted lines on the concrete, and two proper netted goalposts; and a volleyball net at one end. It was a huge area the size of a football pitch. As I stood there, an inmate ran past me jogging. Another was lying down on the ground with his top off, sunbathing, while another prisoner was doing pull-ups on exercise bars. Lovely jubbly, I thought, taking it all in – this is a change. I'd only been on the roof during the National Guard prison searches. I hadn't had much of a view with my face pressed into the ground.

I looked out at the view at the front of the jail. There were gentle hills covered in a thick cluster of trees sloping down to rusty-red fields criss-crossed with narrow roads. To the left was a barrio, a mishmash of crudely made houses, three or four storeys high, each floor jutting out above the other, each building looking like it would topple. I also got a look down to the driveway of the jail, where I'd been in and out to the courts on a prison bus. National Guard troops stood around a hut with corrugated-iron window frames sticking out of pale-blue walls. One guard was texting on his phone.

Security was high. A wall ran around the perimeter at waist height with wire fences about 30 ft high topped with coils of razor-sharp barbed wire. National Guard troops posted at watchtowers dotted around the prison looked down upon us, polishing M16 rifles. They looked like they'd be happy if we made a run for it so they could try out their shooting skills and pick us off the roof like sitting ducks in a blood sport. If I'd ever hoped I'd have a chance of getting out over the walls of Los Teques, it was dashed now. I'd have to think of other ways.

I walked over to an area where there were a couple of gringos – made obvious by their lighter shade of skin and fair hair. I met Bruce, an Aussie, a couple of Yanks and a Canadian. I was dead keen to meet a few new gringos. We started chatting.

'How much you get caught with, Irishman?' asked Bruce straight off.

'Six kilos – got eight years.'

They'd all been caught in Simón Bolívar airport.

'Fuck, man, yeah, eight years,' said Dan, one of the Yanks. 'If we're lucky we can get out in two.' Everyone was thinking that way: apply for parole after 18 months and get out a few months after.

The others took off and I was left there chatting with Bruce. We got on well. We had similar interests, such as rugby and cricket. He was also a big surfer. He was in his early 40s, a few years younger than me, and told me he had left behind a young son and daughter in Australia after he'd got caught in the airport in Maiquetía. I really felt sorry for him. It cut me up that I was away from Daniel and Katie and the rest of my family, but my kids were now in their late teens. Bruce's were only nine and ten years old. It would have eaten me up to be locked up here with children at home that age and not being able to watch them grow up.

'Ain't easy,' he said. 'Take each day as it comes. Start missing your life too much and you'll end up slitting your throat in there.' Bruce suddenly lowered his voice. 'You know, there are ways to get out of here other than waiting around a couple of years to try and get parole.'

My ears pricked up. 'Like what?'

'Get cancer.'

'Get what?' I thought I wasn't hearing him right.

'Cancer,' Bruce continued. He told me himself and a couple of other gringo inmates had hatched a plan to get diagnosed with it. They knew a lawyer who was in cahoots with a doctor who was in cahoots with a judge. You feigned sickness, the external doctor was called in and would diagnose you with cancer, then the lawyer would get the judge to issue a release on humanitarian grounds for the prisoner to be released to an appointed family. Then you'd start chemo in a local hospital. From there, you did a runner. The whole package didn't come cheap, said Bruce. It was ten thousand dollars down and ten thousand after you got out. 'There's a few of us in it – Ryan, a Yankee, got out just a few weeks ago. Slipped out from the hospital into Caracas. Disappeared into the night.'

Now I was really up for it. It was an awful lot of money that I didn't have, but I was all ears. 'Put me down as interested,' I said quickly, 'but I wanna meet this lawyer, I'm not handing over any ten grand to someone I haven't met.'

'He'll visit in the next couple of weeks. Play our cards right, we could be out in a few months.'

I was really excited, but cautiously – I didn't yet know if I could trust Bruce or this lawyer. I'd already heard stories about prisoners paying thousands to solicitors and dodgy officials on the promise of freedom only for the cash to disappear into a black hole. Bruce seemed trustworthy, though. I decided to play it all by ear. So as well as early parole, I now had a Plan B to get out of this Latin dungeon.

Bruce was an intelligent, well-read guy. Before we parted he lent me a non-fiction book set in a jail in Britain in the late 1600s. It was all about how the inmates had to pay to survive on the inside and how the prison was overrun with death and squalor. I later read it, thinking nothing had changed in the prison world in the last few hundred years.

* * *

Roberto showed his cards. A pair of jacks and a pair of queens. 'Hey, I win, my friends, I win. All is mine.' He was sitting playing poker with myself and Eddy.

'So what, mate?' said Eddy. 'One game. One hand. Many more to come.' Roberto gathered up his winnings from the little blue-painted stool we were playing on in the yard: rings off Coke cans.

New Yawk Mike walked over. 'Paul, man, your money's here.'

'Great,' I said, standing up. I stood up and followed him out into Cell 1 where the jefe was sitting on his bed watching his portable TV. He sat up and started counting out a big bundle of notes. Mike punched in the exchange rate of the 350 euro Western Union money my sister had sent me on a chunky calculator the bosses probably used when toting up their coke deals. There were so many zeros I had to squint to read it. The 350 euro actually turned me into a millionaire, something like 2,500,000 bolos. Out of that sum I had to pay the wing 'entry fee' of 200 euro, leaving me with 150 euro for myself – to last me for how long I didn't know.

The bosses converted the money using the bank exchange rate of euro to bolo. The thing was, though, that the euro was worth twice as much on the street rate, which is where the bosses would have changed my money. So I got my 350 euro in bolos at the bank rate and the jefe and his sidekicks pocketed the same amount. Carlos sat beside Fidel, his Colt next to him. I didn't think complaining would get me far.

I then rolled out the plan I had to get out of sleeping in the toilet. 'Mike, tell Fidel I'll pay him the whole entry fee right now if he gets me out of the toilet.' I had to get out of there – waking up on cardboard soaked in piss was driving me mad.

'All of it?' said Mike, his eyes widening. Most lags paid it in dribs and drabs.

'Every bit of it, here and now. Just get me a spot on the cell floor to sleep.' He spoke to Fidel. I watched his eyes widen looking at the cash in the three neat bundles on the bed. A big grin broke across Fidel's face.

'*Sí, no problema,*' he said. I knew he wouldn't mind; we gringos were an endless supply of foreign-exchange reserves for the bosses. *Vacas de leche*, or milk cows, they called us, along with any of the lags they could get an easy flow of cash from. Crack addicts were among their biggest earners.

Fidel handed me over the big pile of notes from the 150 euro in bolos (about the same as a month's salary for a National Guard). Mike then pointed at all the lags in the yard. 'Now listen,' said Mike, 'never give those muthafuckers money. You'll never get it back.' The whole wing would know the gringo had got a Western Union.

The next day I sat in the yard writing my book and diary. It was part of my routine every day. A steady stream of Venos came up to me looking for a loan of *plata*. I just shouted 'fuck off' without taking my head up from my copybook. I was watching my cash. I didn't want to bother my family or friends for money again unless my life or freedom depended on it. I'd make my own money here.

* * *

In the passageway one day I bumped into Fulvio from my Macuto days.

'It's great to see you,' I said, shaking his hand.

'Yes,' he said, smiling.

'So no luck getting out of here through the courts?' I laughed.

'Yes,' he said, 'maybe.' I remembered he spoke little English.

'No worries,' I said, 'see you around.'

He walked off.

In the wing I tracked down Silvio to see what Fulvio's story was. He knew about all the Italians. 'Fulvio, yeah, he's back from Macuto,' said Silvio. He knew he'd been fighting his conviction through the courts.

'What happened to his case?' I said.

'It went nowhere,' he shrugged. 'Never does, but it gave him something to do.'

* * *

Father Pat was in every two weeks. Myself and Billy looked forward to his visits. It was a break from the day-to-day monotony and a chance to have contact with someone normal. He usually came unannounced, knowing we were likely to be there. One afternoon we were called out for the visita with him and filed out to the passageway.

'Hallo Billy, hallo Paul. It's good to see you two boys found each other,' he said, smiling. The padre was always on good form, and I knew it took him an entire day to make the trip out to us on the outskirts of Caracas and back to his barrio.

'Father Pat, great to see you. And Billy, he moved into the wing with me. In Maxima.' We chatted through the usual stuff. We said we were doing all right and keeping our heads down.

'And are you staying away from the drugs?' He looked at both of us, but the question was really for Billy. He knew I didn't do the garden bugs.

'Yeah,' said Billy, 'all of them.'

The padre said nothing, just looked Billy in the eyes. There was a pause and then Father Pat replied, 'OK.'

I took the chance to lighten the moment and asked Father Pat if he could get me the key ingredient for my home brew: yeast. 'We'd like to make a bit of bread, Father.'

'Bread?' he said.

I looked at Billy fighting back a grin.

'Yeah, for the Christmas, we're tired of the stale stuff they have here. We just need a bit of yeast to make it. Can't get it here.'

'I could certainly get my hands on that, yes, very good.' He seemed pleased we were being 'productive' with our time. 'I'll bring that in on the next visit.' With the chat over, Father Pat got down to do the business he came to do: say Mass. He pulled out his trusty Bible and said a few words. I was hoping he wouldn't ask us for a confession to repent any porky pies.

* * *

Inmates who had jobs in the jail signed a special book logging the hours and type of work they did. Just like my Spanish classes did, each working day counted towards time off your sentence. I wanted a job as well to pick up the pace on time that could be chopped off my sentence.

What I would work at, though? I didn't speak enough Spanish to get a job in the kitchen. The same for work such as collecting rubbish, like Macedonia did. Everyone else in Maxima signed on as a cleaner. Tradesmen could sign on as an electrician or plumber if they were doing building work in the wing. I never said I was a plumber; I didn't want to help the bosses with anything. I hated them. I suddenly had a brainwave. I was a writer. To me, that was a job. I just had to convince the director.

I saw Silvio. He was talking in Italian on his mobile phone. He often spoke to his daughter, who lived with her mother, Silvio's ex, in Madrid. He hung up as I walked over to him in the yard. I saw him breathe out a sigh as I got closer. He was emotional, like many were after talking to their family. I should have given him some space and time. I kept going, though.

'Silvio, I want to sign the work book.'

'You need a job first.' He rubbed his hand across his face. He seemed fragile.

'I have one – I'm a writer. My diaries, and I'm writing a book.'

He laughed out loud. 'Paul, that will never work,' said Silvio.

The next day I hounded him again in the yard. 'OK, we'll go up and ask the director. She will probably laugh.'

Fabio, a gay Venezuelan prisoner who did the director's nails, agreed to come with us. We thought he might be a good inroad into getting her to agree. Fabio babbled in Spanish to Silvio in the passageway leading to the director's office. 'He says he thinks she will agree. It's writing, and it's creative. Let's see.'

The director was seated behind her desk. She was well made-up with glossy red lips. Silvio and Fabio explained I wanted to sign the work book, but there were no jobs if you didn't speak Spanish. 'Show her your work, Paul,' said Silvio. I had the few copybooks I'd filled in with diaries and stories and fanned out the pages in front of her.

The director spoke to Silvio, her blonde curls bouncing about. 'What's your story about?' said Silvio.

'About life in Ireland.' I didn't say I was keeping a diary of life in this hellhole.

Silvio interpreted to her. '*Sí*,' she said quickly. No deliberation. Fantastic. Credit to her.

'You can start signing the book,' said Silvio, his eyes wide open.

We stepped out of the office. 'I didn't think you'd get that, Paul,' said Silvio. From then on I signed the black work book in the office opposite the director's. 'Paul Keany – *escritor* [writer].'

* * *

Soon after, I got the brew going with all the ingredients – sugar, rice, water and the yeast from Father Pat – mixed up in the empty ten-litre water bottle. After about a week or so I inspected it and it looked like it had matured. I was sure it had turned into a decent home brew, like rice wine.

'Let's give it a twirl, Billy. See what it tastes like.'

Silvio and Ricardo gathered around. We all had our cups ready, which we usually used for coffee. I opened the lid. A hiss like a pressure pot boiling eased out of the bottle. A foul smell like methane gas sifted out. Silvio turned his nose away.

'Is it ready?' said Billy, excited.

'Looks done to me.'

'When can we try it?'

'No time like the present.' I hoisted up the ten-litre bottle and poured it into Ricardo's coffee mug. The liquid was dark yellow and cloudy, but it settled and cleared a bit. Ricardo lifted up the mug. We all stood watching him. A few of the Veno lags were looking over too. Ricardo took a sip. We were all waiting to hear what he'd say.

'That's fucking sweet,' he said, licking his lips. We all grinned, and I filled up the rest of the coffee mugs and we all had a drop.

'Lovely jubbly,' I said after a mouthful.

'Tasty,' said Billy.

But now I had to go in to Vampy to give him a bit. He'd also helped us out getting some yeast. He was a pest at times but a decent sort. I went into his cell, where he was sitting on the side of his bed. Billy was with me to interpret. I handed Vampy a cup. He took a drink. '*Muy bueno!*' he said, grinning. '*Muy bueno, gringo.*' I offered the jefe a drink, but he waved me off; he wasn't a big boozer. The Chief, though, took a drop and stuck his thumb up in the air. Word got around the wing that the brew was good and I started selling it at five thousand bolos, or one euro, for a litre bottle of the fortified wine. The lags called it *jugo loco*, or crazy juice. Now I had another source of income to get by on. I was determined not to bother my family for money again.

* * *

It was night. I lay down my cardboard on the floor in Cell 1, crammed in with about fifty people on colchonetas on the floor, spread seven across the tight cell. The air was dead and putrid, a thick soup of the body odours of men squashed onto the floor: feet, sweat, bad breath and farts. I rarely had problems sleeping, only there was a Spanish twat squashed up next to me, his leg moving nineteen to the dozen in his sleep. My little spot on the floor wasn't far from the door to the squat toilet. There was no path to it; you had to walk through a sea of bodies in faint light to get there. 'Agh, agh,' you could hear all night, the sounds of men whining after an inmate had stepped on their head or their legs. The *garitas*, or sentries, at the wing door would hop over us with the finesse of a ballet dancer. They were sharp and wide awake; it was the crackheads who stayed up all night smoking stones in the hallway who were the problem – stumbling over us to the toilet, or stomping on your head or your arm. I was actually regretting I'd left the toilet. At least there was a small window there. Cool air blew in at night, better than the stink here. You know things are bad when you miss sleeping on a toilet floor. Billy was in there now in my spot, waiting for a sleeping space to come up on the cell floor.

The next morning in the yard he came out rubbing his head through his mop of mousey-brown hair. I was sitting down on my bucket getting ready for the headcount.

'What's wrong with you?'

'Fidel hit me over the head with his knife.' He took a seat on a paint tin.

'For what?' Billy was a laid-back guy and I couldn't see him upsetting anyone.

'He came into the jacks at night and I was having a go at myself.'

'Ha,' I buckled over laughing. Billy just gave a sheepish shrug. He broke one of the rules in the wing: you don't play with yourself. It made sense. A hundred-odd men having a go at themselves on the cell floor at night wouldn't work.

After morning Spanish classes I went to Maxima and sat in the pantry, watching TV with Billy. It was the usual fare: an action flick, Steven Seagal, Jean-Claude Van Damme, *Rambo*, guns and bombs. All of a sudden Carlos stood in front of me. At 6 ft 2 in., he was towering over me. He started babbling in Spanish. '*Irlandés, cómo te llamas?*'

'What's your name?' said Billy, interpreting.

'Paul,' I said. It was unusual for Carlos to go to talk to a gringo directly but in itself not enough to be alarming. Carlos babbled again.

'Get your tobo and follow him,' said Billy, looking a bit worried for me. It was dawning on me what was going on, but I wasn't sure. Carlos and a lucero followed me into the yard and I grabbed the cooking-oil drum that was my tobo. They then took me by the arm and marched me into Cell 1, past two luceros who stood sentry outside. All the bosses were there: the jefe, Fidel; his two underbosses; and Carlos beside me. I could see three guns: a revolver on top of a bed and two automatics on a table – the kind of things you notice when marched into a closed room. Carlos called out to New Yawk Mike and he came into the cell. Fidel closed the door. My heart raced. Shit. I was in for it.

Carlos started talking. 'He says he has reason to believe you have been selling coke in Maxima,' said Mike, interpreting, 'and to other wings in the prison.'

'Yeah,' I said, casually, deciding to play it cool and dumb. Mike's face dropped. He looked at me like I'd just signed my death warrant. He interpreted back to Carlos. They all looked at each other in disbelief, shaking their heads. Carlos spoke again.

'This is one of the most serious things you can do in the prison,' said Mike. 'You're not allowed to sell drugs anywhere, that's the job of bosses.'

I kept up my dumb and innocent act. 'Mike, when I came in here you gave me a list of dos and don'ts – do this, do that – but you never told me I couldn't do that.' Jimmy's face dropped again. Probably thought I was landing him in it now. And I was taking a chance with my defiance. It mightn't go down well.

Carlos and another boss then started rifling through my tobo, turning the cooking-oil drum upside down. My towel, T-shirts and wash bag all tumbled onto the floor. 'I presume they're looking for the drugs, Mike,' I said. 'They won't find them there.'

'Well, where the fuck are they, man?' he shouted.

'They're in my other tobo.'

'You have two tobos?' he said, his eyebrows raised. It was rare for anyone to have more than one, but I'd been gathering a few possessions after I'd come into a few quid from selling the coke and booze, and I needed more than one bucket.

'Yeah.'

Mike spoke quickly to Carlos. Suddenly the Chief stepped forward, his lips pursed, grabbed me by the arm and marched me into the hall. There was a crackhead sitting on my other tobo, watching Steven Seagal dressed as a chef battling mercenaries with a frying pan.

I tapped the stoner on the shoulder. '*Tobo, tobo mío.*' ('Bucket, my bucket.') I was a bit less panicky as it didn't look like I'd get a bullet, maybe just a beating.

'No,' he said, waving me off, not taking his eyes off the TV. The Chief's fist came out of nowhere and punched him in the side of the head. The stoner went crashing onto the floor. He looked up in shock and rubbed his cheek. The others watching the Seagal flick suddenly turned around. There was better action closer to home. But they looked nervous. On edge. The Chief marched me back into the cell past the sentries holding pipe guns. I was carrying my bucket. The door closed. Carlos grabbed the tobo and they all started rifling through it, my shampoo and toothbrush and everything was getting wrecked. I also had two million bolos in the wash bag, which I didn't want them to find.

'Mike, I can tell them where the coke is.'

'Well, where is it, man?' He interpreted to Carlos, who called me forward. I bent down, picked up the talc bottle at the bottom of the tobo and held it up. They all laughed at the irony of it. It was a well-known Venezuelan brand of talc. Fidel went and ripped a piece of paper off a notebook. He got the talc bottle, opened it and upended it onto the paper. It poured into a nice little mound. Carlos put his finger in it and dabbed a bit on his tongue, while the others watched. A grin broke out on his face. '*Increíble.*' ('Incredible.') The others then dipped their fingers in for a try. It was so pure. Straight away they knew it was top-quality coke I had smuggled in before getting into the prison system.

'Airport. Macuto. Los Teques. Never find,' said Carlos in broken English. He was listing off all the searches I would have gone through at each stage from my arrest at the airport to arriving at Los Teques. I didn't want to tell him Venezuelan security officials were dumb, but that was why it hadn't been found.

Fidel brought over a little set of electronic weighing scales. He carefully lifted up the sheet of paper the coke was piled up on. My fists were clenched. I still wasn't sure what they would do to me. I eyed the revolver nearby on the bed.

'It's 88 grams,' Mike said in disbelief. He spoke to Carlos. 'Because they have this amount of cocaine you're not getting a bullet today.'

I was blessed. I stood there smiling. The bosses were happy with the haul: it was all that had saved me from being killed, my bleeding corpse dumped in the passageway. They knew they could mix it down with horse tranquilliser powder and turn it into three or four times the amount. It'd be enough to keep the wing going for a week and bring them in good money.

Carlos spoke and Mike interpreted. 'He wants to know if anyone else is involved in you selling coke. Was Eddy involved in this?'

'No.'

'Was Silvio involved?'

'No.'

'Was Roberto involved?'

'No.' They knew who my friends were, and they were suspicious of Silvio because he was Italian and thought he was the middleman selling it to the Italians in the Special. The funny thing was that they never asked if Billy was part of the little coke-deal operation. Everyone could see he didn't have much get-up and go.

'No, nobody,' I said, 'nothing to do with any of them. I did it all myself.'

Mike spoke to Carlos. He nodded and said '*todo bien*' ('all good'). They bought it.

'Your punishment is that you'll have to sleep in the toilet. Now get the fuck out of here.'

I walked off quickly. I'd survived my first 'light' without a beating. That was it. Thank God. Mike then marched me out into the yard. On the way, he said, 'You don't know how close you were to a bullet. You are one lucky muthafucker.'

That evening I was telling Silvio, Billy and the boys what happened in the cell. They all sat there on their bucket listening in, amazed. The biggest laugh was over the crackhead who got clocked by the Chief.

A few days later Silvio found out who grassed me in the Special. It turned out Pedro the shopkeeper had too much coke with the ounce, just over twenty-eight grams, I sold him and not enough Italians among the ten or twelve of them to buy it all. To make his investment back he started selling to other inmates in the wing. A couple of lines made its way to the padrino. That was the near-fatal turn of events. Silvio filled me in that the padrino had pulled up Pedro, wanting to know where he'd got a load of charlie in a drought – which seemed to be rare in Los Teques. The jefes zealously guarded the sale of drugs; it was their bread and butter. But Pedro refused to give me up. They then called a light, hauled him into a cell and beat him senseless with bars and bats. Silvio said Pedro only gave me up after they threatened to shoot him. '*El irlandés. Maxima,*' he screamed. They didn't mess around in the Special.

* * *

I was called out for a meeting with the abogado, or lawyer, set up by Bruce. I asked Silvio to interpret and he followed me out to the passageway. We went into a small office where the prison cops usually had their dinner. The smell of stale smoke and sweat hung in the air. The abogado was a slight, polished old gent in his 70s with silver hair. After we exchanged a few niceties he got down to business.

'Bruce spoke to you; you know why I'm here,' he said through Silvio.

'I know.' I was keen to hear his pitch but sceptical – I didn't trust anyone in this country, least of all an ageing lawyer sniffing for 20,000 dollars.

'I ensure you are diagnosed with cancer and in weeks the prison lets you go and live with a family in Caracas, near a hospital. There you will be allowed stay with the family to be near your treatment.'

'I'm interested, yes.'

'You pay 10,000 dollars for the doctor and he says you have cancer, then for the judge. He gets his money, signs the paper and you are free. Then the other 10,000 dollars get you to Colombia, to the border. How do you like that?'

'I like it a lot, but it'd take time to get that kind of money. Come back to me in a month when I've made some calls home.' I was excited but still sceptical. Even if I went ahead with it, getting 20 grand wouldn't be easy. I did have that mate at home, though, who ran a construction business that had done well in the boom years. I was sure he'd lend me the cash.

I stood up, and the lawyer handed me a slip of paper with the details for his bank account in Caracas. 'That's where you send money.'

'OK, we'll be in touch.'

* * *

In the yard there was the usual bit of excitement after one of the cops dropped in *la lista* after dinner and posted it on the wall. One of the lags pulled it down. It was passed hurriedly from one inmate to the other, all huddled out in the yard, pawing at the sheet to see if their name was on it. It was the list of prisoners who had their court hearing coming up or, for the lucky ones, news they'd done their time and would be freed. I stood in the background pacing up and down in the yard for a bit of exercise. The lista didn't bring me any excitement, I knew I was here for eight years and that was that. Court hearings were just red tape.

'Paul, you're in court in the morning,' said Silvio, after hearing one of the lags reading the list call out *el irlandés*. I walked over and had a glance, and there it was all right – 'Paul Keany' in black and white in small typeface. Silvio filled me in on what to do. 'Wear a shirt, trousers and shoes, and bring food and water. You'll be there all day and you'll get nothing to eat or drink.'

Eddy, Roberto, Vito, everybody in fact, was telling me I'd get eight years. That was the minimum sentence for drug trafficking in Venezuela. If you pleaded innocent they'd go down hard on you; you'd be found guilty anyway and could get up to 20 years. I had no intention of saying I didn't do it. I'd been caught and that was that. And Venezuela didn't look like the kind of place I'd get justice in. So I'd plead guilty and do the time – which I hoped would be just two years – then scoot out on early parole.

* * *

After breakfast the next day I threw on my Ireland rugby shirt with the three shamrocks on the crest. It was long-sleeved and did the job as formal clothing, as far as I cared. I stood in the hallway with a couple of other lags. The garita called out 'agua' and a cop appeared at the door. About seven of us filed out and were called to a halt at the bottom of the stairs in the passageway. The cop held a list. '*Nombre,*' ('name') he called out, looking at me. Silvio wasn't there to interpret. '*Inglés,*' I said, shrugging, thinking he asked me for my number and not my name. A few months in Venezuela and I still couldn't answer my name.

'Pa-uww-l, Pa-uww-l Keany,' said the cop. In Spanish they

always stretch out the vowels, such as the u.

'*Sí*,' I said, nodding.

In the driveway outside I was strip-searched, handcuffed and marched onto the bus. I sat there and watched inmates from other wings being led out for the same drill. They were prisoners from wings 1 and 2, equally hated and feared by other cell blocks. They only spoke among themselves. That was one of their rules: they were not allowed to speak to other prisoners, particularly me. Their wings even had their own ten commandments – one was 'thou shalt not speak to a gringo'. I doubted Moses carved that one into stone.

* * *

The courtroom was a bit like the set of *Judge Judy*. It was small, with a few tables and chairs and a modern-looking gallery, which was empty. I sat handcuffed next to four other inmates. Our lawyers sat on the other side of the court. I looked over, saw my interpreter and gave him a nod. He walked over.

'Hello, how are you?' he said.

'Fine. This is all just a formality, right?'

'Yes, a formality.' There wasn't much to say. I didn't really have any questions. It was a done deal; I'd get convicted and that was that.

The judge stepped into the courtroom: a woman in her 60s. She spoke for a few minutes to my interpreter. He then walked over. 'Eight years,' he said, holding up my sentence sheet, pointing to the word *ocho* (eight) on it. My eyes scanned down further and I noticed the amount of cocaine was down over a kilo from the six kilos I'd been caught with in the airport. I knew I'd scooped up about 300 g from my haul after I was caught. The cops must have had the same idea. Cheeky buggers.

The hearing was all over in about four minutes: four minutes to get eight years. To be honest, I was relieved. I'd prepared myself for that. Had it been 15 or 20 years I don't know what I would have done.

Chapter 12

CHRISTMAS UNDER THE STARS

CHRISTMAS WAS UPON US. THE WHOLE WING WAS WHIPPED INTO festive mode. Our special causa had been used to give Maxima a bit of 'Ding Dong Merrily on High'. It was scrubbed up as usual, and for the festive touch a little Christmas tree covered in tinsel and flashing lights was put up in the hallway by the cells. Still, I doubted Santa Claus would pay a visit to Los Teques unless he came in holed up in a tank.

What I was dreading was the visitas. The director had said all families and their partners visiting prisoners could stay for five nights over Christmas. It was another of her new policies to try to make the prison more humane and avoid another massacre like the one that had taken place the Easter before under the last director. The thinking was that giving armed, coked-up murderers and rapists more time with their families would turn them into model inmates. Guns down, all hugs and kisses.

The five-day visit started a couple of days before Christmas. Myself and the other gringo PWVs, as I called us, as well as a few of the Venos, were stashed away behind the curtains for some 15 hours a day. We had to huddle in there sitting on our buckets from about 9 a.m. to 1 or 2 a.m., or whenever the party stopped in the wing. It was non-stop. The stereo was on full-whack with salsa music blaring out all day. The Veno lags partied away with their wives, girlfriends, children, mothers, aunts, the whole lot, dancing, singing and boozing. At night they would all sleep in the three cells, the prisoners taking

167

turns in the few beds to get it on with their missus, and later squeezing the rest of their families onto any beds that were free.

That left us to kip in the only place left – out in the yard under the stars. The music stopping showed they had finished their day's festivities and was the green light for us to come out from behind the curtain and roll out our colchonetas on the ground. We had to scramble off our buckets to get a spot in the half of the yard that was covered with a canopy made out of an old stretched-out plastic sheet. If you didn't get a place there, you were really under the stars. The weather was mostly mild and sunny during the day in Caracas, but at night it could get chilly. I found it hard to sleep, tossing and turning on the ground, wrapping my arms around myself to get warm.

The whole visit thing was really getting me down. It was horrible mental torture: endless sitting on a bucket, groggy, with no proper sleep for days, listening to the lags partying away outside. At times I was worried I'd lose my cool, run out from behind the curtain, grab one of their guns and start blasting at them. Of course they'd shoot back, though, and that'd be it for me – game over. Also, it being Christmas, my mind was drifting off and thinking of my family back home. That was hard. Katie and Dano – I wondered what they'd be doing now. Would they hate me? Still love me? None of my family back home called me over Christmas, but that's the way I wanted it. I had to put my head down in here and just focus on doing the time.

On Christmas Day we sat as usual huddled up all day behind the curtain, with nothing to do other than chat with the boys, Silvio, Ricardo, Billy and others. Many of the lags were doing the usual – snorting coke. I still hadn't touched it. This place was bad enough without the paranoia from coke driving me up the walls even more. Sitting there all day as PWVs, we weren't allowed out to mix with the lags and their families, but from time to time a boss would stick his head in behind the curtain and look at us. I could snatch glances of what was going on out there. I saw a kid pedalling around on a little red tractor. Lights flashing on the small Christmas tree. A couple dancing salsa, swinging their hips and twirling. Later, I saw a troupe of Mexican-style mariachi musicians walk in, decked out in sombreros, tooting away on trumpets and strumming guitars. I thought they must be hard-up for playing a gig in a prison. I had to remind myself it was a jail and not some reality TV show I was in. *Banged Up in Loonyville?*

What really got up the nose of us PWVs about the whole affair was that our special causa was paying for it: presents, decorations, food, bands. Yet we were getting nothing out of it. On Christmas Day itself we thought, great, at least we'll get the decent dinner the jcfc had promised us. That morning we ate the usual breakfast slop in the cantina and then went in behind the curtain. We were looking forward to the Christmas food, but at the usual dinner time of 4 p.m. nothing came. Five p.m., still nothing.

'This is wrong, I tell you,' said Silvio, raging, shaking his fist.

'I know, I'm starving,' I said. My blood was boiling. We were all pissed off. Our money paying for them to have a good time while we sat there miserable and hungry. We were getting merry on the rice wine I'd made, but we still wanted to eat.

At about 7 p.m. one of the lags walked in with 'dinner'. It was some local Venezuelan dish, a large green plantain leaf with a filling inside, served on paper plates with a dollop of vegetables and a small piece of bread the size of a communion host. We looked at each other and back at the plates laden with portions suited for a kids' party.

'What the fuck is this?' I said.

'*Hallaca*,' said Silvio. 'It's a Venezuelan dish they eat at Christmas. This one's vegetarian.'

'You mean we pay a 100,000 causa and don't even get a piece of meat.'

'No, nothing. It is disgraceful I tell you,' he said. The inmates and their visitors had obviously eaten the best themselves. The rage was flaming up inside me. I wanted to go out from behind the curtain and murder the bastards. Merry Christmas me bollocks. The words of the Pogues's 'Fairytale of New York' also came to mind: surrounded by scumbags and maggots, I prayed God it would be my last in Los Teques.

New Year's Eve rolled around a few days later just as fast as Christmas had. After a couple of days of rest from the visitors they were back in for another five-day stay in Hotel Los Teques, and we were huddled up behind the curtain again. It was endless. All we could do all day was chat; other than that we watched DVDs on a little telly the boss brought in. Most were pirate movies dubbed in Spanish. Arnie in *The Terminator*: 'I'll be back,' in Spanish with a Mexican accent. That drew a laugh from the gringos.

On the night of 31 December, Fidel popped his acne-scarred face in behind the curtain. He was handing out goody bags to his loyal coke customers, like a department-store manager saying thanks for your loyal business throughout the year. They were plastic bags with smaller pieces of plastic wrapped up inside into one-gram lines. The usual band of snorters got one each, Billy included; he'd been back on the stuff only a couple of weeks after coming down from the Church. So much for getting clean.

Billy started elbowing me. 'Put your hand out, you'll get a bag, go on.'

'No,' I said, 'he won't give me any – he knows I don't take it.'

'He will, go on.' So I put out my hand for the fun, and lo and behold Fidel did drop me a lucky bag. He stepped out, and we ripped open our goodies and spent the next few hours snorting charlie, using coins to scoop it up to our noses. After a while I was buzzing, waffling away to beat the band, my tongue loosening. We all were. That was why the Venos called coke *perico*, or parrot, which endlessly twitter and chirp.

We heard the lags and their families start counting. '*Diez, nueve* . . .' ('Ten, nine . . .')

'Countdown,' said Billy.

'*Ocho, siete* . . .' ('Eight, seven . . .')

A bigger chorus of voices now. '*Seis, cinco, cuatro* . . .' ('Six, five, four . . .')

We got to our feet. The jefe pulled back the curtain and stood beside us, smiling. '*Gringos, vamos,*' ('Let's go') he said, pointing his gun in the air.

'*Tres, dos, uno.*' ('Three, two, one.')

'Heyyyy,' we all shouted along with the jefe, jumping up and down and hugging each other and shaking hands and laughing. The sky exploded into a cacophony of gunfire. The jefe let off his automatic weapon and shot into the air, *drrr-drrr-drrrrrr*, a flow of bullets pumping into the sky, cartridges spilling onto the ground. The whole prison was crackling with gunfire now. All the wing bosses were shooting off rounds. Carlos was getting into the action too, standing beside us, pulling the trigger of his Colt with a heavy *boom boom*. The sky was also erupting with fireworks, exploding into a kaleidoscope of pinks, purples, blues and reds.

'Happy New Year,' we shouted.

'*Feliz año,*' ('Happy New Year') shouted back the Venos.

It was a rare moment I actually didn't hate the Venezuelans. I was even laughing and dancing with them, the coke and booze putting me on good form. For a few minutes Los Teques was bearable. I actually forgot where I was – but only for a moment. I started jumping up and down, but I knew that I was ringing in the New Year thousands of miles from home, locked up in a circus of monkeys with guns. My life on the line every day.

* * *

On a Sunday shortly after the New Year the visitors were

back in. More endless days behind the curtain and nights sleeping on the ground in the yard. It seemed like the whole prison revolved around them. That so many came in and so often could only mean that life for most in the barrios wasn't much different from in the jail. Guns and drugs.

One night sleeping out in the yard one of the lads was passing around a joint, marijuana sprinkled with crack cocaine. They called it a *ruso*, which meant Russian in Spanish. Supposedly it was smoked in Russian prisons all the time. While I might take the odd snort of coke, crack was another league, and I wanted to steer clear of it. But I was lying on the ground, cold and miserable, trying to sleep. '*Fumas, fumas,*' ('Smoke, smoke') said a Veno, offering me the joint. I took it from him – anything to escape the drudgery. I sucked in a deep drag, filled my lungs and slowly exhaled. In minutes I was out of my wagon. I lay back and felt my legs curling up. I sat up with a fright and looked down at them. They were straight. It was weird. It was my first and last time taking crack. I could see what it did to the stoners. Turned them into zombies. I didn't want to go down that road.

The next day, myself and the gringos were squashed up behind the curtain as usual with the other PWVs. A lucero stuck his head through the plastic curtain. He rattled off a torrent of Spanish.

'It's a *secuestro*,' said Silvio, shaking his head. 'The cycle goes on.' He put his head in his hands and looked like he was going to cry.

'A what? What's that?' I said.

'Secuestro, a kidnapping,' he said. 'They've kidnapped the whole jail.'

'How?' This didn't make sense.

'They put a chain around the gates in the passageway outside. No one gets in or out of the wings. Everyone who's here stays here till it's over. All the families.'

'So another sleepover?'

'Yes, but we can't even go to the canteen to eat. Nothing. Can't leave the wing.'

'This is bullshit. What the hell do they want?'

'Usual thing, Paul. It's about conditions, or getting court cases moving so people can get their hearings and get out or get a sentence. There are people in here for months who've only been charged.'

I couldn't believe it. You were in danger of losing your life in this dump and you might even be innocent of whatever you'd been charged with. What made me even sicker was that the Venos were basically kidnapping their own families as ammunition to get what they wanted.

For eight days it went on. A bit of rice went around the odd time, which had been cooked up on the little stove in the wing. And some mornings coffee was made, which you had if you had a few bolos to pay for it. The families didn't suffer, though. There was a fridge in the hallway in the wing full of frozen food. Meat, chicken, the whole lot. I'm sure the bosses ate well out of it too. There wasn't much to do to pass the time, but I did start writing again with a vengeance: a crime book set in Dublin, as well as my diaries, in a copybook I'd bought from the shop in our cell block. All day we sat behind the curtain and all night we slept in the yard. I hated the visitors and I hated Venos even more now.

When it was finally over I couldn't see anything was different in the jail. It was still crowded, the food was still muck and there didn't seem to be any greater number of inmates getting out to the courts that I could see.

* * *

'*Irlandés, visita.*' It was a lucero, a skinny little guy with curly hair and a thin moustache. I waved him away. Nobody visited me, only Father Pat, and he never came when the prison was open to visitors; he only came outside general-public hours with a special chaplain permission. That way he didn't have to queue up outside with the families and have to be patted down when he got through the gates. The lucero had to be mistaken.

'*A mí no me visitan.*' ('Nobody comes to visit me.') My Spanish was coming on. The lucero stepped out from behind the curtain back into the yard. It was Sunday, and visit day. I was sitting on my bucket behind the curtain, counting the cracks in the wall.

Canario, another lucero, walked in now. He was holding a black revolver.

'*Visita,*' he barked, '*llegate.*' ('Visit, get here now.') He wasn't asking. I shrugged and stood up. I followed him out to the hallway. In front of me stood a guy in his early 30s with blonde hair.

'How ya doing?' he said. 'I'm a friend of Father Pat's.' A Dublin accent. A Paddy.

'How are ya?' I said, intrigued. So the luceros were right; I did have a visitor.

His name was Jeff Farrell, an Irish reporter working out of Caracas. He wanted to hear a bit of my experience for a story. We sat down on a bench and spoke. Farrell had two shopping bags of food. 'Father Pat said I should bring you something.'

'Fair play to you,' I said, shaking his hand.

'The National Guard took a carton of orange juice off me out of one of the bags.'

'They're like that. They say it's the rules, but it's probably just that they like orange juice and don't want to pay for it.' We both laughed.

He asked a lot of questions about life in the prison. I told him about the murders and beatings. His eyes seemed to light up. A reporter got his story.

We spoke a bit more. The scene in the hallway must have been comical for him. The little Christmas tree in the corner was flashing with lights. Latin music was blaring out of a stereo, and a lucero was dancing salsa with a pipe gun dangling from his side. It was great chatting with someone from home. 'I better go,' he said after a while.

'OK, it was good talking. Billy, the other Irish lad, he's off in the canteen. He'll be sorry he missed you. I'll tell him you were in.' I walked Farrell to the wing door. When we got out into the corridor I told him to march behind me up the passageway. 'That way they'll think you're a prisoner and won't hassle you.' I was afraid one of the animals would jump out of Wing 7 and knife him, but I didn't tell him that.

Not long afterwards, he rang me in the wing. 'Any chance you could get your family back home to give me a photo of you for a story for the papers?'

'No way,' I said. The last thing I wanted was my mug all over the papers in Ireland. My family were going through enough grief as it was, I imagined. Weeks later I got word that Farrell had done a story about me on Irish national radio, RTÉ. He just called me 'Paul, from Coolock' – where I live in Dublin. No surname. Fair enough.

Chapter 13

HONOUR AMONG BANDITOS

TROUBLE WAS BREWING. VISITS WERE ON AND WORD WENT AROUND there'd be a blow-up between the wings after the families went home at 4 p.m. What the strife was about we weren't sure. There'd been talk about a shoot-out between the cell blocks for months, so I didn't think anything of it. The root of the row always seemed trivial to me. Often an inmate accused a prisoner from another cell block of checking out his girlfriend on a visit. The visit 'code of conduct' had been breached and *respeto* had to be upheld.

Unpaid drugs debts might also spark trouble between the cell blocks. If, for example, an inmate fled a wing over a bill he couldn't pay for crack or coke and holed up in another cell block, the jefe there would have to force him to honour the debt to his former *padrino*. If he didn't, this was another cause to take up *armas*. It was all about honour. Pride. Saving face. But the worst of all scenarios for the trouble in the air that day would be if one cell-block 'army council' plotted to take over a rival wing. This was grave. It would mean all-out war – a fight to the death. It was all about turf. If a jefe and his henchmen had, say, 150 inmates in their wing, they made cash from the causa and selling drugs to that number. If the bosses took over another wing with the same number of prisoners, the jefe and his sidekicks doubled their lolly. In the end, it was all down to the dinero.

But in that moment we were safe. A blow-up would never happen during visits. The familia was sacred in

Venezuela. That was the rule in Los Teques, and in every prison in Venezuela. If it was broken, it meant death.

When the visitors finally cleared, we PWVs were allowed out from behind the curtain. I started walking around the yard to stretch my legs. I'd been cramped up on my bucket for about eight hours and they felt wobbly.

'There's a good chance there could be trouble, Paul,' said Billy, his brow furrowed. He'd been locked up for a year and knew the telltale signs: the bosses were jittery and on the phone to the jefes in other wings.

I shrugged it off. 'It'll be grand, Billy, all huffing and puffing.'

I continued pacing up and down the yard. I then sat down and started writing my diary, which I was doing daily. I thought some day my tales from Los Teques could be turned into a book. 'Who would believe this place, Paul?' said Silvio. 'Nobody. They will think you made it up.' He was probably right, but I still kept it going.

Something suddenly whistled past my ear. *Zzzzziiipppp*. I spun around and saw a large hole in the door frame next to me. *Zzzzziiipppp*, again. Then it registered: oh shit, we were being fired upon. Automatic gunfire crackled. *Rat-ta-ta, rat-ta-ta*. Bullets pounded into the yard, slamming into the wall and sending up puffs of dust.

'*Nos disparan*,' shouted the Venos, '*nos disparan*.' ('They're shooting at us.')

Inmates from Wing 2 above had an aerial view of our yard and were taking potshots, pointing gun barrels through their cell bars at us. We were sitting ducks in the yard. There was a scramble for the cover of the cells. I jumped to my feet and bolted for the door. I noticed the luceros and the bosses were first through – and they were armed. Big men. One of the lags fell into me, knocking me over in the stampede. My shoulder was shoved into the door frame. I got back on my feet quickly and ran in through the door and into Cell 1. I saw Silvio, Billy, Eddy and Ricardo had taken cover there.

Bullets now pounded into the main wing door. We were being fired upon by inmates from outside in the passageway. It was probably Wing 1. A steady volley of bullets from an automatic weapon. *Drrr-drrrrr*, like a drill whirring into the steel door. I knew it was reinforced, but I was still worried it would give way. My heart was racing. My fists were clenched. I thought these might be my last moments. I'd be killed in a hail of bullets. Katie and Dano, sorry. Ma, Da, sorry. That's all I could think.

Silvio was panicking the most. It didn't help my nerves. 'I tell you, this place is crazy, crazy I tell you. These people, they will never learn.' The bullets still pounding. No, no. If they stormed in they'd kill us first. The white men. The gringos. I was sure.

A lucero armed with a pipe gun ran up to the wall next to us. It divided our cell block and Wing 1, which was beside us. He started barking orders, waving the barrel of his DIY shotgun. I didn't understand. A few of the Venos ran over, got down on their hunkers and put their ears to the wall. '*Llegate, llegate,*' ('Get here, get here') shouted the lucero at me. '*Bombas, bombas.*' Good God. It dawned on me.

'Grenades,' said Billy, his face stiff with fright. Oh Jesus, we were dead.

'This is terrible, terrible,' said Silvio, his lip quivering, 'terrible, I tell you.' He'd been coking up all afternoon and his eyeballs were dancing around in his head. Mad paranoid. The crackheads were even running around screaming, clawing at the walls like loonies. On the ground in fetal positions, scratching at their faces. Their demons coming to life.

'*Llegate, llegate,*' said the lucero again. Jesus, he wanted me to put my ears to the bricks, listening out to see if the inmates in Wing 1 were dropping grenades into the cavities of the wall, planning to blow it up and storm into the wing. I looked at the Venos on their hunkers, horrified. I couldn't believe they were obeying the lucero. If they heard a rustling in the bricks it'd be lights out. They would be blown to bits.

Dumb bastards. The lucero started shouting at me again. '*Llegate, llegate.*' Maybe it was because I was older than the rest and had less living to do.

'No, no,' I said to the lucero, waving him off. He could shoot me if he wanted, I wasn't going.

We stood there, our band of gringos, cowering down on our hunkers when a Veno at the wall jumped back. 'Grenade!' More bullets pounded at the door. On our feet again ready to run to the yard in case they stormed in. Then I heard a volley of bullets slam into the yard, ricocheting off buckets with a ping and flying everywhere. Shells the size of small carrots were scattered on the ground. Good God, it was the National Guard. The verde boys were spraying bullets from the watchtowers, firing into the prison probably for the fun of it.

Fidel ran up to the wing door into the passageway, an Uzi in hand. A few of the luceros and underbosses followed him, slinking in against the wall for cover and scurrying over to the door. The narrow lookout hatch was pulled back. Fidel poked the barrel of the Uzi, fired off a round and crouched down. The other wing returned fire, bullets slamming into the door. The boss took cover and a lucero took over, firing back out. One of them was laughing. I couldn't believe it. I could see they were worried but that they were also enjoying the buzz – like grown-up cowboys and Indians. The bosses continued shooting out into the passageway, firing off rounds then ducking below the hatch. But it was senseless, blind shooting. Monkeys with guns.

I was in a panic. My knees felt weak. I didn't know what to do if the prisoners from Wing 1 stormed in. I didn't have a gun to fight back with.

Minutes ticked by like days. I was exhausted with fear and panic. I looked in Billy's face at one point. Our eyes met, like we knew this might be it. Two Irishmen thousands of miles from home, ending our lives inside the walls of a prison.

The bosses were now running low on ammo. Marksmen they were not. The blind shooting in the passageway was draining their bullets. They ran back and forth from the wing door into the cells, pulling out magazines of cartridges hidden in the insides of a sheet hanging up dividing two beds. I personally didn't care if they were killed, but as long as they had guns and bullets we had a chance of living. In that moment, the causa was worth every penny.

The shooting eased off. A couple of bullets ricocheted out in the yard and a few more sprays of bullets hit the wing door. Then the cell phones started ringing. The bosses were shouting into their mobiles, waving their hands in the air. 'It could be a truce,' said Silvio, listening in. His face, normally tanned, was drained of colour.

The shooting stopped. I gave out a slow, heavy breath. I felt a knot in my stomach loosen. My hands unclenched. The Venos at the wall got off their knees, but the crackheads were still curling into balls on the floor, scratching at their faces.

'I think it is over, oh please God,' said Silvio.

'Jesus, yeah,' said Billy. 'They're probably out of ammo.'

It was coming on to 5 p.m.: time for número. The shoot-out was over, but surely the National Guard wouldn't come in and do a headcount after what had happened? The bosses believed they would. The luceros started shoving us out into the yard. I stepped out, ducking my head left and right, looking up to see whether an inmate would pop his head out over the roof above and start blasting. The ground in the yard was covered in bullet cases, the wall peppered with holes big enough to stick two fingers into.

Luceros started ordering Venos to run around and pick up the bullet cases. They scrambled around the ground, gathering them and dumping them into a rubbish bin. 'They think if they hide them the National Guard won't know they've guns,' said Billy, sniggering. I couldn't believe it, but he was serious.

The bosses started waving at us to take our seats around the wall for the headcount. I noticed they weren't hiding their weapons this time; I could see their handguns poking up from under their shirts.

The troops filed in and started the headcount. Three guards were armed with the usual pump-action shotguns, but there was nothing out of the ordinary. Satisfied no one had escaped in the melee, they pulled out after the número. Not a word said or a search for guns and ammo. Nada. It was as if nothing had happened.

'There might be a baseball game on the telly,' laughed Eddy. He was always one for the one-liners, and he was probably right. They were mad for the sport.

That night, for the first time, a lookout man was put on the door into the yard, watching for any shooters from Wing 2 who might climb down from the roof and blast us as we slept. I walked over to my space on the floor, rolled out my colchoneta and lay down among the carpet of bodies. In minutes I fell into a merciful sleep.

* * *

I was starting to get to know a bit more about Billy and how he got into this mess. He had racked up debts of a few grand with a local dealer in his home town from getting ecstasy and coke on the slate. The dealer told him if he did a drug run for them to Venezuela he could clear them, and he wasn't exactly asking. Holiday in the sun and expenses paid. The holiday worked out all right, but not the run.

'How much were you going to get paid?' I said.

'Three grand.'

'Three grand?' I said, my voice raised. 'Is that all?' I couldn't believe he was carrying three kilos of coke worth over two hundred thousand euro back home for such a small pay-off. The ten grand I was going to get paid wasn't much either, but three grand . . .

'I had a great aul time on the holiday,' said Billy, grinning. He arrived in Caracas and headed off to a beach resort. Palm trees and cocktails. Bikini-clad women.

At the end of the trip he picked up his suitcase with the

'merchandise' in Caracas. He got to the airport, and game over. Barely made it in the front door before the cops moved in and, like me, hauled him off to the antidrogas building on the coast. I didn't ask him if he got a late-night visit from the bugger squad. I'd decided I wouldn't tell anyone what happened to me there, so I couldn't. I was always curious, though, whether others had been raped there too. No one ever said. I knew for sure, though, it didn't happen in Los Teques. The cell-block bosses would probably shoot you if you did that. It proved to me that the National Guard were the lowest scum in Venezuela.

'How long were you there for?'

'A night. Went to court next day.'

'I was there for five days. No food and water.'

Billy had fallen in with the wrong crowd at home. His parents were worried sick about him. They were on the phone constantly to Father Pat, wondering how Billy was, and forever sending him money to bring in to their son. Billy had decent Spanish and could have picked up work in the prison to make a few quid, but he couldn't be bothered. He was a lazy lad, preferring to watch DVDs and snort coke. He wouldn't work on batteries, as the fella says. We talked a lot, but all he was really into was girls.

'What'd you work as at home?' he said, changing the subject.

'Plumber.'

'Ah, be-Jaysus, boy, I was a carpenter. An apprentice. In my second year. Only getting about 100 euro a week. Wasn't enough to keep the lifestyle going.' His habit wasn't in line with his income and he ended up in debt. He was twenty-seven now and had spent two years in Los Teques, the best years of his life trickling down the drain. And there was a chance he mightn't get out alive to live the rest.

Chapter 14

LOCKDOWN

I WAS SURE THERE WOULD BE SOME FALLOUT FROM THE SHOOT-OUT – and there was. A few days later we got the news. It would mean my life getting even smaller. A lucero walked into the yard and stood up on top of a paint tin after número. We all turned to look. He started speaking, but I just stood there clueless as usual. A few minutes later I walked over to Silvio and he filled me in. 'Nobody leaves the wing till further notice, that's what he says.'

'Not even to Spanish classes?'

'Nowhere; we can't go out.' He explained that one of the inmates in Wing 1 got a bullet in the shoot-out. Probably courtesy of the jefes in Maxima who were shooting out of our wing door in their direction. The garita lookout in our cell block had seen one of the lags getting carried out of Wing 1 after the shoot-out ended, slumped over the shoulder of another inmate. He later died of the injuries. This was bad news. Wing 1 would be looking to settle the score. The cell-block bosses knew it, and that's why we had to batten the hatches and lie low.

But still, to me, it was pure bad luck for the guy that he got killed. There was no marksmanship in the shoot-out. The bosses were just all blind shooting. They didn't seem to know that bullets didn't go around corners or through doors and walls.

So now we paid the price with a lockdown. I felt Los Teques starting to get even smaller. Now the only time we could leave the wing was to go to the canteen. The kitchen workers from

185

our wing even had to be escorted from Maxima up the passageway by a cop to get them there safely. Some started sleeping there to avoid the perilous walk back. A shooter could appear from anywhere. I noticed the bread rolls in the mornings were all bow-shaped and flattened – the inmates in the cantina who had no colchonetas there had kipped on bags of rolls the night before.

But despite the lockdown, the killings didn't stop. Executions went on. One morning I was walking back from the canteen with Silvio and a few others and we came across a body on the ground in the passageway. The inmate was lying on his side, his eyes open yet lifeless, his tongue dangling out. It was a weird sight I'll never forget, and nothing like dead bodies you see in movies. A pool of dark blood had formed around his stomach, blotching his vest. He looked like he was in his early 20s and was dressed in shorts. 'Jesus, look,' I said, pointing at him. It was a horrible sight, but I stopped and looked in the same way people slow down to see a traffic accident.

'Keep going,' said Silvio, pushing me on. There wasn't a cop in sight, but if you stuck around you might get blamed for the killing.

We all gathered out in the yard. The lags knew there would be a backlash from the prison chiefs. You didn't just kill somebody without someone asking questions – even in Los Teques. Life was cheap, but if someone was murdered it was a headache for the authorities. Directors didn't like murders on their watch.

The story was that a lucero from Maxima was walking by him and the lag made a gun sign at him with his hand. The lucero had a beef with him from another jail. The next morning, the lucero rammed a knife into his guts. Word was that Fidel the jefe had given the lucero the green light to take out the prisoner who lived in the passageway.

In the yard, one of the underbosses, Gómez, a Veno with buck teeth, stood up on a concrete block and started a speech. I couldn't make it out, but I knew there was heavy shit coming.

I stood beside Eddy. 'What's the story, what's going on?'

'The cops are going to come down and interview us and nobody is to say a word if they know what's good for their health.' Eddy relayed Gómez's words to me. He told us the boss said that in the past a lag was killed and all the inmates in the wing were taken to court and given a six-month sentence on top of their original term – and grounds for parole removed.

'Ah no, no way,' I said.

'Yes way, that's what he says. That's what happens, that's what they do. Gómez says if we stick together and say nobody saw anything we might be all right.' Might be? I couldn't believe it: there was my plan to get out after two years up in the air.

As we expected, the prison cops shortly after burst into the wing and I braced myself. The killing happened when our cell block was out at the canteen, so it was obvious someone from Maxima had knifed the guy. The head cop was there, a little mean guy with a Napoleon complex. He carried the baseball-style bat he always had in hand. The director was there too. Her usual nice-girl vibe was gone. She was pissed off. There was none of her usual chitchat. We were all standing out in the yard. Napoleon called each of the bosses and luceros into the hallway one by one. They stood spreadeagled against the wall. I couldn't properly see in, but I could hear a dull thud as he carried out his usual beating: three swings of his bat full-force into your ass. That way no visible marks were left. And when you were hit you weren't allowed to make a sound. Not a whimper. That was his rule – he'd hit you again till you stopped. None of the bosses made a sound. If you did, you were *maricón*, or gay.

After that we heard nothing more over the killing. It didn't do the lucero's profile any harm in the wing. He went up the ranks and got more respeto from the bosses. He became a bit of a hero and walked around with a swagger.

One thing nobody dared do was rat anyone out. If you did you were a *sapo*, or a grass. This was the lowest form of life. If you were caught grassing you'd get an almighty beating from the bosses and inmates. There were lags in Maxima who bore the scars of talking out of line. One inmate I called the Penguin walked on the sides of his feet, the soles facing in. He plodded around the wing, wobbling from left to right. Word had it he had grassed up an inmate in another prison. Over what we didn't know. His fellow inmates had wreaked their revenge by pinning him down to the ground and holding his arms and legs while others dropped concrete blocks on his feet. He was locked up for rape, so to me the punishment was deserved.

The Penguin wasn't the only inmate walking around with a deformity. Others had their limbs warped from punishment beatings too, but they hadn't necessarily been beaten for being a sapo. Often they fell foul of the bosses and were called in for a session at the wrong end of a baseball bat. There was one lag whose feet were at right angles to his legs waddling around the wing. One day I was in the yard reading a Spanish dictionary that Silvio had lent me and came across the word in Spanish for duck: *pato*. It stuck in my head. 'Silvio, I have a name for your man with the bogey feet – the Duck.' He bent over laughing. And from then on, to us the inmate was the Duck. I never said it to his face, though. Despite being slow on his feet, he was fearsome: he had a short fuse and was always looking for a row. He loved duelling with stakes of wood used as pretend knives – a pastime the Venos loved – grabbing onto his opponent's arm so they couldn't move and he wouldn't fall over, then giving his opponent a good jab.

No one ever asked how the Duck ended up with his feet pointing the wrong direction. It was obvious. He'd got a beating over something in the past. And if you got a bad kicking nobody would treat you in a hurry. There was a prison clinic staffed by inmates and a doctor who came in a couple of days a week, Silvio said. I doubted anyone got first-class medical care there – and I'd later find out at first hand my belief was true.

Beatings were common. One day a prisoner was called in for a luz and we all had to stand in the yard while the bosses dealt with him. He walked out of the jefe's cell after about 15 minutes, hobbling, tear marks streaking down his face. His right leg was concave, like a piano's. He struggled over to a bench in the corner of the yard, sat down and started weeping. His amigos walked over and comforted him. Within a couple of weeks he started walking properly again but with his leg in the shape of a bow.

Another day a new inmate walked out into the yard after his 'induction'. He had no clothes on, only a blanket wrapped around him. That was because, like a lot of them, he'd soiled his trousers over a hiding by the bosses. He limped in and fell onto the ground in the yard, sounds like a baby gurgling coming out of his mouth.

He was no sapo, though. In seconds, word arrived that he was a kiddy fiddler. We knew anyway. New inmates weren't beaten by the 'welcoming party': the bosses waving guns in the faces of the new prisoners. Only the paedophiles got a hiding – that's how we knew the guy was a kiddy fiddler, when we saw he'd been battered. There were about seven or eight paedos in all. I used to shout in their faces, *'molestar ninos'*, which meant child molestors. Most of us did who had children.

* * *

Despite the lockdown, coke was sold as usual. Every evening when the troops pulled out after the headcount a 'light' was called. The jefes fetched their guns and went bagging and tagging one-gram lines of perico. The lucero foot soldiers then went about as usual, dealing it in the yard to inmates out of bumbags on their belts.

The visits went on as usual, too. One morning after the clean-up on the wing, before the families and lovers came in, I was ready for another day behind the curtain sitting on my empty cooking-oil drum. But first I went into the toilet and sat down on the pot. It was an open door and all the lags could see in at you doing your business. I found it uncomfortable; the lack of privacy was something I never got used to. But even though others could see in, you couldn't just walk in if the pot was being used or if someone was having a wash. That was one of the rules. But a Veno walked in past me and started bathing, ladling water over his head from a drum of water in the corner and splashing me.

'Get the fuck out of here,' I shouted.

'No,' he said. I started standing, pulling my trousers up to have a go at him. Before I properly got to my feet, he shoved me. I slammed back into the wall. My glasses fell off and smashed to the ground. Blood rushed to my head. My eyesight was blurry, but I could make him out. He wasn't a big man, a couple of inches smaller than my 5 ft 10 in. height. I lunged forward and wrapped my hands around his throat. His eyes started bulging. The veins in his neck stood out like rivers on a map. He pushed against me, but I had him pinned. '*Mama huevo*, I'll kill you, you little bollocks,' I shouted in his face. I realised it was visit day. Nobody fought then or you were in big trouble.

'Paul, no, wait till after the families leave,' said Silvio. He had run into the toilet and was pulling at my arms. A lucero then ran in after hearing the noise, a pipe gun at his side. He grabbed me and pulled me back.

'Shhh,' he said, nodding back out to the yard. I could hear the voices of women and children. I let my grip go and stood back. I glared at the lucero and said to him through Silvio, 'I want to fight him. After the visit.'

'*No problema*,' said the lucero, glad the struggle was over and I'd calmed down. Silvio looked relieved, breathing heavily.

'Boxing match: me, you, later,' I said to the little runt. He grinned and walked off. I bent down and picked up my glasses. One lens was smashed and the arms bent outwards. They were useless. I fired them onto the ground and kicked the wall.

'Paul, take it easy,' said Silvio. 'We sort this later.' I looked out towards Billy, Ricardo and the others. All I could make out were blurry shapes where faces should be.

'That muthafucker is dead.' I wasn't letting this go.

'You're not going to fight him, are you?' said Billy, not believing I was serious.

'Fucking right I am.'

'It's your right to fight, Paul,' said Silvio. 'That's the way it works.' That was how rows between inmates in Maxima were settled – you took to the gloves.

* * *

Chávez had ordered troops and tanks to the border with Colombia. The whole country was on alert. Colombian pilots had invaded Venezuelan airspace. That was an aggressive move and had to be dealt with, bellowed Chávez. From inside Los Teques, the whole country seemed like a war zone.

The Colombians, however, denied the charge and were puzzled by Chávez's move. I was sitting down in the wing hallway watching the news pan out on CNN, the screen looking fuzzy without my specs. The whole rift between Venezuela and Colombia was at another stage, with the two countries going head to head. Colombia complained that Venezuela's left-leaning government was harbouring FARC (the Revolutionary Armed Forces of Colombia) guerillas in rural hideouts. Chávez fired back at his neighbour, saying their allegation was part of a US conspiracy, paving the way for the Yankees to invade Venezuela from US bases in Colombia in the country's War on Drugs, to supposedly chase the guerillas and then steal Venezeulan oil while they were there.

In the same stories on the TV, Chávez was throwing jabs at the US itself, saying he'd shut off oil supplies to them. CNN rolled out analysts who brushed off the threats, pointing out that the US was Venezuela's biggest customer, and *el presidente* had made such noise before.

Days later, Chávez's whole drama of war and oil ran out of steam and was shown for what it was: hot air. Barrels of oil continued to be shipped north to the US. And foreign correspondents in Venezuela said there wasn't a tank in sight anwhere near the frontier with Colombia.

Way to go, Chávez.

Anyway, local news stations were saying it was all just a ploy to distract Venezuelans from the misery within: supermarket shelves empty of basics, such as dairy foods and chicken; the cost of living soaring in line with Chávez's temper; and bodies piling up in morgues across the country amid rising crime. The revolución was looking dodgy to me.

Overall, I was starting to think life as a 'free man' for many Venezuelans wasn't much better than being banged up in Los Teques.

* * *

There was a buzz in the yard. All the lags had heard that the gringo wanted to go fisticuffs with the Veno. '*Guantes, guantes,*' ('Gloves, gloves') they started shouting. 'Fidel, boxing, boxing,' I shouted over to the padrino, throwing shadow jabs. I was enjoying having the crowd in my thrall.

'Sí,' Fidel said. He called out to a lucero, who came out of the cells with the gloves.

'*Muy bueno,*' ('Very good') I said. I looked around but couldn't see my nemesis. A few of the inmates were gathering around, starting to form a circle.

'You're a spacer, Paul,' said Billy. 'Are you really going to do this?'

'Yep, don't worry, I used to do boxing as a kid.' It was true, I fought for years with a local club in Oxford, England, where I grew up – and did well, taking part in tournaments. But that was a long time ago . . . I slipped my hands into the navy-blue gloves. They were a proper professional pair. A lucero laced me up. More lags gathered. The gringo was about to fight. What was he made of?

I still couldn't see the little runt. Maxima wing wasn't big, so he was obviously in one of the cells. One of the inmates went in looking for him, and I saw them shoving him out into the yard. He saw me gloved up and ready to roll. His eyes opened wide like he'd seen a ghost and he sprinted past me and ran into the toilet. All the prisoners started cheering and laughing. '*Maricón, maricón*' ('Gay, gay'). It was hilarious. They knew he was all talk.

Fidel went down to him. 'Juan,' he said, '*peleas, ahora.*' ('Fight, now.')

'No, no,' he shouted. Maybe the reputation of the fightin' Irish rattled him.

'He won't come out,' said Silvio, smiling. All the inmates were laughing now. All enjoying the drama and fun. Anything to break the boredom.

But I was standing there gloved up and with no one to fight. My adrenalin was pumping and I was charged for action. I started shadow boxing again, pumping out more jabs into the air, enjoying the moment. 'Waay-hayyyy,' the lags were roaring. Carlos walked up to Silvio and spoke, seeing the inmates wanted a bout. 'He wants to know do you want another opponent?' Silvio said.

'Yeah, let's do it.'

'*Sí, no problema,*' said Carlos.

Minutes later a black lad stepped out from the cells into the yard. He was bare-chested, wearing tight shorts and basketball boots. His upper body was rock solid, bulging biceps and defined pecs, and all topped off with a shaved head. He looked like a young Marvin Hagler. It was as if the jefes had a ready-made boxer at their disposal.

'Ha, haha, haha.' The lags started laughing and pointing at me, thinking I was in for it now. So did I. Holy shit, I'm going to get battered, I thought. He was a couple of inches shorter than me but with a wide frame and the body of a brick shithouse. I recognised the lag from the wing. He was always pumping a couple of concrete-block free weights with Ricardo down the back of the yard.

'No, Paul, don't do this,' said Silvio, pleading, being his usual worried self. But I wasn't standing down; if I got beat I got beat: either way, I was gonna fight.

'We'll see how it goes,' I said. No backing down now.

The lucero gloved up the Veno. The human circle was growing and moving in closer. My heart was thumping. The Veno started the fight in a gentlemanly way and we touched gloves. I swung out the first punch: a left jab to his right temple, seeing a gap his gloves hadn't covered. I followed with another left, when he was expecting a right, and clocked him on the head. I saw surprise in his eyes. The old gringo had a proper fight in him. We danced back and forth. I was bouncing on my feet. The Veno threw out a volley of jabs. The crowd gasped. The gringo was going down. 'Go on Paul, go on Paul,' I heard Billy shouting. 'Gringo, gringo,' shouted one of the Venos. The fighter was fast and sharp, but I countered the punches, defending and absorbing his blows with my gloves. I returned a couple more punches, catching him out again, jabbing with a left and then following through with a wide left hook when he expected a right. Thump. He stepped back a bit as if he was getting his balance. He then threw back a couple of fast punches. One got me on the side of the head. I felt the blow, but I was pumping with adrenalin and didn't even feel a twinge. A few minutes had passed. I felt myself tiring. My legs were weakening. I was holding my own, but if the fight went on I was sure I was a goner. My steps became laboured. Both of us started throwing weak blows. I was exhausted and wanted the fight to end.

Carlos stepped out in the yard, hearing the boxing was at a stalemate and wasn't ending any time soon. He stepped into the 'ring' and stood between the two of us. I was relieved. He grabbed our arms and held up our gloves in the air. 'Heyyyyy, heyyyyyy,' shouted the inmates, jumping up and down. We'd given them a good fight to watch. The luceros stepped in and unlaced our gloves, and I shook hands with the Veno.

'Great fight,' said Billy, walking over to me.

'Paul, *campeón, campeón,*' ('champion') said Silvio, clapping me on the back.

I walked over towards a chair in the yard. My legs were getting weaker. I just made it before they gave in and I slumped into the chair. I was covered in sweat. My heart was still thumping. I was breathing heavily, fast like I'd had my head in a bucket of water and was coming up for air. I'm getting too old for this, I was thinking.

But after that moment I held my head high. I wasn't just the four-eyed guy always scribbling in a diary: I was the gringo who could hold his ground.

* * *

The lockdown went on for the best part of three months. Every day was just the same routine. Número. Canteen for breakfast. Hanging around the wing all day. Canteen for more slop in the afternoon. Headcount in the evening. Visits three times a week. It was hard in the beginning, not getting to the roof or to Spanish classes.

After a while, though, I started getting used to it. I became withdrawn. I spent my days in my head, writing my diaries and now banging out a novel about a man whose marriage had broken down. He then moved out from the family home away from his two kids and in with his elderly parents, then started driving a taxi, his head in a bad place. It was loosely based on my own life. I enjoyed going into myself, but I might have been going too far. I was starting to talk to myself. Some of the prisoners were noticing it. 'Paul, you OK?' Silvio or Billy would say, seeing me babbling to myself. 'Yeah, grand.' I think it was just my way of escaping from this world I was in. A world I spent every minute wanting to get out of. I just sat on my bucket by the door in the yard, writing all day. When prisoners came up looking for a cigarillo or plata, my answer was always the same: 'Fuck off.'

I was starting to take a bag of coke a night now. I'd been taking it ever since the jefe gave me a free sample at Christmas. That was a clever move bosses made to get you hooked. Not that I was addicted to it – but it was mixed with what we thought was a horse tranquilliser and it helped me sleep. It also kept the demons away. Numbed the senses. At this stage it was probably the only thing keeping me from going insane.

Chapter 15

GAS ATTACK

LOS TEQUES WAS FALLING DEEPER AND DEEPER INTO THE HANDS OF the cell-block bosses. The lockdown did little. Gunfire still crackled into the night. Executions were rife. Bloody corpses were regularly flung out of wings. The jefes were literally running riot, armed to the teeth as ever: Uzis, revolvers, grenades, the whole lot. The cops and the National Guard were outgunned and outnumbered. They knew it. The whole jail was one big powder keg. Even the passageway cell-block outcasts were still robbing and stabbing to beat the band. A *masacre* was looming. Something had to be done. The prison chiefs knew it.

I woke up in the morning to the shouts of the luceros. '*Levántate, Levántate.*' ('Get up, get up.') Men stood up from the sea of bodies in the cell. I sat up, got on my knees and rolled up my colchoneta. Afterwards, we all gathered out in the yard waiting for the número. Some were still sleeping while sitting on paint tins, dozing. A lucero walked around slapping them with a knife on the head. If you missed your number it pissed off the guards. They might retaliate with a wing search. That would piss off the jefe, who might call you for a 'light' and a session with a baseball bat.

I sat there fighting sleep, listening for the familiar words: for the garita to shout 'verdes' (National Guard troops) or 'aguas' (cops) before scurrying off to sit down on a bucket with the rest of us for the headcount. But they never came.

Mobile phones started ringing. Bosses spoke rapidly. A

torrent of Spanish bounced around the yard. 'Troops,' said Roberto, next to me. 'The army is coming.'

'This sounds like heavy shit,' said Eddy. 'I've never seen them not come in and do the headcount like clockwork in the morning. Something's going on.' He listened in to the bosses on the phones to lags in other wings. 'There's a shit storm coming. One of them says there are three or four army trucks parked at the prison gate. They weren't there last night.'

I braced myself. I didn't know what was coming.

The heavy drone of machine-gun fire exploded. Muffled shots from inside the jail, like the sound of a drill boring into the ground at a distance. My stomach tightened. 'Jesus, what's going on out there?' I asked.

'I think it's the army,' said Silvio, 'moving in on the wing. I don't like this.'

I stood up from the paint tin I was sitting on. Nobody knew what to do; we were standing around looking at each other. Heads ducked in case bullets whizzed down from above into the yard. I walked into the hallway by the cells. I heard the thud of boots in the passageway outside and felt butterflies in my stomach.

'There's going to be gas next, this is what they do,' said Eddy, 'they're going to storm us.' He was a tough guy, but even he looked edgy. This was bad. 'Get something to cover your eyes with.' I heard him, but the words didn't sink in. I didn't know what to do – I just followed the others and ran into the cells. Billy slipped a baseball cap on and ran over and put on the runners he'd left in a corner, dumping his flip-flops. It was the fastest I ever saw him move. I had on jeans, a T-shirt and runners.

'What do we need shoes and that on for?' I said to him.

'We might end up being taken to the roof.'

Shots rang out, a *poot-poot* sound. A grey cylinder the shape and size of a Coke can landed in the hallway. Smoke billowed out like dry ice pumping into a nightclub. I ran into the toilet at the back of the cell with Billy and Silvio. It was poky and looked like it would give better cover. I stood there looking out into the cell. I watched a lucero run over, pick up the gas canister and put it into a black plastic bin bag. Another landed at the other end of the hallway. One inmate ran over and doused it with a bucket of water. It did nothing. Moron, I thought, it was a gas canister not a flame thrower.

Dozens of canisters were fired into the wing from all directions, shooting in through bars from outside in the passageway. A haze of smoke gathered like a thick fog rising.

I stood there not knowing what to do. 'Down, down,' shouted Eddy. 'Get down.' I got onto my knees on the floor in the toilet. The smoke rose. A blanket of smog formed at the ceiling then slowly descended on us. I was in a panic and confused. Everyone was on their knees now in the cell, coughing and spluttering. Nina, the wing dog, was running around wagging her tail and barking. She thought it was a game and we were all playing doggy with her. She started yelping when the fumes got her.

A gas canister suddenly pounded into the toilet and dropped beside me, smoke billowing into my face. I felt my chest tighten. I was sucking for oxygen but not getting any. I grabbed a T-shirt lying on the ground and covered my mouth. But it was useless. My chest heaved, my eyes bulged. I crawled to the toilet and stuck my head in the bowl. I didn't know if I wanted to get sick or throw water on my face. My eyes were burning. I put my head deeper into the bowl. My breathing was getting slower and heavier. I lifted my head up and looked into the wing. I was dazed and felt I was losing consciousness. Through clouds of smoke I could make out bodies all over the ground, twisting, men rubbing at their eyes, coughing and grabbing their throats. I put my head back into the bowl. I was sure I was a goner, my last sight the bottom of a toilet.

I heard something pounding at the wing door, then shouts. I lifted my head and looked over. Through the smoke I saw one of the bosses had opened the door. He wasn't armed.

They weren't tooled up for a fight. '*Vamos, vamos,*' ('Let's go, let's go') shouted the jefe. All I could think of was escaping from the smoke. I got to my feet, stumbled a bit, got my balance and ran for the door. Troops and cops were in the passageway. Gas masks on their faces. Eyes looked out through thick plastic helmets. Upper bodies bulky with bulletproof vests. Oxygen tanks on their backs like characters out of *Ghostbusters*, but with machine guns in hand.

I ran forward, following the other lags. The smoke started to thin out as we approached the driveway at the entrance to the cell blocks. I followed the others up the stairs to the roof. National Guard troops shouted orders. I followed the others and stripped off my clothes, throwing them into a bundle. Men were still rubbing at their eyes, which were roaring red and weeping like scabby tomatoes. I felt my chest loosening up and my breathing clear. I ran over to where I saw other inmates from the Maxima wing spread out on the ground, naked, legs apart. Guards on the roof pushed us forward, shouting. I ran over to the others and lay down, putting my forehead to the ground and my hands on the back of my head.

A soldier walked up and down between the lines of naked prisoners, prodding them with the barrel of his rifle. Some of the lags shouted '*mama huevo*'. The troops replied by slamming gun barrels into their backs, crashing down on their bodies. Gunfire crackled over our heads. I put my face back into the concrete. I felt cold metal around my rear end; a soldier was poking me now with the barrel of his gun, probably looking to see if I had a condom filled with cash up my ass, like many inmates did.

Hours passed. The panic was gone, but I was getting tired and pissed off. The sun was blazing in the sky, too. I felt my head burning. It was obvious a search was going on in the cell blocks, but this was going on longer than usual.

After a while the troops let us get on our feet to get our

clothes. There was a massive bundle by the wall. Some 1,200 naked bodies of all shapes and sizes ran for the pile, goolies dangling and bellies wobbling. I rummaged through, found my jeans and T-shirt, got dressed quickly and slipped on my runners. I was running back to my spot on the ground when I saw Billy coming towards me.

'You made it?'

'Yeah, but this is some kip,' he said.

'Shithole.'

He ran for his clothes and then I saw him lie down near me.

Back on the ground I could see Maleta naked going down to the bundle of clothes. Now I knew why they called him Cuatro Culos (Four Asses). I'd never seen anything like it. His body was everywhere. He had four ass cheeks: two where they were supposed to be and two lumps of flab gathered together on his lower back that looked like another ass. He looked like a stuffed turkey. Some of the lads were giggling looking at him. No matter how bad things were you could still see the funny side, and the laugh helped lighten my mood a bit.

Hours and hours passed. We lay there with our foreheads pressed into the ground. Billy wasn't far behind me and we started talking, turning our faces towards each other. 'Cunts, what's this about? Up here for ages with no food or water. When's it going to end? Where's the humanitarian rights?'

'I know. We must write to Nelson Mandela when we get out.' He laughed.

I waved my hand at the troops to take a leak. I was bursting. A guard waved me over to where some of the lags were pissing against a wall; others were down on their hunkers dumping into plastic bags in front of 1,200 men.

Time ticked away. Blue skies gave way to dusk. We must have been there for eight hours. No food, no water. My tongue was stuck to the bottom of my mouth from the dryness. My belly ached with hunger. We had had no breakfast, nothing.

The troops suddenly started shouting. '*Vayanse.*' ('Go, go.') We were finally getting up. I got to my feet and descended into the prison, down into the wing.

Maxima had been given a good search. Lids had been lifted off buckets, stuff moved around – but the wing wasn't wrecked like the last time. This had been a more precise search, probably done with metal detectors scanning the walls for guns. Fidel called a 'light' and we all had to go into the yard while they checked their weapons stockpile in the cells. They came out later with only a couple of guns and knives, not the usual big arsenal. I reckoned they'd suffered heavy losses – wiped out of just about everything: knives, cash, drugs, the whole lot.

'Another special causa now,' said Billy, sighing, 'I bet you.'

I put my hand up to my head. It was aching, burnt from eight hours under the tropical sun. My fingers nearly sizzled when I touched the spot where my hair was thin. The Venos were mostly dark and weren't hit badly by the sun. Eddy, though, who was pale, was in a bad way. The backs of his legs were roaring red. The next day it was worse. They went all yellow and bubbly, like a cheese and tomato pizza hot out of the oven. They later started cracking with pus weeping out of them. He was walking around like Frankenstein's monster, slowly moving one foot in front of the other so his legs wouldn't crack altogether, his face grimacing. Eddy never complained, though; he was a hardy chap.

Not only had the bosses been wiped out of most of their guns, I suspected their cash had been lifted too. I was sure they were broke. I saw this as an opportunity to get my hands on a bed. There were about 35 bunks and singles, which were coveted by the jefe, his henchmen and favourite inmates, such as Vampy, who tooled them with DIY guns and knives. It wasn't about being able to fork out cash for a bed, it was about waiting for someone to leave or die. But I saw an empty bunk in Cell 1. I was sure the boss would jump at a chance to get some cash. I got on Billy's case to get him to sell the bed space.

'Billy, it's the perfect time to push him on it.'

'OK, let's go.'

Fidel was sitting in his usual place: lying on his bed watching TV. Carlos was on the floor doing push-ups. Billy started speaking. I could only make out *cama*, bed. 'He says he'll have a talk about it, let's go outside.' I knew they wouldn't want to give a gringo mama huevo a bed, but they needed cash. The jefe stood up and the three of us walked into the yard and sat down. Billy spoke to Fidel again. 'He says you can have a bed, but you'll have to pay – and a lot.'

'How much?' I watched Fidel shrug and smile, thinking it'd be some ridiculous sum I could never pay.

'One million bolos, he says,' said Billy. About 200 euro. I knew I had it.

'One million, OK.' I lifted up a small pouch hanging from a necklace on my chest – a Hungarian inmate we called Peter Pan had made it from a shoelace threaded through a jeans pocket. I had kept my cash from selling the coke in the past, and my home brew. I started pulling notes out of the necklace, all neatly folded.

Fidel's eyes widened. No prisoner would normally have that kind of cash.

I handed him the notes and he started counting, shaking his head in disbelief. 'There you go,' I said, handing him the last few bills.

'He says OK, let's go,' said Billy. Billy was happy to stick with the floor. Organising things wasn't one of his strong skills.

We walked back into Cell 1 and Fidel walked me over to the empty bunk, pointing at the top one. '*Es tuya*,' ('It's yours') he said.

I climbed up and dropped onto the mattress. It was a different world. I had a view down to Fidel's telly. I now didn't have to sit in the yard all day. Life was looking up a bit in Los

Teques. For now. I heard the other Veno lags say, '*Gringo: chico, luca, chico, luca,*' a colloquial phrase they used meaning 'rich kid', thinking I'd had a stroke of good luck with the boss to wangle a bed – even if I was paying big bucks for it. I could probably get a goose-feather mattress at home for the same cash – not a smelly bunk bed.

* * *

The pizza topping on Eddy's legs looked like ninth-degree burns. He should have been hospitalised. But no one in the *clínica* thought so, and they just gave him some useless cream. A few days later he was temporarily let go from his job in the kitchen. He was on the shift that cooked for the prison staff; a cop saw the pus weeping from his legs in shorts and pulled up the kitchen boss about it. They didn't want him cooking their food. I couldn't see why – it wasn't like they would dip their bread into his legs.

* * *

I was glad of the bed. I needed it. My back ached in the mornings and for most of the rest of the day from months sleeping all night on a thin cushion on the ground. My bones were sticking into me all night, worse as time went on, and I was getting thinner. How much weight I was losing I had no idea. My jeans told me I was slimmer, though. They were a 34-in. waist and fitted me comfortably before I got locked up in Venezuela. Now I used a piece of plastic cord as a belt to keep them up. The bland diet of porridge, rice and beans was taking its toll on my body.

For weeks I'd seen a group of inmates beavering away with hammers, chisels, drills and welders in the back of Cell 3. They were building a toilet. Soon after the gas attack it was done. I walked in. I looked around, impressed with the set-up: a mirror, a proper wash basin, two urinals, a toilet pot and a tiled floor. All in the honour of the familia visits, of course. It was the first time I'd seen a mirror since Macuto. I'd been shaving with the power of touch for months. I walked over to the mirror, curious about what I looked like. 'Jesus,' I shouted out loud. I started working my fingers around my face, nudging it. My skin was tight on my face. The jowls I'd had hanging around my chin were gone. Not that I'd been fat, but I'd a bit of weight, a Ned Kelly from the few pints and bit of a rounded, fuller face. 'Fucking hell,' I said out loud again. I was shocked. I'd had my head shaved a few days before and had a couple of days' stubble on my face. I thought I looked like my da – and he was 77. About nine months in prison had put decades on me. I was horrified. I didn't know the man who looked back at me.

I ran out of the toilet into the yard. I shouted out at the top of my lungs into the sky, 'Beam me up, Scotty, beam me up,' shaking my fist into the air. Some of the Venos started laughing. The gringo is loco. Roberto looked up from where he was sitting on a bucket playing cards, grinning. He knew what I was on about, that this place was a loony bin sucking our lives away. The sight of myself in the mirror was a reality check. It shoved into my face the fact that my life was slipping away – literally before my eyes.

Chapter 16

ESCAPE PLOTS

AFTER THE GAS ATTACK THINGS WENT BACK TO 'NORMAL'. THE PRISON chiefs opened up the jail again. They believed they'd wiped out the cell-block bosses of enough arms. Los Teques was supposedly safe now. Spanish classes were back on and trips to the roof would start again. I was looking forward to that. I'd been feeling the walls in the wing closing in on me. Now I was more determined than ever to figure out ways to get out of this hole.

On my first spin up to the roof I bumped into Aussie Bruce again.

'Great to be back to normality,' I said.

'Can say that again,' he said. 'Cooped up like chickens down there we were.'

'How you getting on with the cancer?'

'It was on ice with the shutdown. The lawyer's coming back in this week. We're getting it back on the go. You still up for it?'

'Yep.'

'When he's in I'll tell you and you can meet him after me.'

'Right, sounds good. Now I'm going for me walk.' I was still sceptical about giving some lawyer 20,000 dollars to get me out, but it felt good to at least have something going on. I stepped away and started doing my power-walking laps around the roof. It was an exercise routine I'd started before the lockdown. A lap only took two minutes, so I just kept going around in circles for about an hour, sucking the air into my lungs as the sun blazed away over my head.

* * *

Father Pat was shocked at nothing. He was back in on his first visit since the lockdown. Myself and Billy stood out in the passageway, telling him about the shootings and the gas attack. He just nodded his head, listening but not judging. 'Yes, yes, I see, you have to be very careful.' His face always remained neutral.

He handed me a large brown package he had pulled out of his satchel. 'This is for you, from your family.'

'Really?'

'Yes, some letters I think. Dated four months ago in Ireland.'

'Four months?'

'The post is a bit slow here. But you'll see on the letters they arrived in Venezuela only a couple of weeks after they left Ireland. They probably sat in a sorting office in the docks till they sent them on to me.'

Billy stood there nodding. He didn't say much in the meeting. His eyes were sunk into his head and his cheekbones poked out of his face. The weight was falling off him. He was back on the coke, snorting it most of the day, and had lost his appetite. 'I'm just getting a coffee,' he said. He walked off to the canteen.

Father Pat stepped in closer to me and lowered his voice. 'Billy, is he doing OK? He seems very thin and he doesn't look well.'

'He's grand, Father, it's just the food in here.'

'Is he back on the drugs?'

'No, Father, not at all. Long off them.'

'OK,' he nodded, his eyes telling me he didn't believe me. But I couldn't tell him the truth. I knew he was in constant touch with Billy's parents back home and would tell them. I wasn't exactly a moral guardian either – I was doing a line myself every night. Not much but enough to get a bit of a buzz and to help me sleep.

Father Pat slipped me some cash from the Irish Council for Prisoners Overseas fund. They'd come through good with an emergency payment for the bed space I had bought. Although I got it out of cash I'd made from selling coke and booze, I put the charity's money to good use. I started paying a Nigerian inmate in the kitchen to cook my dinners. The best of the food was all sold like this. What was left in the pot was given out to non-paying inmates – the slop I'd been eating for months.

* * *

'Paul, we forgive you no matter what you've done. You're our son and we'll always love you . . .' I was in the wing reading the letter from my mother and father that Father Pat had brought in the package. It was written by my mother. At the end there were a few scribbles from my Da, Paddy. 'Well Paul, sure you might as well stay in Venezuela, meet a nice native girl and settle down. There's no jobs here and nothing to come home to.' Paddy, he always spoke his mind and wasn't one for giving any emotions.

There was a letter from Katie, too. I felt tense as I started to read it, my eyes poring over the words, almost as if they were sucking them in. She was still on the line that I could pay a lawyer and walk out the front door of Los Teques. 'Da, we can still try and get you out. All we need to do is get 20,000 euro and pay a lawyer and you'll be free.' Things had moved on since that letter had been written and in my heart I knew no money would get me out of here. I scanned further down the letter. 'Always love you Da, Katie.' I had a lump in my throat – all the emotions I'd bottled up over leaving her in the lurch back in Dublin stormed back at me.

I also pulled out a few photos of my family that were in the package. My ma, da and Katie in one. The lump in my throat was getting tighter, like a brick chugging down my neck. There were also letters from Sharon and Mick and a photo of them. I also reached into the package and found a set of glasses in a case. Amazing! I slipped them on and started reading the letter from Sharon. 'Thought you might need these,' she wrote. The letters were sharp now and clear-looking through my glasses, it was great. 'The optician just gave me a repeat prescription of your last ones.' Shaz, what a star. I looked over at Roberto on another bucket. His hair was shaved at the side now. It looked sharper to me.

Some of the Veno lags started gathering around, pawing at the letters and photos. '*Familia tuya?*' ('Your family?') I brushed their hands away like I was swatting flies. It was always the same: they wanted to paw at everything; that's why I started to call them chimps. More hands started groping around the package and in seconds the photos and letters were being passed around. One of the Venos studied the letter written in English; others were pointing at my mother and father in the pictures. '*Tú mamá, tú papá?*'

'*Sí,*' I said. I was resigned that they'd get their way and maul them.

Also in the package was a blue and navy hat of the Dublin football team. It was from my mate Cummins. 'Way to go,' I shouted, and put it on.

'Hey, Paul, you go fishing,' Roberto shouted over. 'Fishing hat, no?'

'Dublin team. Irish football. The best.'

There was also a CD in the package that my son Dano had put in. I asked the boss if I could play it on the stereo in the wing. '*Sí, no problema,*' said the boss, waving me off and turning his eyes back to a baseball game on the portable telly beside his bed.

All my gringo mates – Eddy, Henrik from South Africa, Billy, Hanz and so on – sat around out in the yard excited to listen to some European music. 'Come on, Paul, let's turn off that salsa shite and listen,' shouted Eddy.

'Just a minute.' I was on my hunkers fiddling with wires at the back of the stereo to get the speakers working, as no sound was coming out. I finally got it going and fastforwarded through the songs Dano had put on the CD. There was a great collection of Irish rock and pop tunes. One was 'Crazy World' by Dublin rock band Aslan. The guitars and drums kicked off. It was a sombre enough tune and the verse started 'I have fallen down so many times / Don't know why, don't know where', but it went down well, all the lads joining in with the chorus, 'It's a crazy, crazy world.'

'Very fitting,' said Hanz. 'Sums this place up.'

The words also made me think about Katie and how I had left her high and dry back home. 'How can I protect you in this crazy world / It's all right yeah / It's all right.' From behind bars there was nothing I could do to take care of her, that I knew.

* * *

The abogado was pale and gaunt, the skin tight around his face.

'Paul,' he said to me, 'you didn't send any money.' Straight to the point. Silvio was interpreting for me in the cops' office. On the table between myself and the lawyer a bowl was littered with cigarette butts and a beer-bottle top.

'No, and I'm not putting ten grand in your bank till I know this is a sure thing.'

'He says it's sure,' said Silvio, looking from my face to the lawyer's and back like he was watching a tennis match.

'Ask him is he well. He looks terrible. I don't like the look of this.' The lawyer looked ill. I wasn't giving him any money if he was on his last legs.

'You don't think I look well?' said the lawyer, his voice raised.

'No, I don't think you look well at all.' Something was fishy about him. I stood up. 'I'm not going ahead.'

'You not go ahead.'

'No, and you haven't got anyone out yet.'

'I am working on the papers of a German man. He will be out soon, I tell you.'

'OK, if he gets out we'll talk.' I stood up without saying goodbye. I felt the lawyer's eyes watch his vaca de leche walk away.

On the way back to the wing Silvio told me his own freedom was on the cards. 'Paul, I should be going soon, but don't tell anyone,' he confided.

'Jesus, that's magic. So that's why you've been on your phone a lot lately?'

'Yes, to my lawyer, my time is nearly done.' Silvio got just over two years after cops pulled him over in Maiquetía airport on his way home to London and later found he had swallowed a couple of condoms filled with capsules of coke. The rest of us got eight years for trying to smuggle it in our suitcases. It was an oddity in the Venezuelan justice system I couldn't get my head around.

Silvio kept that to himself, though. Among the prisoners, if you were caught trying to smuggle coke after swallowing capsules or stuffed in johnnies you were a maricón. Real men smuggled it in suitcases, apparently.

* * *

Two cops carried a man in a wheelchair into the wing. It was Terry, a Brit from upstairs in the Special wing. The cops and inmates got tired of always lifting him in his wheelchair up and down the stairs to the canteen, and moved him down to Maxima. He was an old guy in his late 50s with white hair and a beard the colour of snow, a dead ringer for Santa Claus.

I'd seen him a few times on his own two feet while I was walking around the roof. He later fell ill in the jail: he collapsed on the ground and the cops carted him off to hospital. He was diagnosed as having had a stroke and came back in a wheelchair. The cash handouts from the UK embassy were good, so he could pay helpers to carry him in and out of the toilet and bathe him. Being locked up in a hellhole prison in Venezuela as a foreigner was one thing, but being banged up in a wheelchair was another. I'd often watch him in his chair: his right side slumped over slightly, and he cradled his right arm with his left. His right eye was also dodgy: it was stiff and didn't move, as if the eyeball had been glued. He had a hard life inside and everyone felt sorry for him. 'Poor Terry.'

I wasn't so sure. As the weeks went on I watched him from the corner of my eye, seeing his right arm move the odd time. I was sure he was pulling a fast one. We spoke a lot and became friends. 'That was some stroke you had, Terry, a stroke of genius.' He started grinning. Sly old bugger.

'You get the right lawyer on the go and things happen,' he smiled.

'Who?'

'Viviana,' he said, 'she's famous in here. Gets things done. Not like the others.' She had put papers through for Terry to get early parole on medical grounds. He was just waiting for the judges to sign his papers and release him to a family in Caracas approved by the courts.

The lawyer's name stuck in my mind. I made a mental note to meet her.

We talked a lot, and as the weeks went on Terry put me on the inside track to his plans. We had long chats, and I told him endlessly I wanted to get out on early parole, which I could apply for after 18 months in jail: that was my plan. I told him I had little faith in the dodgy lawyer getting Bruce and a few others out on cancer.

'Get a stroke,' he said.

'A stroke?'

'Yeah, just like me,' he laughed, grinning from ear to ear.

'You mean you didn't really have one?'

'Not quite: I took a turn and they took me to hospital. But it was only a minor stroke. I knew it. I'd had one before and knew the signs. My right side had already dropped a bit from the stroke I had years ago; my eye had gone stiff as a board then.'

'So what did they do at the hospital here?'

213

'Nothing. A doctor shone a torch in my right eye and it didn't move. I knew it wouldn't, it was like that from before. So he told the prison I'd had a full-blown stroke. I got a solicitor on the go and I'm waiting to get out.'

'You sly old dog,' I said, laughing.

A cop walked in with the lista. Terry tilted his head a bit more to the right.

'It's easy – you pull off a stroke, have a few spasms on the ground. They take you off to the hospital and then you escape.'

'How?' I said, moving in closer.

'Get to hospital and get out.'

'The doctors will know straight away I haven't had a stroke – I can't fool them.'

'Listen, this is how it works. I've been in and out of the hospital in Los Teques town. Once they brought me in during the week, but there was no doctor for days. There are barely any nurses; the families that visit do all the work, cleaning and feeding the patients. No security. They had an armed guard on me, but when the Saturday came he said to me he was taking the weekend off and left.'

'Some security,' I laughed.

'Yes, I was on my own till Monday morning. All you do is get in there on a stroke, and when you see a chance run out the door, have a guy waiting for you in a car outside, have a false passport, and away you go off to the border in Colombia.'

'That easy?'

'Yes, Paul, if I was a younger man I would have left like that.'

'All I need is the passport,' I said, staring at the ground for inspiration.

'That's all.'

Easier said than done.

I had another plan to get out now and was in good spirits. I put my thinking cap on and wondered how I'd get my hands on a passport. I knew my own was in the hands of the authorities, probably with the cops in Interpol. I'd no chance of getting it back. I'd heard of some of the lags paying up to 1,000 dollars to cops who'd promised to get them their passports. But it came to nothing, other than making the cops richer. I wasn't falling into that trap. Silvio was always my port of call for anything I needed. The next day I went up to him in the yard.

'I need a passport.'

'A passport?' His eyes studied me for a moment as if he was about to ask me why, but he didn't. 'Roberto would be your man. He has Italian connections in Caracas who'd know.'

'Right, good idea.' I followed Silvio over to Roberto. He was sitting in a chair in the yard, one of the in-house barbers shaving a little zigzag design in the back of his head. In jail or not, Roberto cared about how he looked. And he seemed to have a bottomless pit of cash for the finer things in prison life. Silvio spoke to him in Italian. 'Passport?' said Roberto, looking at me now, his eyebrows raised. He waved off the barber and the whirr of the electric razor stopped. He fell into deep thought and spoke to Silvio.

'He says yeah, but it'd take time,' said Silvio.

'How long?'

'It could be a week, a month, he can't say yet.'

'How much would it cost me?'

'Two million bolos, he says.'

I thought for a minute, working it out in my head. It was about 400 euro, a lot, but money for old rope if it got me out of this dive. 'Tell him it's a deal. I don't have the cash, but I'll get it.'

'*Sí*,' said Roberto, nodding his head when Silvio interpreted.

The next morning I sat out in the yard scribbling names of people who might lend me some cash. One was a childhood friend who lived in New York and had a good job in banking. I hadn't seen him in a few years, since he'd come home to Dublin for a visit, but we had been good mates and I was confident he'd come through for me. I'd already asked my family for one Western Union – the 350 euro from my sister when I first got to Los Teques – so I didn't want to bother them again. I decided to tap friends. While I was jotting down names it dawned on me that people might be forgetting about me. I'd been banged up for a year now with little contact from anyone, which was what I wanted, but I hoped I wasn't history to people back home altogether.

I now had my own mobile phone, which I'd paid one of the wing bosses to get for me. I paid over the odds to include his commission and a backhander to a cop to smuggle it in. I had also chipped in with a few inmates and a couple of luceros and bought a laptop with a dongle-stick Internet connection. I had the world at my fingertips from right inside the wing, so it was easy for me to put out an SOS to my mates for cash.

* * *

The cop did the headcount in the evening with his usual armed escort of National Guards, one of them with a gruff face ticking off a roll-call sheet on a clipboard. I watched him shake his head at the cop when the roll call was finished. '*Falta de una.*' ('One missing.') It wasn't that unusual. Often Macedonia would be out in the yard where the cops had their cars parked, doing his job on bin duties, and they forgot about him. The headcount was done again, the 140-odd inmates looking wearier this time, sitting on their buckets, the rims digging into their arses.

But the same number turned up again. It looked like I wasn't the only one plotting to get out of Los Teques. The lags started shrugging their shoulders. The troops and the cop pulled out. 'Conejo, Conejo' was on everyone's lips. 'Conejo, the Rabbit,' said Silvio. 'They don't know where he is.' The Rabbit earned his nickname because he had two badly bucked front teeth.

The National Guard troops and the cop shortly after

walked back into the wing. '*Sotea*,' shouted a guard. Conejo, wherever he was, was in deep shit. Not only would the troops and cops be gunning for him, so would the cell-block jefes. His absence at the headcount prompted a search – which the padrinos hated.

The whole prison population was hauled up to the roof, wing by wing. Another headcount was called. But still no Conejo. Reds and oranges started to streak the sky as the sun set. It was getting dark and chilly. All I had on were shorts and a T-shirt. My arse cheeks were going numb sitting on the ground.

I started singing, 'Run rabbit, run rabbit, run, run, run,' and shouting, '"What's up, Doc?" I said, "What's up, Doc?"' The gringo inmates were cracking up laughing. 'Well, where de likkle wabbit go?' I added, mimicking the Walt Disney cartoon. I lost interest in cracking jokes when drizzly rain fell. Everyone was getting tired and irritated. After hours passed, we got the orders to get back to the cells, wing by wing.

I couldn't believe they hadn't found this guy. He didn't seem like a bright spark who had the brains to escape. He had what were known as 'trusted privileges', because in a past life he'd been a mechanic. Most inmates like him were immediately put to work in the driveway by the gate to the jail, fixing the prison fleet of a couple of buses. Often, however, I'd look down from the roof and I could see them, noting them bent over into the engine of one of the prison workers' cars. I could also see they enjoyed perks like fried-chicken fast food and other takeaways courtesy of the troops for fixing their motors. Anyway, it looked like the Conejo had pulled the wool over everyone's eyes.

'Where the hell did he go? Did he escape?' I said to Ricardo.

'No way, he's an idiot.' Dumb? I had thought so, but wasn't so sure now.

The next day it filtered back that the Conejo escaped out the front gate holding onto the bottom of one of the army trucks as it pulled out of the jail. They found him quickly, though, in his mother's house . . . He was bundled into a police car and brought back to Los Teques the next afternoon. I gave him kudos for having the brains to escape, but he didn't have enough to stay hidden when he got out. Still, he had the *cojones* to pull it off.

Not long afterwards, we were hauled up to the roof yet again after the troops were down one on their headcount. 'They say he's one of the prisoners in Wing 1. They think he's still in the jail,' said Eddy, sitting on his hunkers on the roof beside me. For three nights it went on. It didn't make sense. Nobody could hide in the prison for that long. On the fourth day I expected we'd all be called up for another evening under the stars while the cops and troops searched for the inmate. Eddy and Silvio started talking after the headcount in the wing. 'No roof tonight; they found him.'

'Found him where?' I said.

'The cops started looking on the Internet when they couldn't find the guy. They found a video on YouTube made in Wing 1 and saw him.'

'You must be joking me?'

'No, they saw the guy's face. Then you see prisoners' hands holding automatic weapons and shooting his arms and legs off.'

'That's disgusting,' I said. Now I came to think of it, the night before he went missing there had been a burst of gunfire from outside. This must have been the execution.

'It happens, Paul,' said Silvio. 'They are evil people in there.'

'How did they get his body out?' I said.

'The inmates cut up his body and put it into three buckets. The cops went into the wing and found them after seeing the video.' I was sick. These people were more animal and inhumane than I could ever imagine.

Chapter 17

LOVE CALLS

BILLY WAS FOREVER ON A DATING WEBSITE HE COULD ACCESS through his phone. An inmate in the Church, where you're supposed to be a Christian celibate, had put him on to it. He was texting one particular girl back and forth for weeks. I was sitting with Eddy one afternoon in the canteen on visit day and got to see the fruits of Billy's labour.

'Look at the beaut Billy boy's with,' I said. Billy had a knockout of a girl on his arm, grinning from ear to ear like he'd won a million in the lottery.

Eddy swung his head around. 'Gordon Bennett, there's a sight to behold.' The pair of them walked over and sat down on the stone bench next to us. Myself and Eddy were in the canteen on a Sunday visit day playing cards. The director opened it up for us PWVs to go to when the overcrowding got worse than usual.

'*Hola,*' said the girl, smiling. 'I am Angela.' That she was, with an angelic face and long, slick black hair that cascaded down her back. I started calling her Pocahontas. She was a beautiful, slim girl. We all fell in love with her at first sight.

She told us she was 18 and had a child. Most girls in this part of the world of a certain social class did by that age. After a bit of chitchat the pair of them disappeared off to the 'buggies' – the beds in the cells that had each been cordoned off with curtains, like a hospital bed, for the inmates to have a conjugal shag.

That evening both the Venezuelans and the gringos wanted

219

to know where Billy had met his stunning bird. 'Mate, some princess,' said Eddy, 'where'd you get her from?'

'On the phones, a dating site.'

'She's a corker, Billy,' I said. 'But what's she doing with you? – it's like Beauty and the Beast.' All the gringos cracked up laughing. He was a hairy boy, Billy, with woolly shoulders and a carpet of hair on his chest. I used to call him 'Teddy Bear' for his furry body. The Colombian chica, though, was mesmerised by his sparkling green eyes and thought he was cuddly.

The funny thing was that the Veno women hated body hair. The queues for the toilets on the mornings of visits were endless with inmates waiting to shave off their pubic hair and under their arms, getting ready for the arrival of their missus. A few even did their legs. The Venos took their conjugal rights seriously. When their partners brought in their kids I noticed they'd be three and four years old, yet the guy had been locked up for about four years. It was obvious the oats were sown behind bars.

All the gringo lags were getting in on the dating-site act after Billy's top score. Eddy quickly had women on the go coming in to visit him. Billy was also back on it too, fishing to see if he could get something else moving. And he did. He was all excited one Sunday on the morning of visits. 'Another bird, Paul, and she's coming in with her sister,' he said, rubbing his hands together.

'Well, aren't you the man,' I said.

We were sitting in behind the curtains and a lucero came in. 'Billy, *visita.*'

Billy stood up, swaggered over to the curtain and started twitching it for a peek out first. He looked back at me. His face dropped. 'I can't go out there, Paul, she's horrible.'

'What do you mean horrible?'

'The size of the two of them?' We all jumped to our feet and poked our heads out too, like theatre actors peeking out at their audience. There were two girls the size of beached whales stuffed into the plastic chairs for the visits. Venezuelan women were famous for winning Miss World competitions, but this pair would more likely make the Guinness Book of World Records for being the heaviest women in Latin America.

'Hahaha, Billy, you'd better go out,' I said.

He sat down, refusing to budge. 'No, no way.'

Minutes later the lucero came in again. '*Visita, ahora,*' he barked. It was the height of disrespect to leave a visitor waiting.

'Billy, go.'

He shrugged and pushed through the curtains into the yard.

That evening when the visits all went home Billy was still reeling from having the fattest women in Venezuela in to see him. Nobody ever remarked on a visit. It was a no-no and shameful among the Venezuelans. But they made an exception that day. They were bent over double laughing, calling out *fea* (ugly) and *gorda* (fat). Even the jefe was laughing.

'Yeah, funny, haha,' said Billy.

Of course I was interested in getting it on with a girl myself. Months locked up with men didn't do much for a man's sex life, a straight one's at least. There were *putas*, prostitutes, who did the rounds in the prison. I might have been tempted, only they were rotten and pricey. They wanted 100,000 bolos, about 20 euro, for a go of them. No way was I paying that for a quick shag when the same amount of cash would keep me going for a week with food, bottled water and the causa. I might have paid had they been nice and not jail bicycles, but they were.

All the Veno lags were always trying to set me up with a girl. New Yawk Mike even said he'd get me a proper prostitute off the street for about 200,000 bolos, or 40 euro. 'Paul, I can get you a beautiful queen.'

'Right, I'll go for it. Tell me when she's here.' I would have been up for it had he produced the goods, but he didn't. As usual it was *mañana seguro*. Tomorrow for sure.

Apart from that the Venos were always trying to hook up a gringo inmate with one of their family, be it a sister or a niece. Word had it that there was even an inmate up in Mostrico wing who was renting out his mother and his sister for sex to make a few quid. I never knew for sure, but it wouldn't have surprised me. It would have been just another level of sickness among the Venezuelans. What I did know for sure was that there was one lag who set the Maxima boss, Fidel, up with his nineteen-year-old daughter. On visit day they'd disappear into the boss's bed. To me it was shameful that a man would give his daughter up like that, and probably just to score a brownie point with the jefe for an easier life.

The Colombian lad who'd arrived with me in the army bus on the first day in Los Teques once invited me out from behind the curtain on visit day to meet his family. There was his mother, his girlfriend and his cousin. His cousin was *soltera* (single), he said. She was in her early 30s and pretty, with brown eyes and elegant cheekbones. She also spoke some English.

'Where are you from?' she asked.

'Ireland,' I said.

'Yes, Europe, I travel there,' she said, 'but mostly Spain for work. I am a travel agent.' I enjoyed the chat, but I wasn't going to get sucked into making it a regular visit with a trip to the 'buggies'. I didn't want to get sidetracked in jail with women, drugs, drink, nothing. My focus was on getting out and that was that. Aiming for early parole after 18 months and walking out the jail gate.

I did, however, start texting back and forth on the phone with a South African girl who was locked up in the Los Teques women's prison, close to our jail, and I enjoyed the contact. One of the gringo inmates, Henrik from South Africa, had given me her number. He was a tall lad with blonde hair and a heavy beard. He'd got her phone number from one of his countrymen holed up in another wing. The girl's name was Zenolia du Plooy. I later typed her name into a search engine on the laptop I shared with a few of the lads. There were stories all over the South African media about how she'd been caught with cocaine in the airport in Venezuela. After chatting to her, it looked like she had gotten roped into some dodgy caper. After a while the texts fizzled out. I didn't see the point; it wasn't like I could ever visit her.

She told me she had some rare disease and there was no medication for it in Venezuela. Her family had to have it sent over to her every month on a plane and were campaigning for her to be released on humanitarian grounds. Waste of time, I thought; there was no humanity here.

* * *

Straight love wasn't the only kind of romance going on inside Los Teques. The gays in the prison had their own wing under the stairs in the passageway. We called it the Pink Room, or the Fresa (strawberry) wing. There were about 20 or 30 gays. Many didn't have a choice but to be there. In most wings gays were castigated – beaten up and fired into the passageway. Not that they were total fairies that you could push around. Many were in for murder – so cross one and you might not wake up from a night's sleep.

In Maxima they were welcome, along with the outcasts from other wings such as kiddy fiddlers, rapists and ex-cops. Their causa money was good. Most slept together at the end of the cell near my bed, squashed onto the floor.

I actually got on well with the gays. When I was sitting on my bed one day typing on my laptop, one of them, Chico, came up and asked me for a use of it. '*Facebook, por favor.*' He was as camp as Christmas with a high-pitched voice; he'd make gay chat show host Graham Norton look like an alpha male. So I gave him the use of it. In return he gave me a massage. He would light candles around my bunk bed and had all the proper massage oils. He didn't grope where it wasn't wanted. It was actually great – my back and shoulders were always aching. Even though I had my own bed now, sitting on the buckets for hours on end behind the curtains on visit days was killing me, my body scrunched up in there in the small space beside the toilet that was getting more cramped every week. I could probably get a gig in a circus as a contortionist after Los Teques.

I used to teach another gay a few English words. He was taking classes in the jail and was keen to learn. I didn't mind and just taught him a few basics, such as 'what is your name?' One day out in the yard he came over and stood in front of me when I was sitting with Vito and Roberto playing cards. '*Te quiero mucho*,' ('I love you') he said, with his hand on his heart. I burst out laughing along with the lads and he ran off in a sulk.

'Haha, you're in there,' said Billy.

'Not a journey I want to take,' I said.

One day I noticed another gay who had checked into Hotel Los Teques had a shapely rear end like he'd stuffed two small cushions down the back of his trousers. 'He's a nice ass. But it looks a bit odd. How'd he get that?' I said.

'Paid for it,' said Silvio.

'What do you mean?'

'Plastic surgery.' It was huge business with women in Venezuela. Even gays got silicone pumped into their rear end. This lag's ass looked like a double-D cup.

Another day one of the visitors brought in a newspaper, as they always did. Any clippings about gringos caught in the airport with drugs we always read. One story that really caught our interest was a report about a Romanian drug mule who was a transvestite, according to the newspaper. We were all curious about that one.

'I wonder did they get the male or female cops to search him,' laughed Billy. A few days later we got word a totally camp gay had arrived in the jail.

'It's him, it must be him – or it,' laughed Silvio. A few

hours later the Romanian lad walked out into the yard. He was gay all right; he had plucked eyebrows and manicured nails. But a transvestite? We doubted it. The boss gave him a spot down at the back of my cell with the other gays. He was a bit of a lost soul, didn't click with them that well. He'd only a bit of Spanish, which probably didn't help. He was quickly moved up to the Strawberry wing – but not before taking a liking to Ralph, one of the German lads.

'You're in there, Ralph, the gay boy fancies you,' I said.

'Yeah, sure, see how it goes,' he said casually.

'You what?' We all looked at each other, puzzled.

Not long after, Ralph was seen nipping in and out of the Pink Room on his way back and forth to his kitchen job. He wasn't shy about it. 'Best sex I ever had. A man knows what a man wants.' I doubted he was gay or bisexual – just wasn't fussy and wanted a bit of strange.

But the other lags weren't pleased. 'How he could do that?' said Billy, his face scrunched up in disgust.

'Ah, sure, who cares as long as it's only in here,' I said. What happened in prison stayed in prison, I believed.

The cops took a dim view, however. They didn't like the idea that one of the lags who cooked their food was having sex with the gays. A muscular Nigerian guy in the kitchen, Onyeke, told me. He was a wizard with spices and even made the usual prison food of sardines taste good. So he filled me in about Ralph and the aguas plotting to get him out of the kitchen. 'The cops don't like the German playing around with the gay boy. He will lose his job.'

I later told Ralph. The kitchen was one of the best jobs in the prison. You got to eat well and it paid OK with a few bolos. 'Ah, no, it's fine – I know all the cops, they know me,' said Ralph. Maybe – but within weeks he got the boot, and Ralph's fling of passion with the Romanian came to an end.

The director actually loved the Romanian. He picked up Spanish quick and she gave him a job as her runner, flying around with letters and other messages for her. It seemed to me that she liked to surround herself with gays. They were well up the pecking order with the director and got plum office jobs doing admin. She even put three gays who were professional stylists to good use, doing her hair, nails and make-up every morning.

* * *

Terry's lawyer was still on the case to get him released on early parole due to his health. Weeks had passed and nothing had happened, as was often the case with anything to do with the courts in Venezuela. To speed things up, he wanted to send out a message to the powers that be that his health had taken a turn for the worse. He wanted to get to a hospital and get a check-up, and in there he'd act up for the doctors, who'd hopefully tell the prison director he was too ill for jail. He believed then that the judge on his case would get word of this and speed through his release papers. Fat chance, but worth a try.

The problem for Terry, though, was actually getting the prison bosses to organise transporting him to the hospital. The prison ambulance, which I only ever saw once from the roof, parked outside the jail, was apparently never available. We used to see the black hearse on a much more regular basis. So Terry asked me to get on to the British Embassy and ask them to put pressure on the Los Teques director. I thought I might be getting onto dodgy ground, but I agreed. He was an old guy and if Los Teques was hard for me, it was harder for him. I texted a number he gave me for a diplomat, saying Terry's health was 'grave' and he needed to get to hospital, even if it meant in the back of a taxi.

A few hours later one of the women cops, Morelba, stormed into the wing. I was sitting on my bucket scribbling in my diary and looked up. It was Carlos's 'girlfriend', standing there flapping her arms and shouting. Shit. What's going on here? She was shouting again, looking around the wing. Mariano, an inmate who spoke good Spanish, interpreted.

'Who rang the British Embassy for Terry, she wants to know.' I kept my eyes down in my copybook. Again. 'Who rang? You will have to say or we are all in shit.' Terry looked over at me, with eyes saying, 'How will we play this out?'

'OK.' I stood up. 'It was me.'

'*Tú*,' ('You') she shouted.

'Outside now,' said Mariano. I pushed Terry's wheelchair into the passageway. The woman boss stood there, arms folded. A scowl on her face.

'How did you phone the embassy?' said Mariano.

I knew we weren't supposed to have mobiles, so I nodded to the payphone at the end of the passageway. 'The one on the wall.'

She spoke again, her voice louder. 'She wants to know why.' Terry said nothing, just tilting his head more to the right, rolling his eyes.

'The guy's in a wheelchair, he's dying. He's an old guy, he needs help; if I was in his situation I'd like to think someone would do it for me.' My Mother Teresa act didn't wash. I watched her reply to Mariano, shaking her head.

'She says if you do that again she'll fuck you up. You'll be given the bat by the cops. Three slaps on the ass.'

'All right,' I said, shrugging. Morelba turned on her heel and walked off. She still didn't say if she would get Terry to the hospital or not.

* * *

I was back up on the roof doing my walking laps and I spotted Bruce. I wanted to catch up with him about the lawyer and his plan to escape on a cancer ticket.

'Bruce, is the abogado moving the cancer along?'

His usual jolly face was gone. 'He's in having an operation for cancer,' he said. Bruce and a few of the other lads hadn't heard from him for a few weeks and decided to call his office. A secretary answered and told them that he was in hospital recovering from chemotherapy. I couldn't believe it: how's that for a coincidence? Lawyer promises cancer diagnosis then gets cancer. It was taking karma to new levels.

'Do you think it's gonna work out – the plan?'

'It better do. I've paid him 10,000 dollars. I'll kill the old bastard if it doesn't.'

'Let's see how it plays out,' I said, 'Should be OK, probably just a few hiccups.' I had my suspicions but didn't want to rub it in his face that he'd been sold a turkey. I was just glad I hadn't given the old guy money. I didn't trust him from the start.

* * *

Father Pat was in. 'Billy's got a lovely girl,' I said, smiling. I used to talk to him like he was one of the lads down the pub. Billy would look at me like I was mad. He then pulled out a small photo of his Pocahontas, which he carried in his pocket. Father Pat held the passport-size picture and studied her face for a few moments.

'That's a very nice girl, Billy.' He then went off on a sermon. 'Now, Billy, you'll have to respect this girl. Treat her right.' He also told him to be wary. 'Many of these girls are vulnerable, from poor families. You have to be aware of the implications.' The underlying story was that she hoped a 'rich' gringo would take her to Europe. In Billy's head I think he already had her on the plane on the way back to Ireland.

Father Pat said Mass and turned to leave. 'OK, boys, I'll be seeing you soon,' he said. I felt a bunch of rolled-up notes in my palm when we shook hands. 'That's part of the money your friend wired to me. Too dangerous to bring it all in at once.'

'That's fantastic, Father,' I said. He really was a saviour. I was also over the moon that my mate had come through good with the cash for my passport after I had emailed him. Now we'd see if I could skip out of Venezuela with my very own travel documents.

Chapter 18

UNITED NATIONS BEHIND BARS

'PAUL, IRISHMAN, IRISHMAN, THERE'S ANOTHER IRISH.' VITO WAS shouting over to me in the yard. 'Come, a guy from Ireland.' My ears pricked up. Another Paddy? One more Irishman for Father Pat to take care of? He'd have to get himself the honorary consul job soon. I was absorbed in writing my diaries, but I put them down; curiosity about the guy got the better of me.

We shook hands. 'How are you?' he said. I could tell by his accent he was Eastern European. No way his passport had a harp on it.

'Where you from, they all think you're Irish?'

'Poland,' he said, 'but I have been living in Dublin for seven years.'

'Poland, yeah,' I said, 'there's a couple of Polish bars down around Parnell Street.'

'Yes, but I am liking Temple Bars very much,' he said, referring to Dublin's tourist area.

'I'm Paul, by the way.'

'Dimitry.'

He was wearing a Manchester United shirt – my favourite football team. It was the brand-new away strip. 'I'll give you twenty thousand bolos [about four euro] for that.'

'Done,' he said, and we shook on it.

'That'll get you started,' I said. 'Nothing's free here.'

'Yes, I am thinking that. Is no hotel.'

The new lads, when they arrived they had nothing till they got help from their embassy – if at all. Or at least till they got their first Western Union through to pay the jefe the 'entry fee' to stay in the wing. I knew Dimitry needed a few things to get himself started: a bucket, a cup, a bowl and a few toiletries, such as a bar of soap and toothpaste.

'Go and see Macedonia,' I said. 'He sorts out all you lads with the bosses, interpreting for them if they have any problems. Speaks Spanish and Russian.'

'He is Russian?'

'No, from Macedonia.'

'I see. Makes sense his name.' Dimitry didn't seem at all bothered by the wing 'induction', where the jefe and his henchmen would read him the wing bill of rights down a gun barrel.

Later I got to know him better. He'd been living in Castleknock in west Dublin with his sister and had a job in a well-known hardware store chain. He had been making good money but got laid off. He was approached by some gang to do a drug run, but he didn't say who he was working for. No one ever did. We all guarded ourselves like that. You were afraid something might happen to your family if you fingered whoever you'd been working for back home.

Dimitry was one of the growing number of gringos in Los Teques. What had been around 200 was reaching up to 300, we guessed, out of about 1,200 prisoners. Every week another few arrived. Soon enough, I thought, we could apply to the United Nations for status: the Gringos' Republic of Los Teques. Dozens of countries had an 'ambassador' here: Poland, Lithuania, Estonia, South Africa, Mexico, Colombia, the United States, Germany, France, Ireland, Macedonia, Turkey, Libya, Israel, Nigeria, Australia and so on. All caught at the airport. The cops there were getting good at sniffing out packages of coke stuffed in suitcases and collaring jittery gringos who'd swallowed johnnies packed with capsules of coke.

There was no shortage of characters among them. José was one, a Spaniard whom we all liked. He was a real clown, always out in the yard like a street entertainer: singing and dancing, and juggling oranges and lemons. One afternoon when a luz was called we all piled out into the yard to play statues, staring at the back wall while the bosses went to take out their guns. José had been in the wing only a few days and didn't know the drill, and was bathing himself in the toilet area in the cells. The bosses ran in and dragged him out. He ran running into the yard naked, the lags kicking him up the bare ass.

He was the village idiot, but I could see he was intelligent. And, like every clown, he had a sad story behind the jokes and laughs. He was born into a rich family in Madrid but broke away from them and started up a business that went bust. He then found himself living rough on the streets. Like all of us, he was approached to do a drug run and make 'easy money'.

Another quirky sort was an old Polish guy. He was a fat little fellow with a scrunched-up wrinkly face. I called him Mr Magoo. He was 67 and looked it. 'What's he doing in here?' I said, puzzled when I first saw him. I couldn't believe there was a guy this old locked up for being a drug mule. Despite his senior years, he was mad into the crack cocaine. He suffered from depression and you could tell he wasn't right in the head. Roberto and a few of the others used to dress him up in hats for a laugh, and he'd parade up and down the yard like he was in a fashion show. It was sad, really – he was an old guy who'd already been locked up for four years. By this stage he should have been released on humanitarian grounds, or at least on parole, given his age, but he hadn't. He probably didn't have the know-how to get somebody in his embassy, or back home, on the case.

There were a couple of Krauts who lived up to their stereotype as being dour. One looked like a typical old-style German to me: he had a moustache, trimmed and curved down at the edges around his upper lip like handlebars. He reminded me of Kaiser Wilhelm II, the German emperor during the First World War. He was a fair bit older than me, in his 50s. I didn't like him much; he seemed pompous. Despite the fact that all us foreigners were locked up for drug smuggling, he thought he was better than us all.

'The Gypsy' was a name we gave one Romanian lad. Like many Romanians of his social class, he went to nearby Italy looking for work but fell on hard times there and got roped into doing a drug run. One of the Italians in the wing used to slag him. 'Go home, you Romanian bastard – taking our jobs.' But it was just a laugh – I doubted any lobbying groups in Italy were campaigning for equal rights for foreign and local drug mules.

Most of the gringos had the same story. They had lost their job and were approached to do a 'holiday in the sun'. The few quid was a big carrot. One Polish guy, Vladimir, had been working in the north of England. He had great work as a gardener and lived with his English girlfriend. But he lost his job, hit hard times and got roped into doing a cocaine run. One day he was sitting out in the yard next to me with his head in his hands. 'Paul, what am I after doing? What am I after doing? I had a great life and a beautiful girl.' Most of the young lads used to tell me their woes, seeing me as someone to talk to, probably because I was older. I didn't mind listening to their problems; it was a chance to forget my own for a while.

Vladimir's story was common. The rise in the number of foreigners coming into the prison started in the early months of 2010, which was in line with the recession biting hard back in Europe. Almost all of the drug mules coming into the prison were first-time drug runners, many of whom had lost their jobs in the downturn and were offered a 'holiday in the sun' to do a drug run to Venezuela. I thought the recession was a bonus for the drug dealers. They could walk into any pub or dole office back in Europe and take their pick of would-be mules. Offer them the going rate, between 5,000 and 10,000 euro, which to someone on the dole who'd fallen on hard times was a lot. But it was a good investment for anyone hiring them. If the mule smuggled back four or five kilos of cocaine, it could be mixed with sodium or something to double the volume; the coke would then have a street value of up to 500,000 euro.

Although most drug mules banged up in 2010 were first-timers, that's not to say there weren't seasoned mules too. Many of the Spaniards and Italians had been doing it for years. The Spanish, the biggest foreign contingency in the prison, numbering about 70, seemed to me to behave like drug running was their national pastime. And for some reason they were all crackheads. For many of the South Africans, too, it was their fourth or fifth run before they'd got caught in the airport in Caracas. And they had done time before, and would likely mule again.

One long-termer in Maxima was an old South African guy. He'd been in for four years. I put him down as between 60 and 65. He said he'd been working on oil rigs for years before returning home, hitting hard times and getting roped into a drug run. Like other South Africans, he said he got nothing from his embassy. He hadn't a bean and walked around all day asking for 'cigarillo, cigarillo'.

Most of the lags gave him one. You couldn't help but feel sorry for him, a weary old guy locked up far from home. He had a crazy look in his eye, and he probably was. He was filthy stinking, too; he rarely washed and had messy hair. The jefes often shoved him into the toilet area, forcing him to have a wash, or paying the in-house barber to give him a haircut, so he'd look respectable in front of their families on visit days.

The South African walked up to me one day. 'Look, look, my invention. It will make me millions.' He pulled out a bundle of folded-up pieces of paper from his pocket covered with squiggles and drawings, an idea he said he'd come up with on the oil rigs that would speed up the drilling process. He told anyone who'd listen, then quickly pocketed the pieces of paper containing his coveted invention in case you'd steal them. I couldn't help but feel sorry for him. He'd lost his marbles.

He saw me with my phone one day and got on my case to contact the British Embassy so he could ask them to represent him. That way he could get a few quid. Being from a commonwealth country, he had a decent chance, and if they did agree to represent him, it meant a little money from a prisoners-abroad welfare charity in the UK. I agreed and dialled a number he gave me.

'Good afternoon, British Embassy,' said a girl in the Caracas office. It was a novelty to hear a posh English accent: I was only used to hearing Eddy's Mancunian twang, like listening to an extra in *Coronation Street* going to the 'Rovers'.

I told her about the old guy's request to get represented as a Briton. 'Yes, we heard about him a long time ago. We'll look into it. Can we call you on this number?'

'Yes,' I said. It was no surprise to them that an inmate was ringing from his own mobile. 'And he should have been out a long time ago; he's done two years more than most.'

Weeks later he did get a visit from British Embassy officials, but I never found out if he got help. He didn't say, and I didn't ask, not wanting to get involved with him if I could help it. He was later finally released on parole, and after a short stay in a halfway house I heard he was living rough on the streets of Caracas. Poor old guy: he probably died there, living under a bridge or in a cardboard box in the street.

* * *

Some fared better than others inside when it came to getting looked after by their embassies. The Brits seemed to do well, getting a decent payout from a prisoners' charity at home. The Spanish did OK, too. The Italians were on a good number. They had good credit rating, too, running up tabs in the shop and with the bosses for perico. They had no problem getting it all on the slate; everyone knew they were good for it. I often watched Silvio coming back from his monthly meeting with his embassy official. He'd walk straight in to see the padrino and pay his coke bill, then would go to the Chief in the shop and square with him for food, coffee and other bits.

It was an Italian priest representing their embassy who came to visit them. A bonus for the Italians was that he gave them a big hamper of food every month. They'd walk back into the wing after the visit with goodies like fresh ham and cheese wrapped in fancy paper. It was weird; it seemed like their embassy was rewarding them for being drug mules.

They weren't the best off, though. There was an Israeli locked up in a private cell upstairs in the jail – the only inmate to be on his own. We reckoned he must have been minted and paying a boss big money for it – but out of his own pocket, I guessed. I doubted any embassy was that generous. He rarely came out. I only saw him once, beady eyes poking out of a gaunt, bearded face. He looked a bit like Che Guevara.

Other nationalities were on the margins and got little or nothing as far as I could see: the Nigerians, Eastern Europeans, Turks, a Chinaman and so on. The Latino foreigners also didn't seem to get a peso. Colombians, Mexicans, Ecuadorians – nada. They all had to work. Everyone could find their niche if they had to. There were jobs in the kitchen, but they were only for Spanish speakers. If you were an English speaker and getting nothing from your embassy, such as the South Africans, you were really looking at work in the wing for other inmates, such as hand washing their clothes or cooking food for the jefe and his henchmen, which many did.

As for myself and Billy, the Irish, we got nothing from the embassy. Zero. Like Billy, I got one visit from the consul after I was caught. That was that. In fairness, he was only an honorary consul and it was a voluntary job. They didn't get paid. The nearest embassy that covered Venezuela was in

Mexico. A plane trip there took about five hours, about the same as a flight to Ireland. But despite the distance, they were plugging away behind the scenes. They had papers on the go for Billy to be repatriated back to Ireland to serve the remainder of his time there. He would make history – the first Paddy to be repatriated from Venezuela. The Department of Foreign Affairs had also partly funded the pot of cash for the one-off payment we both got from the Irish Council for Prisoners Overseas, dished out to us on the ground by Father Pat.

The influx of gringos into Los Teques seemed to be down to the Venos making strides in catching foreigners trying to smuggle coke through Simón Bolívar airport. For years it was seen as – and was – an easy touch, according to some of the gringo mules in Los Teques who'd been smuggling coke through there for years. The airport was now crawling with sniffer dogs, something I hadn't seen when I was caught.

Passenger profiling was big too. Gringo males travelling solo were almost always pulled up by the cops, questioned and searched. Most, like Billy, were nabbed as they stepped through the front door. Cases searched and bingo, the bags of white coke were found. Others also swallowed it in condoms. Up to six at a time full of capsules of coke up to half a kilo could be taken. One Nigerian inmate, Arikawe, an enormous bodybuilder, said he had swallowed a kilo before he got caught. But this large amount was rare. The cops would march them to a toilet in the airport and wait for hours till it passed. They were hardly pros, though, if people like me could smuggle out thousands of euros' worth of coke from their seized haul in a talcum-powder bottle.

Overall, though, it seemed everybody was getting caught. Nabbed and then paraded in front of the cameras. Mug shot in the papers. Another gringo bites the dust. More 'great' work by the Venezuelan security at the airport.

But it was all window-dressing. Father Pat filled us in on the news on the outside world, and I learned other bits from the newspapers brought in by families on the visits. One story raging in the press was about a report released by US anti-drugs chiefs saying Venezuela was the prime route for coke smuggled from Colombia to Europe. They said over 200 tonnes of the stuff passed through the country every year. The bulk of the charlie was flown in by light aircraft from neighbouring Colombia, often onto military airstrips deep in remote areas in Venezuela. So it didn't take a bright spark to figure out who in Venezuela was behind that. Chávez, not one to take a kicking from the US, went on TV with his usual chant: 'Yankees go home.' He put his words into action and booted out the US's anti-drugs officers.

* * *

Terry got word he had a court hearing. This had happened many times before: he was carted off to the courthouse and the judge never heard his case. This time he was sure it was different. 'I can feel it, Paul,' he said. 'They will let me out of here this time.'

'See you later, Terry,' I said, giving him a wink. 'See you around.' A helper he paid to take care of him then wheeled him out of the wing.

'*Mañana seguro*,' ('Tomorrow for sure') he said, laughing. He never came back from the courthouse that night. Rather than feeling down about someone going free while I was still stuck in Los Teques, I was in high spirits. It gave me a lift seeing him get out. Made me think that some day not so far off I'd get out of this dump too.

* * *

It was March. St Patrick's Day was looming. A few weeks before, a few of the boys were on to me to mark it. 'Paul, Paddy's Day, we'll have to have a few drinks,' said Aussie Bruce. All the lads were looking forward to drowning the shamrock with an Irishman. The pressure was on to fly the flag for Ireland and put on a bit of entertainment, so I rolled up my sleeves and spent a couple of weeks making a bucket of home brew: about 18 litres of liquor we called jugo loco. I ran around gathering the ingredients – yeast, sugar and so on – and got to work, brewing up the booze in my empty cooking-oil drum.

When it was ready I put out the word: 'Right, Paddy's Day in the canteen at midday.' I slowly walked up the passageway to the rancho and ran the gauntlet of cops, my arm straining under the weight of the 18 litres of booze. Normally during the run-up to Venezuelan national holidays the cops would check all the buckets going to the canteen to see if there was illicit booze – but they weren't clued in to any Irish ones.

A good few of us got together with myself and Billy, including Hanz, three South Africans – Dieter, Henrik and Capetown – and Tibor, an inmate from Hungary. Tibor had white skin the colour of snow and walked with his right foot dragging slightly. I presumed it was something he had been born with, but I wasn't going to ask him in case he was offended. To fly the Irish colours I wore my trusted green rugby shirt, which I still had, and my Dublin hat with the light-blue and navy-blue stripes – the team colours of Dublin's GAA Irish football team. Billy wasn't into dressing up and wore nothing special for the occasion. I supposed his pale Paddy skin was Irish enough for the festivities.

The drink did the trick and we all got merry, sliding out the bucket from under the table and ladling in our coffee mugs for a refill. I sang out a few traditional Irish tunes, from 'The Fields of Athenry' to 'Molly Malone'. In between we played cards and did a couple of lines of coke. The craic was great and I was doing my bit to mark Paddy's Day, thousands of miles from home locked up with armed loonies in a circus behind bars.

At the end of the afternoon myself and Billy stumbled back to the wing with an empty bucket for the número. I felt light-headed from the coke and booze. Shortly after the headcount

I climbed into my bunk bed and put my head on the pillow. I looked back on the day. I'd enjoyed the craic, but I'd never been more homesick. All I could think about was wanting to be back down at the pub with my mates having a pint.

Only the month before I'd rung in my second birthday in Los Teques. I was 45 when I was banged up; now I was 47. I was getting older, and my kids and family were starting to become distant memories. I did speak to my son, Dano, a bit on the phone, however. But despite asking my family to get my daughter Katie to call, she didn't. I hadn't heard from her in over a year and a half. I let you down Katie, sorry, was all I could think. I lay there in bed, twisting and turning. Sleep then saved me and wrenched me off into a less painful world.

* * *

I walked over to Roberto with Silvio. He was sitting on the lower bed of a bunk, being one of only two non-Venezuelan prisoners to have a bed – me being the other.

'Tell him I have the cash,' I said, 'the two million bolos for the passport.'

Silvio interpreted. 'He says OK, you pay him and he'll start making calls.'

'Great.' I got the cash from a friend back home. I'd sent him an email asking him to wire 1,000 euro to Father Pat's Western Union account. In a couple of weeks he came through. Brilliant. Father Pat brought it in to me in dribs and drabs over a few visits. He changed it on the black market and I got about ten million bolos for it.

The next day Silvio had news. 'Roberto has things to say about your passport.'

'Good.' I jumped off my bucket next to the door of the yard where I always sat.

'He says he can have a passport for you soon, a Dutch one.'

'Dutch?' I said. My brow furrowed into a knot.

'Yes, there are Dutch colony islands off the coast of Venezuela.'

'Oh yeah.' I remembered Silvio pointing out Aruba on the map in the classroom.

'OK, he has the money,' Silvio told Roberto, 'but we need a photo.'

'How are we going to do that in here?'

'We will sort something.' I decided to change my appearance. I thought it was better that I looked nothing like my original passport. I had visions of that photo being used as a mug shot in a 'Wanted' poster in Venezuela if I went on the run. The next day I sat in the yard and paid one of the in-house barbers a few bolos to shave my head. I also retired my razor and within a week had a decent enough beard.

'OK,' said Silvio, 'it's back on. Roberto has made some calls.'

'Paul, sit,' said Roberto. 'We doing passport photo now,' he said, grinning.

'Do I need to wear clogs and eat Edam cheese?'

'Is what?' he said, puzzled.

'Nothing, just joking.'

I sat down beside him on the bunk bed. Roberto then hung down a sheet over the wall behind me as a background for the photo. He stood up off the bed holding his phone at me, a BlackBerry – only the best for Roberto.

'OK, Paul, stay still.' *Click*. 'It is done, look.'

I sat forward and studied the photo. It was a picture of a bald guy with a gaunt face and a beard. I looked like Robinson Crusoe on chemo. Perfect. Nothing like me and, although the photo looked a bit blurry, it would do the job.

As soon as I got the passport I'd pull off a stroke. Colombia, here I come!

Chapter 19

RUSSIAN MAFIA HIT

THE BOOZE WAS FLOWING OUT IN THE CANTEEN AGAIN. THIS TIME IT was in honour of Bruce's birthday. Rum and Cokes, no cheap home brew for him. Myself and Vito were enjoying this rare treat, filling our coffee mugs from the bottle of rum under the table. We were well on, giggling and laughing, then cupping our hands to our mouths when a cop popped his head into the canteen wondering if there was a party or something. When he disappeared I steadied my hand under the stone bench and filled our cups with another round. But the rum, a local tipple in Venezuela, where it was cheap and popular, was running low. We needed to do something to keep the party going.

By chance, Gary the Russian walked in with bottles of homemade brew, doing the rounds with *agua loco* (crazy water) on the Sunday afternoon when visits were around to get some sales. They made dozens of bottles of it in the Special. It was clear liquid and didn't arouse the suspicion of the cops. I waved him over.

'Paul, you want to buy?' he said, looking down his pointy nose, which was a bit like a gerbil's. He had a shifty look and a face that brought to mind a Russian pimp, with bloodshot eyes that were sunk into the back of his head. Any deeper and you could stick your fingers in and pick up his head like a bowling ball.

'Yeah, how much?'

'It's 40,000 bolos,' he said.

'Right, give me one.'

He slipped his hand into a plastic bag and gave me the booze in a litre water bottle. I passed a 20,000-bolo note into his hand. He put it into his pocket and left without looking at it. I had lent him a 20 before and he had never paid it back. Now he had, and he'd soon realise it.

The following Sunday Gary was back down in the canteen on his rounds. 'Paul, you only gave me 20,000 bolos last week. The bottle was 40,000.'

'Gary, you owed me 20,000 from before and you never paid it. Well, now you have.' He had stayed in Maxima when he first arrived. He racked up debts on the slate with coke, food in the shop and loans. When he knew the boss was about to call him in for a chat and break his legs he fled to the Special wing upstairs.

'Paul, it is not my money; it is my boss's money.'

'I don't give a flying fuck. You owed me 20 and now I have it,' I said, walking past him. Swine thought he could shaft me for a few notes and get away with it.

The lads in Maxima got wind of my tiff with Gary and were joking I should be on the lookout for a reprisal. 'Watch it with the Russkys, Paul,' said Billy. Gary's boss was Fyodor, another Russian, who was forming a loose coalition of inmates in the Special wing from the former Soviet states and its satellites: Poles, Lithuanians, Latvians, Slovakians, Romanians and so on.

'The Russian mafia might be after you,' said Eddy, joking. But the word was the Veno cell-block bosses were watching the Russian gringo daring to set himself up as a boss. The fear was he might try to build up arms and take over a wing. Only a Veno could become a jefe – it was their country and their rules. Cross their line and you'd pay the price.

I was back up on the roof doing my laps and taking in the view. I watched the National Guard troops in the watchtowers: one was chatting away on a mobile phone, standing next to a machine gun propped up on a tripod; in the other tower the soldier was chewing gum and polishing his tinted sunglasses with the sleeve of his uniform. Down below I saw the cesspit of prison rubbish. I also saw the fat mechanic lag from Maxima – he was fast asleep, sitting on the ground, his chin slumped on his chest.

Fyodor the Russian suddenly stood in my path. He was tall, at 6 ft 4 in., with sharp Slavic cheekbones. He was a good six inches inches taller than me. 'Paul, you owe me money,' he said, looking down at me. 'Do you have it?'

'Are you on about this as well?' We squared up to each other with our eyes. There were always luceros from each wing on the roof, knives at the ready – so if it came to it the luceros from Maxima would step in and cut Fyodor up. 'I've already told Gary. He owed me 20,000 and now I have it and that's that.'

'The other 20,000 you should have paid is mine.' His eyes locked on me and he moved his upper body forward slightly, trying to crowd me with his height. It was starting to bore me.

'Gary owed me 20 from before. What goes around comes around.' I moved around him and continued walking. I didn't know it then, but Fyodor put out a hit on me.

* * *

'Alllll rrrigghtttt Paullly, alllll rrrrrighhhhht.' It was my mate Cummins from Dublin on the phone, shouting over a din of what sounded like people roaring. 'We're at the Man United game in Old Trafford.' That explained it. 'We won, we're having a great time.'

It was a Champions League game. I knew because I was watching it on the telly in the wing. 'I know, I'm looking at it here,' I shouted back.

'We're having a great time, a great time.' He was there with the lads from home, all Manchester United fans.

'A good one, Cummins,' I shouted down the phone. I was pretending I was happy to hear from them. But I hated those calls. The lads also often rang me when they were out boozing.

I don't know what they were thinking. They meant well, keeping me in the loop, but it just reminded me of where I was and where I wanted to be. Pure torture.

It also reminded me of how disconnected I was from my family. I might have been only at the end of a mobile phone, but to my family and friends I felt I was out of sight and out of mind. A few calls a year and that was it. Not that I blamed them for that; it's just the way it was. I didn't want the calls anyway. It only messed with my head. I preferred to pretend the outside world didn't exist till I was back in it.

After the chat I sat back down on my bucket in the hallway in the wing to watch the rest of the game. All the gringos were crowded around the telly: Spanish, Italians, British and so on. Few Venos bothered with it. Baseball was their game.

* * *

For weeks the lags had been working away building a second floor over one half of the yard. Every few days I'd be called out to help carry in materials. There was a truck parked in the driveway at the pedestrian entrance to the cell blocks. One of the lags standing on the back of the lorry lowered down a bag of cement onto my shoulder and I lugged it back to the wing. It was like Sunday afternoon at a B&Q hardware shop.

Carlos turned the small floor area into a gym when it was finished. He had a ripped physique; you could drop a penny into the grooves of his six-pack. He put in a proper treadmill, a couple of exercise bikes, free weights and a bench press. Eddy got the job of managing it. A Lithuanian lad who was a graffiti artist gave the place a bit of colour. He got to work with his aerosol cans and streaked the walls with urban-style painting of skyscrapers and yellow New York-style cabs.

It wasn't Eddy's only job. He started up a little business as a tattoo artist. One of the lags smuggled in a proper batch of needles for him. His work was popular, and between that and the job in the gym, it gave him a way to focus himself since he had started to ease off the crack cocaine. Inmates came down from other wings for a bit of his artwork on their skin, from flaming dragons to Chinese characters.

I started working out for two hours over four mornings a week. I was thin, but in weeks I was fit and hard. I was lifting the weights with the determination of a man on a mission. Fitness was part of my escape plan. I stood there sweating, doing bench presses and bar-bell curls with visions of the National Guard chasing me through the jungle as I bolted for freedom over the border into Colombia. One more rep, one more, I was saying in my head. I wanted to be mentally and physically fit for the journey ahead. I was doing very little coke and I was eating extra *avena* (porridge) in the morning, buying packets of it from the kitchen and making it in the wing with cold water.

* * *

I was on my march around the roof again. Bruce's head popped up from the stairway and he emerged wearing a yellow T-shirt, shorts and flip-flops. 'Dressed for the barbie, mate?' I said, laughing. He didn't smile.

'Paul: the lawyer, he's dead.'

'Dead?'

'Yes, the lawyer, the guy getting us out on cancer – he's gone.' Bruce looked like he was about to cry . . . but it wasn't due to grief.

'How'd you find out?'

'We didn't hear from him for weeks and we called his secretary. She said, "Sorry, but he passed away with cancer." He died from cancer. Can you believe it? He tries to get us out on cancer and he gets it himself. Old bastard.'

'And you paid him all your money?'

'All the down payment.' He couldn't bring himself to say 10,000 dollars.

'Bad score,' I said.

'That muthafucker, can you believe it?' he said, shaking his head. 'He took my money and did nothing.'

'Terrible, Bruce.' There wasn't much I could do to console him. However, I was curious whether others had got out on the cancer diagnosis and asked Bruce.

'A German, and the secretary says the cases are on the go for two others to get out on humanitarian grounds because their papers were already on the way to the judge. But they can't put any more through.' He turned his eyes away from me.

'Sorry to hear that, Bruce. Really am.' I reckoned the old lawyer knew he was dying of cancer when he got the scam going to get inmates out on humanitarian grounds. He got one or two out to make it look real, and the rest, I'd say he was using their cash to leave a nest egg for whoever he was leaving behind. I just thanked my lucky stars I hadn't paid the old guy a cent. Anyway, that he died of cancer while trying to get prisoners out on it to me was poetic justice.

As for my other plan to get out after faking a stroke, it was all down to Roberto first getting me the false passport. Months had passed since I'd paid Roberto for it. I'd been on to him all the time. '*Mañana seguro*' was the answer. After a while I'd given up chasing him for it. I liked Roberto, and he had been in the click with myself and Silvio, his fellow Itie. But he had since been made up into a lucero and kept his distance a bit. I suppose he had to. You couldn't push lags around the wing and be their mate at the same time.

My plan to fake a stroke after falling unconscious with an overdose of sleeping tablets turned out the same. Nada. I couldn't get hold of any. In Los Teques you could get crack, cocaine, hash, guns, weapons and hookers. Anything under the sun, really, if you had the cash. For some reason, though, no one could get me half a dozen sleeping tablets. I figured that'd be enough to knock me out for a few hours and get carted off to hospital. In there I'd come through and disappear out a window on my way to Colombia with a new passport.

It looked like I could scratch off getting out of Los Teques with a stroke. I got a bit down about it all, but there was nothing I could do.

* * *

A cop walked into the yard with la lista. The lags huddled around, wondering if they were going to the courts or, better, getting out. The agua then said something about Silvio I couldn't make out.

'Silvio, he will go free,' said Vito, smiling, sitting on his bucket next to me wearing an Italian football top.

'Wow.' I stood up, went over and clapped Silvio on the back. 'Great news.'

'Yes, fantastic I tell you,' he said.

'When do you get out?'

'Now.'

'That quick?' I said, my voice raised a notch.

'Yes, I get my things and go.' In his eyes I could see the sparkle of a free man. We embraced and shook hands. 'Paul, I'll see you, see you in London,' he said, our hands still locked.

'Yes, Silvio,' I said, 'and I want free tickets to the best movies in town.'

Billy shouted over. 'Good luck, *mama huevo*,' he said, laughing. Silvio then did the rounds, saying goodbye to all his *compañeros*. It was a strange feeling, saying goodbye to Silvio. He'd been a big part of my life in jail. Over the months we'd faced death twice in two shoot-outs, wondering whether we would get out alive to see our friends and family. Now he was leaving. I watched him walk off, then run to the wing door through a gauntlet of inmates lashing out with their legs, cheering and clapping. Even Carlos, Fidel and the other bosses came out to give him a boot. But it was all in good spirits. That was how they gave you a send-off in Los Teques – with a friendly kick up the arse.

Silvio stooped down to fit out the wing door and disappeared into the passageway. I watched the door close behind him, wanting to be in his shoes. But my thoughts became clearer. Watching Silvio go free was proof you could get out. Liberty wasn't some far-flung hope – it was real. I was more resolved to get out of Los Teques as soon as I could. I had my eye on getting out in just two years, not four or five.

* * *

I shuffled the deck and dealt out a hand to Henrik and another South African, suitably named Capetown. The cards skimmed along the top of the stone bench over crumbs and bits of rice. It was Sunday morning, just a couple of hours after breakfast in the canteen.

Capetown suddenly opened his mouth like he was about to scream. Nothing came out. He just pointed behind me, his face frozen. I turned around and went to stand up. I put my arm up to defend myself. I could feel something was coming and felt a wallop on my head. The room started spinning. An inmate was standing over me with a big rusty knife like something used on a trawler to gut a fish. I touched the top of my head and felt wetness, then put my fingers in front of my face and saw the tips were red.

Henrik was around by my side in a flash with the other South African and they pushed the guy away. The boss of the kitchen jumped over the counter with a machete he used for chopping meat and ran over. The two of them dragged the inmate with the knife off and out into the passageway. A woman sitting at another bench with a Veno inmate put her hands over her daughter's face and pulled her into her side.

I sat there dazed. 'Paul, you're OK, you're OK, it's only a scratch,' said Henrik, standing over me and looking at my head. 'He only broke the skin.'

'Did you see the size of that knife? Tried to crack my head open like a melon.'

'But he didn't,' he said. 'Get that cleaned in the wing and you'll be fine. But you're one lucky man. If you hadn't turned around when you did we'd be picking up your brains with our fingers.'

The boss of the kitchen was roaring and shouting, waving his machete. The guy who tried to knife me was gone now. Where, I didn't know.

Henrik walked with me back to the wing. I was weak from the shock. We fished out the first-aid box under Mariano's bed. He saw a trickle of blood on my forehead. 'What happened?' he said. 'What happened?'

'Don't know. Some bastard, I think from the Special, tried to cut my head open.' Henrik started dabbing my head with some cotton swabs.

The word came back later that Fyodor the Russian had paid a lucero from the Special wing to do a hit on me. The Russky was trying to send out a message to me, and others, over the 20,000 bolos he believed I owed him: don't fuck with me. The lucero got boozed up to give him Dutch courage, knowing anyone who started a fight in front of the visitors was a marked man. He was never seen again. We heard he was shot in both legs and transferred to another prison. I didn't see Fyodor for weeks. When I did, I was up on the roof doing my laps around the wall. He started walking with me and chatting as if nothing had happened. He had his comeuppance, though: his face was all puffed up like the Elephant Man's and he was cradling his right arm, and this was weeks after his botched 'hit'. I could only imagine what he looked like straight after the beating.

The boss of his wing sent him a message: our country, our rules. An eye for an eye. Fyodor was actually lucky: the number of killings was going down in the jail and disputes were sorted with baseball bats and boots rather than bullets. Otherwise Fyodor would have been on his way back to Russia in a box, a message to his family: 'From Venezuela with love.' As for me, I'd survived my second attack. Like a cat with nine lives, I was hoping I'd seven left. A prison riot was looming. I'd need them.

Chapter 20

DEATH AND DISEASE

THE LETTERS PAINTED IN BLOOD WERE STREAKED ACROSS THE WALL in the passageway. Jaggedy and scrawled, a bit like the way 'Red Rum' was written in the movie *The Shining*. On the ground outside the infirmary office there was a small pool of dark blood, like burgundy. It was a ghoulish sight to take in as we walked past on our way to breakfast in the canteen, slowing down our pace to look while the chitchat between us faded. When I got closer I saw the writing spelled out 'Antonio', probably the name of a prisoner.

Earlier, lying in bed, I had heard a lucero do the wake-up call then shouting *'mira, mira'* ('look, look') and running over to the jefe. I got up a few minutes later, not sure what the commotion was all about. I saw a few spots of blood on the floor next to one of the colchonetas near the toilet at the back of the cell.

It turned out Antonio was an inmate. He had cut his throat during the night and slowly bled to death lying on the ground on his colchoneta. If they'd written his name on the wall in the passageway as a joke or out of respect in a ritual way I didn't know.

It wasn't hard to see why someone would take their life in Los Teques, so it wasn't much talked about. But if cutting your own throat was one way to end your life, there were also the perils of getting hit by a stray bullet or being knifed out in the passageways. Falling ill was another way you might go out in a box. And many did.

Another morning an inmate looked like he was being

stubborn and not getting up off his colchoneta while the rest of us got to our feet. A few of the lags went over to look. His body lay there lifeless. One of the luceros felt the veins in his wrist. '*Nada.*' Four of us lifted him up, each grabbing an arm and a leg, and carried him out to the hallway. We left him there for the cops to collect like he was a bag of rubbish. When the troops marched in for the número the headcount was down by one. '*Muerto,*' ('Dead') the cop shouted. The National Guard scribbled onto a paper on his clipboard, and the cop went on with the count. There was no minute's silence. We felt sorry for him. A few said he was a 'nice guy' and 'what a pity', but after five minutes I'd forgotten about it. I wasn't shedding any tears. Nobody was. To me, he'd just escaped – but in a box.

He'd been withering away in front of our eyes for weeks, so we weren't surprised he had died in his sleep in the middle of the night. But what rattled me was that when the Venezuelan guy had arrived in Maxima a couple of months back he was a tall, fit guy in his early 30s – a good ten to fifteen years younger than me.

A few months later he started having spasms. He'd fall down and his body would start shaking violently, like he was possessed by a demon. His face and eyes then started puffing up. Then the weight started falling off him, making him gaunt, with a skeletal frame. He was in and out of hospital over a period of about two months. Eventually he couldn't walk and was put in a wheelchair. He ended up back sleeping on the floor. It turned out he had some infection of the nervous system. He was gay and often chatted with the kiddy fiddlers – one of the few who did. The rumour was he'd had Aids, but I never knew for sure.

There were rounds of jabs given out against serious infections, doled out by a team of nurses and doctors armed with needles the length of bicycle spokes. From time to time the army of white coats came in, cops in tow. On the first morning I went there was a nurse at the front holding a long, thin needle like a small javelin. 'Good Jesus,' I thought. Some of the lags were trying to get out of the queue at the sight of it, the luceros shoving them back into line. We stood with our sleeves pulled up above one shoulder. One lad, Porto (from Portugal, naturally), was panicking. He had a bit of English. 'Needles, I don't like, not for me.' Some of the inmates started laughing. He got more jittery as he moved up the queue, getting closer to where the three nurses were standing and his turn.

I watched the nurse slam the needle into his shoulder like she was jabbing an ice pick into a bag of cubes. Porto turned his head away, grinning and bearing it. On the fourth jab, he crumpled to the floor. The nurses carried him over to a bench and he came through with the lags laughing and hollering maricón at him.

I got my jabs and walked away. Four pinpricks soon swelled up into a mound on my arm. I was given a little card that showed what I'd been immunised against – all in Spanish. I thought it was for malaria or some other tropical disease; I didn't understand or care and threw it in the bin. If I died in here it'd be from a bullet or a knife, not the plague.

Ruut, a Dutch inmate, was another prisoner whose health had declined. He was in his late 50s and had a bald head the shape of a melon, a big belly and man boobs. I called him 'the Buddha'. His right shin had become infected with some flesh-eating disorder. His leg looked like someone had ripped the skin off his right shin – and not with any precision. The mad thing was that the colour of the flesh and skin was a charcoal grey and black. The shin had swollen, too, and looked like an elephant's leg.

What started out as a small mark like a scrape spread out across his shin in a matter of weeks and looked like a mushroom cloud after a nuclear-bomb explosion. He was treated in the infirmary in the jail for a while and given daily bandages, after it got so bad he could only walk with the help of a crutch. After a while it got worse and he was shipped off to the military hospital next to Los Teques jail. I was sure he'd be sorted there and we wouldn't see him again. He'd served a good four years and was due to be sent back to Holland to serve the rest of his time at home, like most Dutch prisoners. It was a deal their officials had drawn up with the local government, like many embassies in Venezuela did for their nationals locked up there.

In weeks Ruut was back. 'Great there, nice nurses, nice food,' he said, smiling.

'Thought you'd be in Holland. So what are you doing back here?'

'They can only treat you for a short time, then you have to leave.' He went back to the infirmary for daily treatment on his leg, but they were tired of him and weren't bothered. They seemed to have it in their heads that they would help you for a while and then that was that, you were on your own. So Ruut asked me to take over and do his nursing.

'Please, Paul, I'd be very grateful. Those morons in there just brush me off.'

'Sure. Course I will.' He was a nice guy – I would have felt bad saying no.

Myself and Ruut got on well. We spoke a lot. It was great to talk to someone older and wiser, and not just the usual bunch of gringo kids decades younger than me.

The first day nursing him I put his leg up on mine and slowly peeled off the rotten, septic bandages. I nearly got sick. The smell was putrid, like rotten meat left in a butcher's bin. How his leg got infected we didn't know. He was a diabetic, which was probably part of the reason. Or he'd probably got a small cut and dirt got into it.

Twice a day I put fresh bandages on and he was beaming because of the help. I went to the infirmary to get the materials every day. Some days there was none. Medical supplies used to come in once a month, so if you were ill around that time they might be able to help you, but towards the end of the month you were screwed. I reckoned a medic was selling the drugs and materials, probably one of the lags who helped out in there. All I could do was roll off the bandages and turn them around, so the side soiled with blood was on the outside. Some of the gays also gave me cotton swabs they used for their make-up, which I used to clean Ruut's wound. The gays were good like that.

But Ruut also needed antibiotics and there was rarely much in that line in the infirmary. I had to go to the shop in the wing and buy an antibiotic they sold there. They were little white tablets that I crumbled between my fingers into powder and then tapped out across Ruut's shin before wrapping up the bandages over it. It wasn't pretty work, but I didn't mind doing it. Penance for my sins and all that.

His leg didn't seem to get any worse over the weeks, but it wasn't getting any better. One morning I took pictures of it on my mobile phone and emailed them off to his son back in Holland. The photos were like something you'd see in a medical journal: a hideous lump of damaged flesh that reminded me a bit of a slab of meat in a kebab shop, the lower end tapering where the chefs had sliced it off. The plan was that Ruut's son would send the pictures to the Dutch Embassy in Caracas and get them to put pressure on the authorities in Venezuela. All going well, Ruut would get released to serve his time in Holland. We heard they only did a week there before being freed.

I woke up one morning not long after and noticed a large spot on my thigh. Jesus, I thought. Maybe I had Ruut's flesh-eating bug? I'd be bound to Maxima for years with a gammy leg, my plans to flee Venezuela through the jungles to Colombia up in smoke. I started scratching the spot, digging my nails into it in the hope it would go away. 'Don't, don't do that,' said Mariano. 'It's from a spider. It lays the egg inside. It'll only get worse if you scratch. Leave it till it's big enough to cut out.' So a spider had laid its eggs inside me. Great, I was going to be a daddy spider. At least it didn't look like flesh would start to roll off my legs like Ruut.

A couple of weeks passed and the bite grew into the size of

a small egg, by which time I could hardly walk. It was time to get it cut out. I went down to the infirmary. In the past they had treated you in a basic dedicated clinic, but it had been turned into a wing when prisoner numbers hit the roof and space started running out. So I went into the office next to it. In my head it wasn't a place you'd get better in. Any time I saw it I thought about the prisoners whose bodies were carried in after they had been shot, stabbed, beaten to death or having cut their own throats or even blown themselves up with grenades. There was rarely a doctor in it, anyway. Only a nurse, sometimes – usually one of the prisoners who had first-aid experience.

Mariano came with me to the infirmary to interpret, his lanky legs swaggering up the passageway. 'The problem is getting a doctor, Paul. If he comes it's on Tuesday.'

'Today's Monday.'

'I know, so that's the problem. But I said *if* he comes – often he doesn't.'

'There's no point in going then.'

'Yes, there's a point. If you wait you may have spiderwebs in your leg by the time you get to see him. There are prisoners who are nurses there; they do all the work.'

'Are they qualified?' I was starting to have second thoughts.

'Probably not, but they have experience. The only guy to avoid is the Butcher from Amsterdam.'

'The what?' I was really getting nervous now.

'A Dutch guy. He walks around with a white coat and a stethoscope. He's not a doctor at all. He pretends. He's a crackhead and sells all the medicine in the infirmary to prisoners so he can buy a few stones.' I didn't want to hear any more.

In the infirmary it was a nurse inmate all right, but he seemed OK. I'd take my chances. He sat me on the side of a bed and started squeezing pus out of the bite, then sterilised and swabbed it. 'Jesus,' I shouted, nearly hitting the roof. I looked at him making an incision the shape of a cross in it with a scalpel. 'Agh,' I cried out. 'Have you not got an anaesthetic or painkillers or something?'

'*No, nada,*' he said, with a look that said he was wondering why I would even ask such a thing.

I sat there while he poked around in my thigh with a blade. John Wayne might have had a stick to bite on when a fellow cowboy cut a bullet out of him and a shot of whiskey to drown the pain. I got nothing. I just sat there clenching my teeth. I had to go back three days in a row before it had all been cut out.

But after a while the wound cleared up, the scar all but disappeared and there was no sign of any baby spiders practising their web-spinning inside my thigh. The only other health problem I'd had till then was that half the time I couldn't eat. I was suffering with mouth ulcers. Bumps like little white pinheads were popping up inside my mouth and on my tongue. I could barely take in food. When it was really bad, I could only eat the odd ice-pop I got out of the shop, sucking on it, the coolness giving a bit of relief.

* * *

'Dear Paul, thank you very much for sending me those pictures. I will do what I can to push our embassy to get my father out of there,' Ruut's son wrote back in an email. Weeks passed and there was no word from the Dutch Embassy. Ruut would have to sit tight, suffer and count the days to his release, hoping his leg didn't fall off in the meantime.

* * *

A big cheer went up in the yard. 'Hhhhheeeyyy.' A group of both gringos and Venos were shaking each other's hands and waving their arms in the air.

'He's dead, did you hear?' said Hanz, beaming.

'Who's dead?' I said.

'McKenzie was killed. Shot up. Couple of hours after getting out of Macuto.'

'Yeah? How?' I was only curious and wouldn't be sending any wreaths.

'He got day release at the end of his sentence. He was gunned down only a few hours after getting out on the streets.' Hanz started jumping and cheering now.

McKenzie's fate didn't surprise me. He wasn't exactly popular in Macuto. What struck me was how so many were jumping up and down in the yard, cheering. Venos and gringos. More prisoners had passed through Macuto than I knew, and many had had a taste of McKenzie's machete, poked into their ribs as he robbed them of all they had.

* * *

If your body didn't let you down in Los Teques, your mind might. One day a new Veno inmate walked out into the yard. He was a big tall black guy. He stood still for ages with his bottom lip quivering, crippled with fright – or something else. He wouldn't speak to anyone. Wouldn't move. It was clear he wasn't right in the head. Later, during the número, I saw one of the luceros help him over to a bucket and sit him down for the roll call. He was on another planet and didn't know what was going on.

'This man doesn't need a prison, he needs a mental hospital. A blind man can see that,' I said to the lads, Billy and Eddy.

'I know,' said Eddy. 'It's not right. Shouldn't be here.' A few days later he was gone: I heard he was moved to the Church wing. Months later I saw him working in the canteen serving food. He'd put on weight and seemed clued in to the world. Months of morning prayer and discipline away from booze and the fear of violence must have sorted him out. Just as well; in Los Teques you could barely get a hold of a doctor let alone a psychiatrist.

He wasn't the only one affected by mental torture. For

months I'd watched Billy go into a steady spiral of depression. He started having spasms like mini fits. We'd be sitting there talking to him and his arms would bolt forward with his hands stretched out, shaking, and his face froze. 'Billy, Billy Scissorhands,' I said, roaring with laughter. It was obvious he was suffering from some sort of stress disorder, and although I was joking I think it helped lighten the moment for him.

I knew what was going on. It was slowly dawning on him that his lawyer wasn't doing anything for him. I'd seen him on the phone only a few nights before the spasms, roaring and shouting into the phone. All I could hear was 'fuck' this and 'fuck' that, while he paced around in circles. I didn't want to bother him, but he later told me what was happening. His lawyer had phoned him demanding another 5,000 euro or he couldn't do anything more with his case in trying to get him out on early release. This was after Billy's family had already pumped about 14,000 euro into him. Billy wasn't quick off the mark, but he was finally realising the abogado was taking him and his family to the cleaners. He'd have to find another way to get out. To me, the lawyer was a tonic salesman. Buy me and I'll cure all ailments. He'd been fooling Billy and his family for about three years now. In fairness to them, the lawyer was a smooth talker. He even had the wool pulled over Father Pat's eyes. But he hadn't fooled me – he might have had the gift of the gab, but I'd smelled his bullshit.

Billy soon got another lawyer on the go, one recommended by Vito. He finally copped he was wasting his time with his original abogado. 'It's the only thing I can do,' Billy told me. 'The guy hasn't done anything.' I could see the despair in his eyes. 'Vito is raving about this woman, Viviana. Says she does great work and gets results, and she can get me out on parole because I've done over three years now.'

'Sounds like the right thing, Billy,' I said. 'You have to try someone else now.' I realised it was the same woman who got Terry out, so I knew he was on to something good.

Macalou, a French-Algerian, had also hired Viviana. He

was completely paralysed, wheelchair-bound. He couldn't even hold a cup. He had arrived in Los Teques on his two feet but then got struck by some muscular disorder. Luckily for him he had a few quid to pay an inmate to feed him, bathe him and bring him to the toilet. He was about my age, a slim guy with a huge smile, which he wore all day despite being stuck in a wheelchair inside Los Teques. We got on great and spoke a lot.

Viviana said she could get him out on humanitarian grounds. She even organised a court case with a judge to hear his case. But when a cop came into the wing and said there was an *ambulancia* waiting to take him, he pulled out. There were gringo lags who, no matter how bad Los Teques was, didn't find it easy to go home and face whatever their demons were – or just had nothing to go home to. Many were drug addicts whose family and friends had long given up on them. Others just enjoyed the steady supply of crack and coke, morning, noon and night – a false paradise they slipped into.

I never spoke to Macalou about turning down the court case. I knew it was a personal thing, and there were some things no inmate wanted to talk about, no matter how well you got on with them.

I asked him about Viviana, though. I was hearing yet more good things about her work. 'A wonderful woman,' smiled Macalou, his white teeth gleaming, with a couple of gaps between them like the black keys on a piano.

I was intrigued by the lawyer. I wanted to find out more, to see if she could help get me out of here on parole. What I didn't know then was I'd soon need her legal help not for that but to pressure the prison chiefs into getting me to the local hospital in an ambulance.

Chapter 21

MAÑANA NEVER COMES

THE GUN WAS SHOT JUST OVER MY RIGHT SHOULDER, LEVEL WITH MY ear. The crack of the rounds of bullets caught me by surprise. I jolted to the left from where I was sitting on my bucket. My back hit the wall and I lost my balance and toppled over. I only stopped myself from landing on the ground by pushing out my left hand. I sat up, dazed, rebalanced myself, and fixed my glasses, which were to the side. There was a mad buzzing sensation in my right ear. Then a hollow sound with air whistling inside, like my eardrum had sucked in a tornado. Then it went numb.

A few inmates were sitting in front of me, laughing, watching me nearly fall over. I looked up and there was Carlos holding one of his specials: an Uzi. He was grinning, too. They all thought this was hilarious, great fun – look, we gave the gringo a scare and he hit the deck. He had just fired off a round in honour of a boss from another wing who was getting his *libertad* and going free. A gunfire salute to show respect to a fellow jefe. Normally you could see the bosses coming into the yard with their guns to give a dozen-shot salute. This caught me on the hop. My ear was sore for days and I could barely hear. I was telling the others, going around with my hand clutching my right ear. It was Thursday, but I had to wait till Tuesday to see the *médico* in the infirmary – the only day he was scheduled to come in. He was a fat lazy bastard so I wasn't expecting much. When the day came I went up to Mariano, as usual, to get him to interpret.

'Mariano, you have to come with me to the doctor. My ear, it's in bits.'

'Yes, I'll help,' he said, but his face showed no concern. A lot of people said they weren't doing well, but you never really took any notice.

In the infirmary office, the woman cop was there, Morelba. She swivelled around on a chair from a desk where she was filling in some forms. As soon as she saw it was me, her face stiffened. She'd never liked me, remembering it was me who had phoned the British Embassy to hassle her into getting Terry out to the hospital.

Mariano spoke and I listened to Morelba's curt reply in Spanish, her eyes looking me up and down as if I was taking up valuable space. 'She says wait five minutes and the doctor will be here,' said Mariano. He had perfect English as he'd grown up in New York.

The doctor we called El Gordo (Fat Man) walked into the office, a stethoscope hanging over his chest. It was probably so people thought he was a proper doctor. I doubted he was.

'Tell him what's wrong,' said Mariano.

'*No oigo,*' ('I can't hear') I said, pointing at my ear. 'Pain, here.' He nodded at me to sit down. He then took out a narrow pocket-sized black torch, flicked on the light and bent over to the side of my head, his belly doubling up as he did.

El Gordo spoke to Mariano as he inspected my ear. 'He says it's dirt,' said Mariano. 'You need to clean it out.'

'Then why doesn't he?'

'He says he has no syringes. He says another day.'

'Great place this. Tell him I said he's a stupid bastard.'

'Probably best I don't.'

The doctor handed me a small bottle of liquid. 'They're drops,' said Mariano. 'Use them twice a day and it'll clear up the dirt in your ears, that's what he says.'

In the wing I sat down on the side of my bunk next to the gays, who were taking turns brushing each other's hair. I tilted my head to the left and squeezed a few drops into my right ear.

A couple of hours later, jolts of pain were surging around my skull. I felt like the drops had seeped through my eardrum and into my brain. The pain started at my right ear and shot across to the top of my skull, my body jumping every time in a mini spasm. It was like getting electric-shock treatment. I put my hands on the sides of my head and squeezed in a vain effort to stop the pain.

Over the next few days I was still taking the drops, but the pain got worse. My jaw started feeling tight and I couldn't move it properly. The Nigerian in the kitchen, Onyeke, was still bringing down dinners to me in the evening, but I could only open my mouth wide enough to fork in a bit of rice, and I couldn't chew well. I started giving my dinners to Billy. Then the pain got worse and my jaw almost seized up. I was now down to taking in soft food: a cup of porridge for breakfast and liquids for the rest of the day.

'These drops are making me worse,' I said to Billy, shoving him over another dinner Onyeke had brought from the canteen in the afternoon. The words were garbled, barely getting out, like I was talking with balls of cotton shoved in my mouth. 'I'm in bits with a headache. They're killing me. I need to go to the hospital.'

Billy's eyes widened, as if in that moment he knew I was in a bad way and wasn't making a song and dance out of a little headache.

'What about the drops – still taking them?'

'I ditched them a couple of days ago. Were doing nothin'.'

'You will not get an ambulance, Paul,' he said, putting his plate of food down on his lap. 'You won't get it.' He had been around Los Teques for a good three years now and knew the score. But it wasn't what I wanted to hear.

More days went on and the surges of pain were still shooting from my right ear to the top of my head. It felt like a corkscrew twisting into my cranium. I was worried I had some kind of brain infection. I'd seen others go like this, such as the Venezuelan who started off ill and losing weight, then got worse and ended up in a wheelchair before croaking in the middle of the night. I started to think, this is it, Paul, your number's up. You're a goner.

I walked over to Hanz after the evening número. He was at the cards table up in the gym, a professional felt table the bosses had smuggled in. 'Hanz, I need you to do something for me. I want to write some letters home.' He looked at me, puzzled. I was always writing on my own – why would I need help? I knew the others didn't know how bad I was.

'What kind of letters?'

'Goodbye letters to my family.'

'No, Paul, you serious?'

'Yes, I need this done,' I said, standing there over the table as he lowered his hand, not caring now the others saw his play.

We walked back to my bed and I sat down. I handed my laptop over to him. I'd bought out the shares of the others who had owned it with me when they were short of cash, and was making a little money renting it back to them, and others, to use. 'I need one for my mother and father and two others for Katie and Dano, my kids, and another for my nephew Michael.' I lay back, closed my eyes and started dictating.

'Dear Mam and Dad, I'm really sorry,' I started, listening to Hanz's fingers tapping on the keyboard. 'I didn't think it would come to this. I was sure I'd get out of here. But if you're reading this it's because I'm dead.'

Hanz's fingers stopped tapping. I opened my eyelids. They felt heavy, like lumps of lead. As I opened my eyes, Hanz's face slowly emerged, his mouth open. 'OK, Paul, I'm sure you'll get through this.'

'Just type, Hanz, this is important to me.' I closed my eyes again and went on. 'Firstly, I want to tell you all how much I love you. You, my parents, Katie and Daniel, Sharon . . .' I finished that open letter to all my family then did one separate email for each of them. Hanz then connected to the Internet with the dongle stick in the USB port and stored the typed letters as saved drafts in his personal email account. 'Send them to my nephew, Michael, he'll know what to do if anything happens to me and will pass them on to the rest of my family.'

'OK, Paul, but I'm sure you're going to pull through.'

'Listen, I might not last – just send them on if I don't.'

My health didn't get any better. A couple of days later I was sitting in the yard on my bucket by the door into the hallway. A luz had been called and the bosses were hiding their guns before número. I sat there with my hand on my ear, rocking back and forth like a loony with the pain. Then the sharp jolt kicked into my ear, shot across to the top of my head and seemed to explode. I jumped up from the bucket. 'Arggggh, arghhhhhh,' I shouted, my arms stretched out, shaking. 'Arrgggggggh, argggggggggh.' I ran around in circles like a chicken that had had its head cut off, screaming like I was possessed, then I ran into the hallway by the cells. My head was tilting from side to side and the wall in the room and the face of a lucero were spinning in front of me as my eyes rolled back in my head. I was possessed like a man in a crazy house.

'No, you can't be here,' said the lucero, a Colombian who had the face of a 19-year-old, and probably was. He was waving his hands at me like he was signalling to a plane above. Normally with a search on you'd get a beating for not staying in the yard. But seeing me flailing around waving my arms they knew there was something wrong.

Two weeks went on and I was still racked with fits of pain in my head. I was still barely eating because of the pain in my jaw. I was losing weight and felt weak.

Vito came up to me in the yard. He knew I was in bad shape. He put his hand on my shoulder. 'Paul, this lawyer I was telling you about, Viviana, she can help you with your pains.' I'd met her briefly before, through Vito, in the office upstairs one day after meeting with Father Pat, but I hadn't spoken to her for long. I'd been meaning to get her on board as my lawyer. She had got Terry out on early parole, and Vito said if anyone could get me out on the same ticket, she could. Then I got sidetracked after Carlos blasted his gun next to my ear.

'How can she help me with the pains?'

'You need an ambulance,' he said, speaking softly. 'Go to the hospital. She can help you. She has many contacts.'

'Right, let's do it.' I didn't need much persuasion.

'Good, I will organise all. She is coming to see me on Thursday and I will bring you. You talk and you see.'

It was Viviana who got a court order to put pressure on the prison chiefs to get Macalou an ambulance so he could appear in front of a judge and have his case to be released on humanitarian grounds heard. I had been impressed and was hopeful I'd get sorted with an ambulance. In the end Macalou refused to budge an inch out of Maxima, but that wasn't the lawyer's fault.

'This woman is really good,' said Vito, as we walked past one of the vermin crackheads in the passageway. His eyes looked like he had woven red threads through the whites. If I was on my own I'd have been on edge. 'She can get everything started to get you out of here on early parole.' I felt good about this lawyer and I hadn't even met her. 'She works for the people 110 per cent,' continued Vito, 'and she knows people, many contacts out there.'

We walked into the new office for official visits – it made a change from standing in the passageway. There were four tables. On one side were the lawyers, and inmates were on the other. It wasn't hard to tell which was which. Not many inmates wore suits.

At the last table on the right sat a woman, alone. 'There, there is Viviana. At that table. The right.' My eyes nearly popped out of my head. She was a good-looking bird, wearing tight trousers and a low-cut top. She had luscious long, dark hair and her make-up was all done, with red lipstick. I guessed she was in her 40s.

'*Hola*,' she said to Vito, standing up and kissing him on both cheeks in the Latin style, then doing the same to me. I picked up a subtle perfume and savoured it. Nice smells were rare in jail. I had to pick myself up off the floor. It had been well over a year and a half since I'd come that close to such a beautiful woman, or any female, really. Next to us, the lags with their lawyers looked over, glancing at Viviana.

Vito and Viviana spoke in rapid Spanish and I took in the sight of the room. In the corner a cop sat in a chair, cradling a shotgun like Deputy Dawg. He had a thick black handlebar moustache and was dozing in and out of sleep, his chin on his chest. He had on a wide-brimmed hat like a sombrero and looked like a Mexican bandito you'd see in a spaghetti western.

'OK, Paul,' said Vito, turning to me. 'I told her you wanted to meet her before deciding she's your lawyer. She says yes, she will be your solicitor. What do you say?'

I lifted my eyes up from her chest to her face. '*Sí*, yes,' I said, 'let's go with her. I have a good feeling about this.'

'I told her about the pains in your ear and your head,' said Vito. 'She says she can get you a court order and force the prison director to get you an ambulance.'

'Great,' I said, smiling at Viviana. I was feeling better already. 'And could she get me antibiotics for my ear? They've nothing to give me here.'

They spoke in rapid Spanish again. I didn't understand, and was almost deaf in my right ear anyway, which didn't help. The few words that made it in churned around in my head like clothes in a washing machine.

'OK, let's do it,' said Vito, 'just some formalities first.' Viviana took some papers out of her bag. 'Sign them,' said Vito, 'and she's your solicitor.' There was no pen. Viviana stood up, walked over to a ledge and brought back a sponge soaked in black ink. I pressed my thumb into it and dabbed it on the paper.

'Ask her can she get me out of here on early parole,' I said to Vito.

I watched Viviana nod her head. 'She says you're in the best of hands.'

With Macalou she got results; other lawyers, like Billy's last solicitor, took your money and pretended to work behind the scenes but did nothing. Vito said Viviana's price was 1,000 euro. A bargain, I thought, compared to the 10,000 dollars Bruce had paid his lawyer for pulling a stroke, or the 14,000 euro Billy had pumped into his useless abogado who did nothing.

* * *

'It went well, great, it looks good.' Billy was just back from a court hearing on his parole that Viviana had sorted out.

'Will you get out?'

'Don't know for sure, but Viviana thinks it looks good.'

'What about the exam, when will you do it?' There was also a psychological test you had to pass in Spanish before you could qualify for parole.

'I failed it. But Father Pat stood up and told the judge he'd vouch for me on the outside, that I'd stay with him and he had a friend who'd organised a job for me as a gardener.'

'A gardener?'

'Yeah, in a college. The guy's a lecturer there or something. You have to have work set up: that's one of the conditions of the parole.'

I was glad somebody had good news and was getting somewhere with the system.

I texted Father Pat as soon as I got back to the wing. I wanted him to meet Viviana and pay her with the cash one of my mates back home had wired to his account for me from months before.

'Yes, Paul,' he wrote back, 'will do.'

The pains and electric-shock-like jolts that pierced my head went on. All the lags knew I was in pain with my right ear now. They saw me forever rocking back and forth with my hand gripped around my ear. It didn't help that the Venos were always coming up and flicking at my ear like it was some joke, wanting to touch my earlobe out of curiosity or something. I had to swat their arms away. 'Chimps, fuck off,' I shouted. One idiot even stuck his finger in my ear and I nearly hit the roof. I got my hands on some cotton wool and shoved a clump in my ear. That was a sign to the chimps to say 'please fuck off'. They never bothered me after that.

Word got around I was desperate to get a trip out to the hospital for a check-up. As always, the cogs turned inside the Venos' heads, as they schemed up ways to make money. 'Paul,' said Billy, 'one of them says there's a guard who'll take you to the hospital in his own car for two hundred thousand bolos [about forty euro].' No matter how bad I was, I wasn't going down that road. Nothing ever came of giving cops money.

'Tell him I said "fuck off".'

'Fair enough – you're probably right.'

Soon after I got word through from Father Pat that Viviana had got the court order requesting that the prison heads get me an ambulance and bring me to hospital – and this was within a week of meeting her. I was impressed. This woman meant business.

The next day my name was on la lista. 'Paul Keany – ambulancia.' My spirits started to pick up and I felt a little better, despite being in bits with the pain. It looked like I'd get a real doctor the next day and in a hospital that had proper medicine in it.

In the morning I followed the inmates being escorted by the cops out the gate to where the buses were waiting to ship them off to court or to other jails. It was 8 a.m. and I took a seat on the stone steps next to the barred gate into the driveway, where a cop sat. I watched two buses pull off, spluttering out thick fumes. I then put my head between my legs, gripping my ear in agony.

At 9 a.m. there was no sign of the ambulance. Or at 10

a.m. Or at 11 a.m. 'Hospital, *ambulancia*,' I said to the cop, an old guy with dirty fingernails and hairy wrists.

'*Mas tarde*,' ('Later') he said.

By 2 p.m. it was time to go back inside. The cop escorted me back to the wing.

'No *ambulancia*?' I said again, shrugging.

'*Mañana seguro*.'

For the next 14 days I sat out on the stone steps. No ambulance came. All I could do was sit there all day and look out through the bars at the activity, watching Macedonia lug bags of rubbish about, lawyers coming in to meet their clients. It was all boring. One day, though, I did notice something interesting. I saw the boss from the Mostrico wing walking along with his dog. He walked up to the gate, where a national troop was on guard. He slipped a bag off his shoulder and the soldier handed him another bag back. They exchanged bags without saying a word and the jefe walked back with his dog, whistling as if he was just out on a leisurely stroll. It was obvious what was going on. The wing jefe was handing over cash for drugs or guns.

The next day I was back on the stone steps again, massaging my head trying to get the pain away. The painkillers I bought in the shop or jabs I got in my ass from the inmate medics worked for a while but wore off after a couple of hours. I was starting to wake up in the middle of the night with pains like electric shocks in my head.

A cop in charge of transport for prisoners walked up to me.

'Maxima, *regresas*,' ('Maxima, go back') he said.

'When will the ambulance come?' I asked in Spanish.

'*En la tarde, te llamamos*.' ('This afternoon, we'll call you.') I doubted it, but I didn't have much choice but to go.

The next morning Vito walked out with me to the gate where I sat.

'The ambulance, it didn't arrive?' I said to the cop.

Vito interpreted. 'Yes, it came yesterday.'

'What do you mean it came yesterday?' I said, nearly hitting the roof.

'It came; where were you?'

'I was in the wing, where you told me to go!'

'No, we were looking for you there.'

My blood boiled over. '*Mentiroso*,' ('Liar') I said, a word I'd learned the night before. '*Mentiroso*, you muthafucking lying bastard.' I was shouting now. The cop stood back and held his hands out. Vito stepped in between the two of us.

'Paul, no, no, this could be very dangerous, talking to the cops like this.'

'Bastard, liar,' I said, then calmed down.

'It will get you nowhere, getting angry.' He was right. I gave up.

* * *

I was texting Father Pat every day. 'Still no ambulance, waste of time.' I was still barely eating because of the pain in my jaw. I was losing more weight and had to tighten the rope-belt around my waist even more to keep my jeans up.

A few days later Father Pat was back in to visit me and we spoke in the special office upstairs. He said he had rung the female cop, Morelba, in the infirmary to put pressure on her and get me to hospital in an ambulance for a check-up.

'She said it's only a European with a headache. That's what she said to me.' He stood there shaking his head, and for the first time I detected a trace of anger in his voice. I had told him my symptoms, the jolts of pain. His brow furrowed like old leather; I could see he was worried about me. He didn't want one of the Irish boys dying on his watch. One of his own. He had been on to the Irish consulate about getting on the case and forcing the jail to get me an ambulance and a trip to the hospital.

I nodded. 'If that's what it takes, that's what it takes. They might listen to that. But if it doesn't work could you try to get me some antibiotics for now?'

'Let's do that.' I listed off what was wrong and he wrote down 'pain' and 'bloody ear wax' in a little notebook he kept in his satchel. 'I'll tell Viviana,' said Father Pat. 'She said last night on the phone she had a good friend who was a doctor. I'm meeting her this evening to give her your money.'

The next day Father Pat was back with a bottle of tablets in his hand. We spoke only for a few minutes. 'Take them back with you, get a glass of water and start them. Viviana's doctor gave them to her after I told her your symptoms.'

I didn't waste time. I shook his hand and nodded. It was a thank you and a sign of respect to the Father, and I blessed myself. 'Right, I'm gone.'

In two days I felt like a new man. I started dancing out in the yard. 'Heyy, heyyyy.' I was doing a little jig, lifting my knees up like Michael Flatley in *Riverdance*. The Venos were staring at me like I was mad. After four or five days the pain cleared up and one evening my jaw started to loosen. I was starving then – I had only been eating rice and was looking forward to a steak dinner for lunch the next day, which I'd pay a lag to cook.

* * *

The next morning I sat on my bucket next to the yard door for the headcount. The cops and the army marched out after the número and I was feeling like a million dollars. The whistling was gone from my ear and I could talk without feeling like someone had stuck a crowbar in my jawbone. But I was still starving. I could already smell and taste the ladle of porridge that was waiting for me in the canteen for *desayuno* (breakfast).

The bosses suddenly stood up in front of us all. What's going on here? I thought. They rarely made any announcements after the headcount in the morning. An underboss wearing khaki shorts and a red bandana started talking. My Spanish was a bit better than it had been and I understood more. But at that moment I wished I hadn't. The words I picked up spun around my head and I felt dizzy. *Huelga de hambre* (hunger strike).

I couldn't believe it. I put my head in my hands and started saying out loud, 'No, no, it can't be, no.' The bosses, in their infinite wisdom, had called a food ban.

'When does the madness in this place stop?' I said to Eddy. 'What's it about?'

'The cops, they reneged on their promises after the kidnappings. They're still taking cash and cigarettes off the visitors.'

So the days went on without a bite of food. My stomach thought my throat had been slit. All we could eat were the few boiled sweets that were passed around, and drink water and some coffee. You couldn't eat or the bosses would shoot or stab you. It was that simple. The worst thing was I hadn't eaten properly for a long time, not since the pain like electric shocks started in my head and my jaw seized up.

The first few days were painful. My belly groaned. You were used to getting your two meals a day – and now nothing. On the fourth and fifth day I started feeling my ribcage, and was able to poke my fingers into the bones, something I hadn't done since I was a nipper. I was already thin. I was about 13 stone when I was locked up. Now I'd say I was down to about ten stone, or less. So I didn't have much weight to lose.

'What's it going to be like after ten days?' I said to the others.

On the seventh evening of the strike I walked to my bed and sat down. My legs felt like it was a struggle to carry my upper body. I flopped down on my bed. The world around me started to swirl. The sounds of voices trailed off, like people were talking miles away. The yellow light from bare bulbs threw faded light on walls that looked like they had jaundice, spiderwebs clung to corners, everything seemed to be sucked away into a blackness that fell around me.

Then nothing.

I woke up the next morning. I'd been out for about 12 hours. I opened my mouth. It was dry and my tongue was stiff, like it was some kind of alien object. Everyone was up and a lucero was doing the wake-up rounds, nudging and kicking bodies on the ground. I dragged myself out on weak legs to the yard. Dazed, bleary-eyed, confused. I sat on a bucket. The cops came in and did the headcount.

I struggled back to my bunk. Then I heard someone singing out in the yard. There were a couple of voices, then more. It was some Venezuelan song. I walked out and saw a load of Venos standing on their buckets and all singing now, waving towels back and forth and singing at the top of their lungs.

'The national anthem, mate, that's what that is,' said Eddy, seeing me looking puzzled. 'The hunger strike. It's over.'

I turned back to watch the Venos singing. It was like being at a football game, with the towels they were waving like fans holding up their team colours. The sound of it was weird, over 1,000 inmates singing their anthem, their voices echoing through the whole prison and all singing in time. At the end of it they started shouting and clapping and roaring, 'Venezuela, Venezuela.'

Later, at about 5 p.m., I found out there was no dinner planned for that day as the strike had been called off all of a sudden. I actually didn't care. I wasn't bothered about food. The interest was gone. It was a weird feeling. A few of the lags went down to the back of the yard and pulled out the containers where dry food had been locked away for the strike. They started pulling out biscuits and crackers, getting stuck into anything they could.

I felt it had been touch and go in the last few weeks. Just as I was pulling through after the infection in my ear, I thought the hunger strike would wipe me out. I was afraid I'd get so skinny, like the crackheads, that Billy and the boys would have to report me missing.

But not everyone survived. The few inmates who had diet problems were moved to live in the canteen during the hunger strike. That way they got their regular meals, such as for Ruut, who was diabetic. Macalou, the French-Algerian, went out too in his wheelchair but had taken a turn and died. I was devastated by the news. I got on really well with him. I loved his infectious laugh. We often spoke for hours.

I was mad, too. Only a few months before he had had a chance to get out of Venezuela on humanitarian grounds and had chosen not to. His twisted body had now probably been turfed into some unmarked grave in the hillsides of Los Teques. No wreath or loved ones to shed tears. That he died in the jail wasn't just a story. Viviana later confirmed it to me.

On the upside from the hunger strike, the prison authorities started upping the ante with court cases and psychological exams to get people who qualified for early release out on parole. More court cases had been one of the demands made by the cell-block bosses during the hunger strike – and the prison chiefs were living up to their promises. In the past, only one or two prisoners a week were getting out. Now it was about ten. It was music to my ears. Between that good news and getting my diet back on track, within weeks I was fitter and healthier and back in the gym. Strong in body and mind, ready for my mission to get out on parole – and one day home.

Chapter 22

BLOODY SUNDAY

THE DIRECTOR WAS STILL TRYING TO BE THE BEST FRIEND OF THE inmates. She was going even further with her policy to make the jail more visitor friendly. An 'open house' for families and partners. *Mi casa es tú casa*. Murderers, rapists and bank robbers, now happy, would then put down their guns and settle rows with a handshake. That was the thinking in her 'infinite wisdom'. She had already allowed visitors to stay over during holidays such as Christmas and Easter – now she opened the prison for overnight stays every Saturday. The inmates took the meaning of visits to new heights and put on a disco every Saturday night. All aboard to boogie.

I had taken to sleeping on a colchoneta on the floor of the Maxima wing's gym with cotton wool shoved in my ears to try to get some sleep on Saturday nights. The music from the party went on until the early hours of Sunday morning. Eddy had been doing the same and would stretch out on another colchoneta. I had to give up my bed to the inmates in the wing who had visitors in so they could spend the night there; Eddy had to give up his place on the floor.

We spent our evenings in the gym watching DVDs on my laptop, such as *The Godfather*, a favourite we viewed over and over. The violence in it was like a tea party compared to Los Teques, though.

On the second week of the disco I was sitting down on the gym floor chatting with Eddy and doodling around on the Internet on my laptop. Music was pounding out from the roof above. Billy's mop of mousey-brown hair appeared as he walked up the stairs into the gym, his hands in his pockets.

'That sounds mental. Let's go and try it out,' he said.

'Nah, not for me.' It wasn't my cup of tea. I was too long in the tooth for discos.

'Come on, Pauly.'

'Nah.'

'Come on, just once.'

'All right, I'll just have a look.' Anything to keep him happy. Eddy and two South African lads agreed to come along as well.

We walked out onto the roof. Dance music pumped out of giant speakers the size of wardrobes. Multicoloured lights twirled in a collage of colours: purples, blues, reds, yellows, all spinning and streaming out to the night sky. A DJ was spinning discs at a turntable. Bodies grooved to reggaeton music, crude pop songs with jungle rhythms. A mass of limbs grooved. Hips swinging. Shoulders shaking.

The National Guard troops were up in the watchtower, machine guns at hand. They didn't seem bothered that hundreds of the prisoners were partying away on the roof. A typical Saturday night in a Venezuelan jail. I suppose if any trouble broke out they could just open fire and pick off their targets like shooting at alien invaders in a video game. There was barbed wire coiled around 30-foot-high fences around the perimeter. Nobody was going anywhere anyway.

As well as a disco, the inmates had also turned the roof into a place to bed down for the night. A rope was hung across the entire width of the roof, about 100 ft across. The prisoners then tied other ropes off this main rope and cordoned off little areas with curtains. It looked like a giant open-air hospital ward. Here they put their colchonetas on the ground and spent the night sleeping there with their missus. On the right beside the football pitch there was even a four-man tent set up.

I stood there taking in the whole sight: murderers, bank robbers and kidnappers, all with guns, all coked up and boozing. In my gut I knew this was going to go sour. 'I don't like it one little bit, lads,' I said. 'This could get messy. All you need is a row breaking out and the boyos pull out their Uzis and start blasting.' I didn't actually see any guns on show, but I knew they were close by.

'Come on, Pauly, it'll be grand,' said Billy. 'We'll just stay for a while.' We sat down on the ground, our backs to the wall by the basketball court. We smoked a bit of weed, snorted a few lines. It loosened the tongue and we chatted for hours. The entertainment was good, though. The place was pumping. Inmates and their girlfriends were hopping around and doing twirls and twists like professional salsa dancers. Dancing was like breathing to the Venezuelans; it was just natural. I looked over at the DJ spinning discs on a turntable. He was dressed in a shiny tracksuit and had his hair in short dreadlocks, which were poking out of a baseball cap he wore back to front. 'He's one of the top DJs in Caracas,' said Eddy. 'I heard them talking about him during the week.'

'He wouldn't come cheap,' I said. 'I suppose we're paying for him.'

'No doubts about it. Right out of the causa.'

The other boys were all fired up about organising their own 'room' on the roof. 'This is deadly,' said Billy. 'We could get a tent in and crash out here on the Saturdays. Get stoned and do a few lines and then a few feet of a walk back to the tent to sleep. Better than the floor of the yard.'

Dieter was up for it too. 'Yeah,' he said, 'great. Let's do it.'

A light rain started and swept across the roof. I enjoyed the dampness on my face. The rain was rare enough.

* * *

The next Saturday the disco was called off. The cell-block jefes probably couldn't get a hold of any big-name DJs. They were probably on another leg of a tour of the country's jails. The bosses put their thinking caps on and decided to have an indoor disco in the Special wing. It kicked off at 10 p.m. that Saturday. We went up to the roof, which had a bird's-eye view down into the entrance to the wing. I couldn't see in properly; it was dark and strobe lights were flickering. Billy was standing beside me, peering down.

'I bet there's going to be literally murder there tonight,' I said.

'I know. Looks dodgy,' said Billy. 'Wouldn't touch it.' The whole concept of a disco in a wing was mind-boggling. You knew there had to be trouble. A cocktail of booze, coke and guns – it was a ticking time bomb.

Billy, Dieter and a few others had set up a tent on the roof. Even though there was no Saturday Night Fever that evening, all the families and partners of the inmates still came in for the *pernocta*, the sleepover. It was about 11 at night and I left them to it and went down to the gym to sleep on the floor.

The next morning I was sitting at my laptop writing away, catching up on my diaries. I was writing about the disco and how I'd expected a gun battle to kick off but it hadn't. There was word there might be trouble because of a row that had broken out in the Special-wing disco the night before. But nobody knew what it was about. Billy still hadn't come back from his camping adventure up on the roof and was probably asleep in the tent, so I couldn't ask him. There was never trouble during the visits, so if gunfire started it would only happen after the visitors went home at 4 p.m. That's what I wrote in my diary. There were now about 1,500 inmates in the prison, and another 500 or so visitors, we guessed, who came in every Saturday night. The jail was heaving.

Suddenly a volley of shots burst out. The sounds came from the roof. Another round went off. The gunfire was coming from the Special wing, which was above our wing. There was a stampede in the Maxima yard below the gym mezzanine. Women and children screamed, racing for the cover of the cells. The building rumbled. Everybody was fleeing. Thousands of feet on the move. I bolted behind a weights machine. More gunfire. I put my laptop down on the floor and kept my head low. Eddy was next to me with his arm around a girl who was in visiting him. She was crying and shaking.

From where I was crouched I could hear inmates jumping from the roof down onto the yard area of the Special wing, on the floor above Maxima. Then I heard shooting from higher up. I was sure it was coming from the roof. Billy, was he still there?

More gunfire erupted. A body sailed through the air up above. I watched it fall like it was in slow motion. The top of his head was pointed towards me. He didn't make a sound or have his hands out to protect himself. He looked already dead. His body landed with a dull thud on the ground by the door into our cells, a good 20-ft drop from above. Blood splattered out onto the wall where the top of the inmate's head crashed. Women visitors screamed in the wing.

'Paul, we gotta get out of here,' shouted Eddy over the gunfire. 'Into the cells.'

'I know.' Another burst of shots was fired from above. I covered my head with my hands. Bullets slammed through the roof of the gym. Jesus. After a minute I looked up. Little holes had been formed in the flimsy corrugated-iron roof. Eddy was right: we had to get out of here. I was sure we weren't being targeted. They were stray bullets but still deadly.

The yard was empty now. A lucero appeared at the door into the cells and waved us over. 'Ven, ven.' ('Come, come.')

'Eddy, you go. Take the chica inside. I'll take my chances here.'

'You're mad,' he said. 'Come with us.' The girl had her head down resting on his arm, making gentle sobs.

'Ven, ven,' the lucero shouted again.

'I'm going, Paul. I have to get her inside.'

'Go, I'll be all right.'

Eddy dashed down the steps with the girl, almost dragging

her on the run through the yard like she was a rag doll in his arms. There was about 20 ft to cover to the cell-block door. No way was I running that. The gunfire was blazing again from the Special wing above. Bullets sounded like they were coming from all directions. Stray shots pinged around the yard. The lucero was still calling at me. I waved him off. I'd probably be in trouble for going against their orders. I didn't care. I wasn't running through a hail of bullets.

I crouched down on the ground and started typing on my laptop. What was I doing? My senses were alive with fear. I wanted to capture the gunfire and the panic in words. A war correspondent on the front line: 'Paul Keany reports from the battlefield'. The bullets were now raining down on the corrugated-iron roof. It sounded like a clatter of hailstones. Jesus. No. A few pierced through, turning it into a colander, but most missed. I was sure the shelter was still safer than attempting the run.

An hour later the gunfire was still blazing down from the Special wing. What was it about? Nobody started trouble on a visit day. Honour thy familia: that was the rule. It didn't make sense. And Billy – was he caught up in the gunfire? Had he been killed? What would I tell Father Pat? What would I tell his parents?

I had done more than enough writing and closed my laptop. I had to get out of here. I knew it. Usually the gunfire went on for a few minutes – never a couple of hours. Soon the shooting slowed into a few sporadic volleys. I still wasn't running the 20 ft to the wing. There was an area below the gym mezzanine where the prisoners sat behind the curtains during visits. It had solid walls and a concrete roof. I'd be safer there. I hid my laptop under a towel on the ground and set off.

I ran down the stairs. My eyes darted up to the roof. No gun barrels. I put my head down and ran. At the bottom of the steps I made a run behind the curtains.

There were about 20 lags in there who had been trapped

since the gunfire started. One of them jumped back when he saw me. They thought I was a shooter. William, a South African, looked at me. 'Jesus,' he shouted, his eyes wide with fright. 'What are you trying to do, scare us to death? And where were you?' The colour had drained from his face. The Venos were all on their feet, pacing back and forth. One held a cross that hung from his neck and was whispering a prayer to himself.

'Up in the gym,' I said.

'I'm staying in here,' he said. 'The run into the cells is too far. It's too dangerous without cover.'

'I know, I'm doing the same. But the shooting, it seems to have stopped.'

'They'll be at it again,' he said. 'Wait for the storm.' Willy had been locked up for four years. He'd been through a few gun battles.

I was bursting to empty my bowels. I'd been holding it for hours. I ran into the toilet in an inner room beside us. I sat on the pot. Minutes later more gunfire crackled again from up above. I heard bullets ping around the yard. There was a stampede into the toilet. A solid mass of bodies. One of them knocked me over and I fell off the pot. 'Jaysus,' I shouted, 'what are you at?' They were running for cover behind me, in a narrow area in between the toilet back wall and a further wall behind. The bullets flying around the yard could easily ricochet through the curtains and then it would be game over.

I got up off the ground, cleaned myself and pulled up my trousers.

'Paul, get in here, now,' said William. I ran around and stood with them, my hands holding onto the rough concrete of the wall. We were all squashed in. The fear was palpable. About 20 men were breathing heavily. Jittery. Hearts pounding. I was crouched down in a dark, damp toilet, the smell of the leavings of men in my nostrils. It wasn't a situation I'd ever expected to find myself in in my life.

Another hour passed and the volleys of fire died down.

Myself and William and the Venos got out of the toilet and went back to standing beside the buckets behind the curtain. 'I think we should try to get out of here now,' said William. 'It's our best chance. There have been no shots for a good half an hour.'

'*Es seguro*,' ('It's safe') shouted a lucero at the yard door. '*Correte!*' ('Run!')

William pulled back the curtain slightly and peeked out. 'Leg it,' he said. He bolted off towards the cells and I ran behind him almost like his shadow. My eyes darted up to the roof. No sign of gun barrels peeping over. Another few feet. I skipped over the body on the ground. The guy was covered in a sheet with red blotches. Bare legs, all twisted, sticking out of blue shorts. I almost jumped through the wing door. I put my head forward like a sprinter running across a finish line.

Inside, my eyes adjusted to the darkness of the cells. A woman in her 20s was sitting on the side of a bed rocking a baby back and forth in her arms. A trail of mascara streaked from her eyes. 'When can we get out, when can we get out?' the families were saying to the bosses. That was all I could hear. There was no sign of the cops. They were always the first to go missing when gunfire broke out. I saw Eddy sitting on the side of a bed with his arms around his girlfriend. She was bawling, her head snuggled into his shoulder. She was a fragile, petite girl, educated, with great English – one of the better girls Eddy met through a dating website.

'You made it, mate,' said Eddy. 'I was worried. I had to go, couldn't stay there.'

'I know, don't worry. I made my choice to stay.'

'This is terrible.' There was a moment of silence as he seemed to gather his thoughts. 'It was mad. I was waiting to get out of the gym and boom-boom-boom.'

'What about the lads up on the roof?' I said. 'I wonder if they're all right.'

'I dunno,' he said. 'Ask the bosses. They're all on the phones.'

'No. I'm not talking to them.' Even though the Maxima jefes weren't involved in the shooting, to me most were the same class of vermin that had started the trouble. I looked at them pacing around, ears to their phones, chatting to bosses in other wings. They all had guns out in front of the visitors, like peacocks showing their plumes. One was walking around with a gun in each hand like he was Rambo; another I noticed had two grenades, each hanging by a thin string from the breast of his jacket. I thought we were more in danger from one falling off than any warring inmates in other wings.

Another hour passed. There was loud banging on the door. '*Abre, abre*,' ('Open, open') shouted a voice from outside. Jesus, who's that? Everybody jumped. The lookout man slid back the bolt. What's he doing? I looked around, ready to run. A cop stood at the door, a pistol in his hand. Phew. They knew Maxima wasn't behind any of the shoot-outs, because we were the workers' wing. Most of the lags in Maxima had jobs in the jail, either in the kitchens or doing maintenance work such as hauling out rubbish, mopping floors and so on. In the other wings, most of them sat about doing nothing all day. The devil makes work for idle hands and all that. In the eyes of the prison officials, we in Maxima were the peaceful wing. The bosses in Maxima shot back if fired upon, but they didn't go picking a gun battle. So I knew the cops weren't looking to mete out any vengeance on us, thank God.

The cop stood with one foot in the passageway and one in the wing. He called off the visitas. Inmates threw their arms around their women and children and said goodbye, then the families ran into the passageway where the cop shouted, '*Correte, correte*.' ('Run, run.')

About an hour later, Billy and the other gringo lads appeared at the wing door. Pale faces. Shaken. The cop ushered them in. 'Jaysus, you made it,' I said to Billy.

'We did, boy, we did.' I was relieved beyond all imagination. Billy had his whole life ahead of him – no young man should see the end of his days in this hellhole.

'It was awful up there, awful,' added Dieter, who had been with them in their makeshift tent. 'We didn't know if we would live.'

'I was woken up by the shooting,' said Billy, talking quickly. 'There were holes all over the top of the tent.' He stopped and caught his breath. 'If we hadn't been sleeping we'd be dead.' His eyes widened as if his last words had just jumped back into his head and he'd understood them for the first time. Part of me laughed inside. Billy's fondness of lying down probably saved his life.

'We had to run,' said Dieter, shifting on his feet as he spoke.

'It was awful,' said Billy. 'Porto was the first to run out. Bullets lashed into his legs and he fell back. One of the prisoners walked over and shot him in the head. He was screaming at them, "No, no." There was nothing we could do.'

'Jesus,' I said. It was only just dawning on me how bad it must have been up there. My spot in the gym seemed peaceful in comparison. I knew I'd done well to steer clear of the roof and the disco.

'We were thinking should we stay or go,' said Dieter. 'We had to go. After a few minutes the shooters were piling up on the roof from Wing 1.'

'We ran off,' said Billy, 'to the stairwell down to the Special and Mostrico wings. There were machine guns pointing in at us. Bullets flying everywhere.' He stopped again to catch his breath. 'We just had to run.' They took refuge in the Special. The inmates there knew gringos weren't behind the shooting and let them take cover.

'What was it all about?' I asked.

'We don't know,' said Billy. 'Something about a row in the disco. Then we ran out of the wing when a cop came after the shooting ended. Down in the passageways outside. It was horrible. Full of bodies, Paul, full of them.'

'How many? Dead or hurt?' I said.

'Loads, we walked about 50 metres and there were bodies

all the way. Some covered with sheets. Must have been dead. Others had visitors looking after them, wrapping bandages around them. Blood, blood everywhere.' Billy, I knew he was already a bit unstable and this might put him over the edge altogether. 'It was an awful sight.'

'All right, Billy, all right,' I said. 'I get the picture.' I knew this was bad for the injured. There was never a doctor in on a Sunday in the jail, and likely not in the clinic in Los Teques town either. I also knew from my own experience there probably wasn't a jail ambulance available to get them there.

Vito started shouting. He had been part of the stampede that ran from the yard into the safety of the wing when the gunfire started. 'These people, these fucking people – when will it be over? All this war. Fighting. Shooting. When will it be over?'

The talk soon changed. What would happen now? 'The Black Cops,' said Billy, 'they'll be in. They'll sort these boyos out.'

I was told they were an elite unit called the Guardia Negra, or 'Black Cops', but I didn't know if that was an official name or just what the prisoners called them. We all went out for número as usual a few hours later, at 5 p.m. The main cop, Napoleon, came into the wing, a truncheon hanging from his belt. He was with three other aguas and a dark, slim guy in his 50s with curly black hair. He was dressed in a cream-coloured jacket over a low-necked T-shirt that showed the top of his chest. A sharp-looking guy. Reminded me of Sonny Crockett from *Miami Vice*.

'That's him,' said Billy. 'That's the boss guy.' Billy was already familiar with the Guardia Negra. He'd been in the prison a couple of years before, when the Black Cops had stormed the jail during the last *masacre* and more than ten inmates were reported killed.

The Black Cop boss walked up and down the yard while a cop counted us one by one, doing the usual número. All the bosses in our wing had their guns hidden, stashed in holes in the wall and in false floors, I imagined. The National Guard weren't edgy doing the count, and the Black Cop boss had his hands in his pockets. They knew we hadn't started the Gunfight at the O.K. Corral. We were the workers' wing; they knew that.

Later I saw the rest of the Black Cops, a motley crew of what I believed were mercenaries. One wore a pirate bandana emblazoned with a skull and crossbones, black combats and a T-shirt, and had a sword strapped on his back. He looked like a ninja. Another wore a baseball cap and black jeans. Another had six guns sticking out of holsters all over his body, strapped to his arms, legs and waist. One of them had the handle of a knife, gleaming white like ivory, in his ankle boot. They all had bullet belts around their waists and slung over their shoulders and carried heavy machine guns. They didn't look afraid to use them. There were seven of them, each with his own individual look, so we called them the A-Team and the Magnificent Seven. They were mean-looking guys, and I was sure they had carte blanche to kill. No questions asked.

But I didn't hear another shot fired in the jail. All the cell-block bosses knew that these boys meant business and had long ago put down their arms.

The next morning I stepped out into the passageway to go the canteen for breakfast. The passageway was spotless. There was only the smell of disinfectant.

In the days that followed, I heard the A-Team swooped into all the other wings and removed about 60 prisoners, going from cell block to cell block standing down the 'army council' of bosses, underbosses and luceros. They were all identified, bundled into prison vans and whisked off to other jails. A bullet in the head awaited many of them. They'd broken the code in the Venezuelan jail system: you don't start trouble on visit days. The familia was sacred. The price for putting the inmates' loved ones in danger was paid with your life.

Word was the National Guard in the watchtowers had

been taking photos of the asesinos on the roof, but I didn't know if the troops even fired a round. Their job was to make sure no one escaped. You could be shot to death inside for all they cared.

A few days later the visitors came back in as if nothing had happened. I couldn't believe it. One of them brought in a newspaper, which ran a big story about the Los Teques riot. I got a hold of it and my eyes scanned across a headline of one of the reports: '*Domingo de Sangre*', or Bloody Sunday. According to the story, six were killed and eighteen injured, including three visitors. One newspaper said two women were among the dead, meaning they were visitors too – somebody's mother, wife or girlfriend. Ambulances brought the dead and injured to hospitals, it said. We heard most were ferried to the hospital in Los Teques town in private cars or any way they could. I'd say it was like the injured bought a lottery ticket on the way, by hoping a doctor would be on call when they got there. The slain inmates were in their early 20s to early 30s. We were sure a lot more lost their lives and were hurt that day. We later heard that three or four had died from their injuries in hospital, bringing the death toll to at least ten.

There were two reasons given for the riot that led to the bloodshed. One was that a cell-block jefe had invited a group of prostitutes for the fiesta. A bunch of lags got boisterous and tried to seduce them (presumably without paying) and other inmates came to 'rescue' the chicas hired for the night's entertainment, sparking a row between the two groups of prisoners. Guns were used to settle it the next day.

In another – more believable – account, a prisoner had made 'inappropriate' comments about another inmate's wife being dressed 'provocatively' in the disco, a tiff that later ignited the bloodshed. The word in Maxima was that the guy from Wing 1 who made the offending comments was a cell-block jefe. He had been invited to the husband's cell block, in Wing 2, the next morning by the boss of that wing 'for a chat'. As a peace gesture, he turned up unarmed and without his henchmen, a rarity for a boss, believing nothing would happen to him on a visit day. He was wrong. An asesino was waiting for him and shot him in the head to settle the row. The shooting show then kicked off when the compadres of the slain jefe came out guns blazing in retaliation.

The National Guard were also criticised in a comment piece in the press for not being up to the job of keeping the peace in jails. The writer was on the money there. The opinion article, by a prisoner-welfare group, also said Los Teques was built for 350 but housed 1,800. That meant there were about 400 more inmates than I thought there were.

For now, however, there was peace in the jail. It was great. The Magnificent Seven stood armed to the teeth in the passageways and escorted the cops in for every headcount. I knew no gun battles would break out with them around. The director and all her cohorts went missing, sidelined, for the weeks the Black Cops were in charge. For five weeks there wasn't a prisoner with a gun in sight.

We were all shepherded up to the roof, wing by wing, for a few hours each night. The Magnificent Seven and their search team went about with metal detectors, sweeping the walls looking for guns, grenades and ammo. The bosses were wiped out of most of their weapons and were down to just a few knives and a couple of pistols and revolvers. But, like always, it'd only be a matter of time before they'd build up another arsenal.

I knew more than ever that I had to get out of this prison. I would not let these animals take my life, my bloody body lying on the floor in the passageway, covered with a sheet. Shipped back to my family in Ireland in a box. I would not die behind the walls of Los Teques. I had plans afoot to get out of here.

Chapter 23

PAROLE? SÍ, SEÑOR

IT FELT LIKE AN INTERROGATION. BUT I HAD TO ANSWER THE QUESTION. And properly. It meant I had a ch nce at getting parole after 18 months. Or serving the full eight years. No way. I'll answer. I'll tell the truth. That's what you're supposed to do. Isn't it?

'Why were you a drug mule?' There it was again.

'For the *dinero*, the money,' I said. A roar of laughter broke out.

'Aha. No. That is the wrong answer. Under no circumstances say you did it for the money.' I was sitting in a classroom full of gringos. The man who asked me the question was a small tubby guy. He was our new Spanish teacher. He wasn't interested in teaching verbs, though. He was giving us the low-down on how to pass the psychological exam and get parole.

'Then what do we say?' said Hanz, who was next to me. We were sitting in the classroom where Silvio used to teach us Spanish and escape routes to Colombia.

'There are a number of things you can say,' said Guatemala, the teacher, who, naturally, was from Guatemala. 'You can say you were depressed. That you were going through a difficult time. But never say you did it for the money. Anyone who says that fails. Always.

'Now, the second important question: what have you learned from your crime and time in jail?' he asked us. He had lived in Canada and spoke perfect English.

'Not to get caught the next time,' said Dieter. We all laughed.

'Aha, no. You will be sure to fail. That I can guarantee. You must say you have learned not to do drugs any more and have learned the errors of your ways. And talk about how much you love your family: how you miss them and are sorry you brought this trouble upon them, and that you made a stupid mistake.'

I was scribbling all the prepared answers into a notebook. The others were doing the same – I never noticed them being so attentive in any of Silvio's Spanish classes.

'But there is a caveat,' continued Guatemala. 'You have to be careful. When you get parole you will be released to work in Venezuela to finish your sentence. So you don't want the examiner thinking that you'll jump on the plane home the minute you get released. No no,' he said, wagging his finger back and forth like a windscreen wiper. 'You must say that you are looking forward to working in the community in Venezuela, to making a contribution to society here. So you're letting the examiner know you want to set up a life in Caracas. That's what they want to hear.'

He finished going through the standard first few questions we would be asked in the oral exam. '*Como se llama?*' ('What's your name?') '*Cuál es su apellido?*' ('What is your surname?') '*Tus padres estan vivos?*' ('Are your parents alive?') '*Cuál es el nombre de tú papa?*' ('What is your father's name?') '*Como se llama tú mama?*' ('What is your mother's name?') I could learn the first five off by heart in Spanish, but the order of the other ninety-odd questions was never the same, said Guatemala. Pity, I thought.

The director's office was just downstairs. I wondered what she would think if she knew we were preparing for the psychological test to get out on parole. But I supposed that in a way it was a Spanish class.

'Now,' continued Guatemala, 'the next day we will focus on the drawings.'

'What do you mean drawings?' I said. 'It's not an art exam.' Eddy broke out laughing, stabbing his pen in the wooden desk in time with his giggles.

'Yes, very good, Paul,' said Guatemala. 'You are right. But we are not drawing masterpieces of the Flemish tradition, just simple matchstick men of your families. That'll be all today. Now, if you walk past the director's office later, please try to speak Spanish. Say *hola*, at least.'

* * *

The prison was back to 'normal'. The A-Team had done their job by clearing out the bosses and luceros in the other wings who were behind kicking off the prison shoot-out. They'd also cleared out the Maxima bosses of their heavy-duty weapons; they were just down to a few handguns and knives. But it wouldn't be long before they, and all the other cell-block bosses, would rearm. An insight from Silvio came to mind: 'There will be kidnappings, hunger strikes, then a riot. Things get better, then they will go back to the same.' One big vicious circle.

* * *

'It's happening, it's happening,' said Billy, a grin stretched across his face like someone had cleaved his cheeks apart.

'What's happening?' I said, standing beside him in the yard.

'I'm going free. I just got the call from Viviana. The judge signed the papers.'

'That's amazing news, Billy.' I put my hand on his shoulder. 'Brilliant.' His release documents had been in the courts for weeks waiting for the judge to approve them. Every few days a court usher rang Viviana looking for a bribe to speed them along. Viviana told Billy about this but advised him not to pay. Nothing happened, and over the weeks he fell into a deep depression. But now he was going free. 'Where do you go now?' I asked.

'Some halfway house for a few days before I can move in with Father Pat.'

He ran over to his bucket and handed out T-shirts and clothes he didn't want to the lads. Most of the boyos stood there, Eddy, Dieter, Hanz and so on. Billy then slipped on the same small rucksack he'd arrived with in the wing. 'Lads, I'm off.' A big cheer went up. He cautiously headed to the wing door. A few luceros lashed out with the friendly goodbye kicks, but none connected. Billy bolted. I'd never seen him move so fast.

I was happy for him. We all were. Just like when Silvio was freed, Billy's release showed the system worked. One day it would be our turn.

* * *

Today we had an art class with a twist. 'OK, guys, listen up,' said Guatemala. 'In the first class we practised for the oral questions. Now we're learning how to draw.' Again, the class was full. There were about 30 of us. 'When you finish all the oral questions the examiner will ask you to do a drawing. You'll have to draw yourself, your mother and father, and where you live.' He picked up a marker on a ledge on a blackboard behind him and started to draw a picture. 'Now, here's a house. Two windows. A little chimney with smoke. And here's your mother and father standing outside. Just be simple.' He drew two matchstick characters of a woman and a man in front of the house next to a tree.

We all broke out laughing. 'You gotta be joking?' shouted out Eddy. 'We'll be locked up again for being too stupid to live on the outside.'

'Ah, laugh you may, but this is how it works. I heard it from prison workers who look at the finished exams before they are filed. They see what fails and what doesn't. Now, back to the drawing. The mother,' Guatemala said, pointing at the matchstick character on the board, 'she has to have a skirt and shoes, and hands. And fingers. Always draw in fingers.' The mother matchstick character was now more ridiculous. Guatemala drew giant fat fingers like she had bananas growing out of her wrists. It was like a Picasso gone wrong. 'You must draw yourself in here, standing between your mother and father, here in the middle.' He put his marker down. 'Now it's your turn. Get your pens and paper and start drawing. But don't copy me. Just make sure it's a simple house with your mother and father outside. Don't forget the tree, and put yourself in front of the mother and father. That's it. Get drawing.'

I doodled away in my copybook. On the cover there was a kid on a BMX bike cycling under a rainbow. It was fitting for the class. I scribbled a house and a few swirls of smoke at the chimney. It reminded me of being five years of age all over again and being in the Irish Catholic school in Oxford run by the nuns.

After about five minutes we all turned in our works of art. Guatemala went through them one by one. It was like a playschool class for adults. 'Yes, good, good,' he said, holding each one up in front of the class. 'Yes, this one is perfect,' he said of another, where the mother had curlers in her hair and was wearing an apron. 'Yes, good, Paul, very good.'

'Where's my gold star?'

'I want one as well,' said Eddy.

Jokes aside, the main part of the exam was the oral part and it was in Spanish. I knew I hadn't a hope in hell of getting through it. I had been putting in a fair bit of work in the past few months reading newspapers that came in on visit days, and there were a couple of verb books knocking around the wing. So I could read Spanish a bit, but I could hardly speak it at all. When the Venos spoke to me I barely understood. '*Qué?*' I'd say, shrugging. '*Mama huevo*,' was the usual reply I got. I was the gringo who barely had a word of Spanish. In the psychological exam it wasn't like I could bring in Hanz or Vito to interpret, as if I was going in to see the boss to ask him permission to use the gym or something. You were only allowed to bring in a qualified interpreter. And the system wasn't always organised enough to arrange one. I would need an act of God to pass. If I didn't, it'd be another 18 months before I could try for parole again. I couldn't let that happen.

* * *

Viviana was in on one of her visits. I went up with Vito to see her in the office upstairs. Deputy Dawg was sitting in his chair snoring again, his shotgun resting on his belly. I was worried someone would drop a cup or something and he'd wake up and start blasting us out of fright.

Viviana stood up and kissed me on both cheeks. We all sat down. 'Nice work with Billy, getting him out,' I said, smiling. 'Tell her I said that,' I said to Vito.

'She says thank you,' he said, 'and she is happy to be of service.'

'Brilliant.'

'She wants to talk about your parole,' said Vito. 'She says you've done the 18 months to qualify, and she's looked at the work books you've been signing for writing your book. She says she can put you in for the exam now and it'll come through in a couple of months.'

'A couple of months? That soon?'

Vito went back to Viviana and spoke. 'Yes, that soon, and if you pass it you'd be out about a month after.' I couldn't believe it. I wanted to jump up in joy. But I'd seen too many gringos, such as Billy, fall into a spiral of depression when they didn't get out as quickly or as easily as they'd been told. But this was different. Viviana had come up with the goods for Billy, true to her word.

'Unbelievable, means I could be out before Christmas.' I sat there grinning.

'Yes, she says it's very possible.'

'But the exam: I'll never pass it.'

'Viviana says she has faith in you.'

She might have believed in me, but I was still anxious. From then on it was at the front of my mind all the time. How was I going to pass? I knew some had paid a cop to pull it off, but that almost always came to nothing and inmates were still failed. But I knew Bruce had passed it and decided to hunt him down for a chat. On my next trip up to the roof I caught up with him. 'Bruce, the psychological exam to get out on parole, I heard you passed it?' I said while I was on my fast walk.

'Yep, two weeks ago. Just waiting for the judge to sign my release papers.'

'How'd you do it?' I knew Bruce's Spanish wasn't great, like most gringos.

'Simple. You hand the money over and it's done.'

'No way?'

'Yes, five million bolos [about 1,000 euro] I paid. I could have spoken Chinese for all the examiner cared. Money in the bag for them.'

'I'm gonna have to think about this. I don't trust those cops.'

'Just hand the money over and it's done.'

'I'll have to think first about where to get it from.' Bruce walked off and I continued alone on my laps. I passed a few of the luceros from the Maxima wing playing football. When I looked closer I couldn't believe it – they were all there. All the bosses. Gómez, now the new jefe after Fidel had been released a few weeks before, his two underbosses and all the henchmen. There were supposed to be at least a few of them guarding the wing at all times. That's what we were paying the causa for. Chancers.

Chapter 24

CAP IN HAND

Riley – how's it going, me old pal,

Now a letter that starts off like this should be disregarded immediately, as you should know what's coming next.

Yes, you guessed it, Riley, it's a good old begging letter, but it's for a good cause: the Paul Keany Getting Out of Prison Fund, set up by yours truly, of course, with donations being made from all over the world.

Right, let's get down to the serious nitty gritty, as you know I'm due to sit an exam soon, but with my Spanish the way it is I don't hold out too much hope. Now a few quid in the right direction could change all that.

All I was waiting for was the right person to pay off and the right time. So now I have the person and basically they want 10,000,000 bolos. Now I know it sounds a lot, but it is actually equal to USD 1,000, depending on the exchange rate on the black market here.

Now this isn't 100 per cent yet, I just need to know if you can meet my demands, then if it comes up I'll let you know straight away and send you an account number. It's to an Irish priest, Father Pat, and thank God for him, that's all I can say.

I know times are tough with the old recession, so if you can't handle it then no problem – just let me know as soon as you can so I can put me begging hat back on. You know what they say, Riley – a friend in need is a pain in the arse. Well, it's true.

The truth is I hate writing this letter, but it has to be done.

As I said at the beginning of this letter, it should be ripped up and disregarded, but thanks for reading.

Talk to you soon.

Paul

Riley came through with the cash quickly, as did my other mates. A deposit into Father Pat's account. Fair play to them. Mates I owed my life to. Vito was telling me I wouldn't need to pay anyone off to pass the Spanish exam, but I couldn't take any chances. My freedom depended on it. Even if I didn't use it for bribes, the cash would come in handy to keep me going in Caracas if I got out on parole.

Viviana was in a couple of times a week. Vito was in constant touch with her and translated for other Italians who didn't have any Spanish. So he kept me filled in if there was anything to report on my case.

'Paul, you need to come upstairs,' he said, smiling. 'Viviana wants to talk to you. She has good news.'

'What kind of news?' I said.

'It's best she tells you.'

She was sitting in the office waiting for me.

'*Hola,*' I said.

'Paul,' she said, smiling. My eyes hovered over her parted red lips.

Vito spoke to her and turned to me. 'You're on the short list for the exam.'

'What's that mean exactly?' Viviana was nodding at me and smiling.

'In two to three weeks you do the exam,' said Vito. 'You'll be called.'

'What about my Spanish? Do I pay someone to pass?'

He turned to Viviana. 'No, don't pay.'

'You sure?'

'That's what she says,' he said, smiling – as happy for me going free as I was. I still didn't know how I was going to pass the exam, though. Not without bribing someone. But I decided to trust Viviana's judgement. She'd got Billy out, after all.

'Lovely jubbly.'

Over time, prison life was becoming more bearable, knowing there was light at the end of the tunnel. But I was careful not to get too hopeful and bottled up my emotions as best as I could. I wasn't setting myself up for a fall if things didn't pan out.

* * *

The days blurred into one another. The exam was looming. I tried not to worry about it, but one day Vito walked up to me. He had just got a text message from Viviana. 'Paul, she says you don't exist.'

'Don't exist?'

'In the courts, she went to start your papers; they say you don't exist.'

'That's a good start,' I said. Viviana had gone with the prisoner number the Los Teques officials had given her for me, but there was no record of the number in the courts. The same thing had happened to Billy, so I wasn't feeling too panicky.

'Don't worry. Viviana, she fix everything,' said Vito.

It showed me how important it was to get a lawyer on the case to get things moving. I couldn't rely on the Venezuelan 'mañana seguro' policy, or I'd probably end up serving my full eight years.

In the evening, Guatemala came down and sat beside me on the bed. He had the psychological test sample papers with him. 'OK, Paul, I know your exam is coming up soon. I can practise a few questions with you.'

'I need it. How'd you think I'll do?'

'Doing it in Spanish?' he said, his eyebrows raised.

'Yeah.'

'You're screwed, man,' he said, laughing.

'Thanks.' We went over the questions I could memorise. I knew I could ask for a translator, and I did that with Viviana. I remembered Silvio had told me in the past he knew of one English speaker who'd got an interpreter organised, so it could be done. But there was no guarantee the examining board would bother with the trouble of getting one.

'*Como te llamas?*' said Guatemala.

'Paul Keany,' I answered.

'How was your childhood?' That would take more than a few memorised phrases to answer.

'*Bueno,*' ('Good') I said. We both laughed. 'I don't have a chance,' I said.

* * *

Viviana was true to her word. Almost three weeks to the day I'd met her, I got news of the exam. Vito walked up to my bed. 'Paul, exam, this morning,' he said, smiling.

'Right,' I said, letting out a deep sigh.

'You do good, my friend, no worry,' he said, clapping me on the shoulder.

* * *

I stood outside the office for the exam next to a barred gate that led to the driveway outside. A cop sat down on a wooden stool on guard. There were three of us waiting. Hours passed for my turn. It was like being in detention for school.

A while later a woman stepped out of the office and walked up to me and said, 'You're the one who speaks English and needs an interpreter?'

'Yes,' I said, my eyes sucking in the sight before me: she was blonde and blue-eyed with tanned skin. She looked more like a Swedish blonde bombshell than a Venezuelan.

'I'm the interpreter. I've lived in England, so you've nothing to worry about.'

'Good,' I said, smiling. This was fantastic news.

A few minutes later Carlos walked by and spotted me standing by the office where the exams were always held. '*Tú, examen hoy?*' ('You, exam today?') he said, his eyebrows raised so high his brow furrowed.

'*Sí,*' I said.

'*No aprobas,*' ('You won't pass') he said, laughing. '*No español.*' ('No Spanish.')

'*Traductor, inglés perfecto,*' ('Translator, perfect English') I said, pointing to the office behind with my thumb.

'Ah,' he said, smiling, '*bueno, gringo.*'

The interpreter stepped out after a prisoner sitting the exam came out. I was last in, at about 2 p.m. 'Please, come in.' Inside, another woman sat behind a desk. 'You can sit there,' said the translator, pointing at a chair in front of the table. I pulled it out and sat down. I needed a miracle to pass. With the interpreter on board, I might have it.

'*Buenas tardes,*' ('Good afternoon') said the lady, a slight woman in her 40s.

'*Buenas tardes,*' I replied nervously.

'OK, we'll just start with the questions,' said the interpreter. 'They'll be simple stuff, your name, where you're from, that kind of thing. I'll translate them all.'

'I'll say as much as I can in Spanish,' I said. I wanted to make it look good at least, show them I had a little bit of the language.

'Oh, no problem,' she said. 'If you prefer.'

The examiner ran through the few questions I knew. 'What is your first name?', 'What is your second name?', 'Are your parents alive?' and so on. I answered them all in Spanish, while the woman scribbled into a notepad in front of her.

Then came the question I'd been waiting for. 'Your crime, why did you do it?'

'I'd been going through a bad time in my life,' I said, starting the speech I'd rehearsed for weeks in my head. 'I'd split up with my wife and I was very depressed.' This was true, but it had happened about 15 years ago. 'I needed to get away for a while,' I went on, 'so when I was asked to go to Venezuela I said why not.'

I then sold myself as the model prisoner. I was totally reformed, never did drugs and was remorseful about what I had done. And I was hoping my kids would come and visit me in Caracas if I got out on parole – but that I knew I couldn't go back to Ireland for another five years. I ticked off all the boxes Guatemala had told me about.

I also explained I had a job organised as an electrician's helper. It was actually with Viviana's ex-husband, who was an electrical engineer. I also told her I would stay with Father Pat, an Irish priest who I had come to know through his visiting me in Los Teques.

'Very good, Paul,' said the interpreter. 'And your relationship with your parents: would you say it is good?'

'Yes, great,' I said. 'My old man ran the house with an iron fist when I was a kid, but there was lots of love.'

'Good,' said the interpreter, nodding, then speaking to the examiner. I was now braced for the art materials to come out. The examiner opened a drawer, handed me a sheet of paper and a crayon and spoke. 'Now, Paul,' said the interpreter, 'we'd like you to draw a picture of your family. Nothing serious, just a simple picture. Of your house when you were a child, and you standing outside it with your parents.' There it was: Guatemala was on the money.

'Yes, OK,' I said. I drew exactly what Guatemala had said in the classes. I put myself as a matchstick child next to two matchstick characters of my parents: my da smoking a pipe and my mother wearing an apron, and me in the middle in front of them. We were all standing outside a little three-bed house.

I looked up from the drawing when I finished it and noticed

the examiner's eyes staring intently at the picture and nodding her head. I handed it to her and she spoke to the interpreter.

'Paul, very good,' said the interpreter. 'That's all for now. We have finished the test and the examiner will be in touch with your lawyer regarding the examination.'

That was it. Two hours after it had begun it was all over.

'Thank you,' I said, and stood up.

I stepped into the passageway. The door closed. I breathed out a sigh of relief.

In the wing, I was grinning from ear to ear. I knew it had gone well. Vito ran up. 'Paul, the exam – did you do it in English?'

'Yeah, almost all of it.'

'I don't believe it,' he said, grinning. 'See, I told you Viviana was good.'

Now I just had to play the waiting game and see if I would pass. I didn't have to wait long. A week later Vito came back with amazing news.

'Paul, you passed, you passed. Viviana just told me.'

'Really?' I said.

'You're on your way home, Paul, the *examen* is good.'

'Lovely jubbly,' I said, rubbing my hands together.

But I didn't want to get too excited. I'd seen too many gringos go down that road, like Billy, only to end up waiting for weeks, and even months, before they put their foot outside the jail door.

The days ticked on. Vito was in constant touch with Viviana. He came up to me one Thursday. 'Paul, I think you are going on Monday,' he said, beaming. I couldn't believe it; I still wouldn't accept it was true till it happened.

A week passed. Then another. Still no sign of the exam results. I was starting to lose my temper easily. I was getting ratty with the Venos. I'd always tolerated their stupidity. Now things like having to stand in the yard for hours in silence while the bosses hid their guns was driving me mad. I wanted to run up and slap one in the face. I knew if I did I'd get my legs broken by the bosses and I wouldn't be running out of the jail in a hurry. Even with Vito I was getting short-tempered.

'Paul, tomorrow, tomorrow you go free,' he said again a week later.

'Tell it to my ass,' I shouted out at him. Quickly I apologised. 'Sorry, Vito, it's just this shit.'

'Is OK, Paul, is the system.' He knew how frustrated I was.

During the next few weeks, waiting to hear when I'd get out, I spent hours on my own all day just lying on my bed, becoming withdrawn. I didn't want to talk to anyone.

Bruce had been out about a month and was texting me almost every day, which made it worse. 'Paul, cold beers tonight in Caracas?' He knew I was due to go free any day and we'd planned to meet up on my first night. He'd offered me a room for the night on the couch in the hotel room where he was staying.

'Not tonight, Bruce,' I wrote back. 'Still waiting.' Freedom was taunting me.

Chapter 25

GET ME OUTTA HERE

THE WEEKS PASSED AND I WAS STILL LOCKED UP. STILL NO NEWS OF my parole release date. Every day was another let-down. The papers for my freedom were in front of the judge waiting to be signed. That was it. All it took was a judge to read my papers and scribble their name at the bottom. '*Mañana seguro.*' ('Tomorrow for sure.') That was what still kept me behind bars.

On a visit day I walked out of the wing and went up to the canteen. It was about 10 a.m. and I knew it'd be quiet. I slept badly the night before, tossing and turning, wondering if I would ever get out. When? When? Would I ever see my family again? How would I live for five years on parole in Caracas? I hated Venezuela and just about everybody in it. I stretched out on one of the stone benches and quickly fell into a deep sleep.

Shortly after, I felt myself rocking from side to side like I was on a boat on choppy waters. I opened my eyes. There was a hand on my shoulder. I looked up. It was Vito. 'Paul, you have the freedom. You go today.'

'How do you know?' I said, ready to snap at him.

'In a few hours. The judge signed the papers.'

I stood up and shook his hand. 'If it's true, this is amazing.'

'Yes, it's true.' Vito left and I sat alone on the bench, shifting back and forth. I couldn't sit still. I decided to go back to the wing. I still wasn't 100 per cent sure I was going. I needed confirmation.

Back in the wing Roberto walked up to me. 'Paul, inside.

307

Come.' I followed him to the bed area. He had a bunk next to me. I leaned against the frame. 'It is true, you are going. We were told by the people upstairs.'

'That's fantastic. Fantastic.' I let my doubts slip away. It was happening. I wanted to scream for joy. But I wouldn't let myself go till I had my foot outside the jail.

Roberto handed me an envelope. It was the remainder of the two million bolos I'd paid him for the Dutch passport, a scheme that came to nothing. He'd been paying me back in dribs and drabs. 'Is the last of it, Paul. Sorry it did not happen.'

'It's OK, Roberto,' I said.

At my bed I sorted my belongings. My cooking-oil drum and a few things: a pair of jeans and a few toiletries – soap and toothpaste. It was stuff I knew I'd need in a special halfway house, where I'd have to stay for at least a week, so I shoved them into a small bag. I had already slipped my computer out with Viviana a few weeks before. Prisoners often robbed you when they knew you were getting out. The laptop, the months of diaries and photos it contained, was too precious to me.

Roberto came back. I held my Dublin Irish football-team hat. He'd always liked it. I handed it to him. 'The fishing hat, Paul – for me?'

'Yes, all yours. Enjoy. Catch me a few sharks here.' He laughed. We stood there and just looked at each other. The silence lingered. But there seemed to be an understanding passing between us. It had been a long journey for the two of us. We both dealt with being locked up here differently. I kept my head down. Roberto got into the circle of bosses. But we both sought the same thing: survival.

We embraced. 'You take care, my friend.'

'You too,' I said.

I carried my few belongings out to the yard, where all my gringo mates were. I picked up my Irish rugby shirt and handed it to Dieter. He was always going on about Irish music and sport, and the craic, and always remarked on the shirt.

'That's for you,' I said.

'Super, Paul, super,' he said, holding it up. 'This means a lot to me.' All the lads were there: Hanz, Eddy, Dieter, Vito. I stood there looking at them all. We'd been through the full gamut of Los Teques together – we'd faced death, dodged bullets and knife attacks, and even starved together. I detested Los Teques, and everything in it, but these people I would never forget. And now one of us was going free – me. Everyone enjoyed that moment. It made them realise they would actually get out some day too.

'Keep the faith out there, buddy,' said Eddy and we embraced.

Vito stepped in. 'It's great to see you going. Keep it good, no more holidays with drugs in suitcases.'

I laughed. 'No more, all over.'

'And don't forget,' he said. 'I have a taxi coming for you with my Italian friend who lives close.'

I embraced all the lads and shook their hands. A big cheer went up. 'Heyyyyyy.'

'Lads, I'm outta here.' And I turned and walked, step, by step, by step . . . Neither of the bosses, Gómez nor Carlos, were out in the hallway. Probably inside bagging coke. I walked up to the wing door. A *lucero* slid the bolt back. '*Adiós, gringo,*' he said.

'*Adiós,*' I said.

* * *

A soldier stepped out of the shadows at the prison gate. He rattled his keys in a smaller door in the gate and pushed it out. Here we go, I thought. The moment of truth.

I stepped through. I was free.

There was a guy waiting outside. I knew it was probably Vito's Italian friend. '*Amigo,* Vito,' I said, pointing at my chest.

'You want taxi?' said the Italian. A jeep was parked across the road.

'Yes, for me,' I said.

'OK, now you go. Come.' I followed him. He pulled open the passenger door at the front. 'You go here.' The driver gestured me into the front seat. I could just make out his profile. There was little illumination from the streetlights.

'Back,' I said. 'I'll go there.' I had business to take care of. I had about 1,000 euro in bolos in a condom up my rear end, which I needed to fish out. The door shut. I waved at the Italian guy through the window and he walked off to the driver's door. Nice work, Vito, I thought. Man of his word with the taxi. The engine rumbled into life. The driver sped off down winding dark roads. His headlights were off. Probably didn't work. I didn't want to ask. I didn't care. I reached down inside my trousers and felt the rubber and fished out my money. Then I looked out the back window at the prison where I'd spent the best part of my captivity of two years, two months and twenty-three days. I could only make out the walls and the watchtower. It got smaller and smaller and then faded to a shadowy blur.

* * *

It was over an hour's drive to the upmarket district of Altamira in Caracas, where I was due to meet Bruce for dinner. The driver couldn't find the address and drove around in circles. I looked out the window, staring at the life outside. Motorists pulling up in cars at a McDonald's drive-through. Waiters in dickybows bringing pizza to diners in sidewalk cafes. All the simple things I hadn't seen in so long.

'Here, I'll walk from here.' I saw a building I recognised and knew the restaurant was close. This was the area where I'd spent my last day of freedom before I went to the airport, more than two years ago. It felt strange.

I paid the driver and walked into the restaurant. I saw

Bruce down at the back sitting at a table. 'All right, Bruce,' I shouted down, waving.

'You Irish bastard. You made it.' He stood up and threw his arms around me. He introduced me to his girlfriend. She was in her 30s and nicely dressed in smart clothes. 'What do you want?' he said.

'A freedom beer.'

I put a bottle of Polar Ice to my lips, took a sip and let it swish around my mouth. I ate a steak meal and devoured the succulent beef. After a few hours of more drinks and catching up I was bleary-eyed and tired. We walked back to Bruce's hotel.

On the way we passed through the main plaza. I saw all the sights I'd seen when I'd stayed here over two years ago. The stone fountain at the centre where water gurgled. Courting couples canoodling. The whole thing gave me déjà vu. It was weird.

'It's just here, the hotel.' Bruce snapped me out of my daydream.

'Here. See that hotel beside it?' I said, pointing to the hotel next to his. It was a four-storey building with white balconies. I couldn't believe I was seeing it. Another experience of déjà vu. It was where Damo, the lad from the Dublin gang, gave me the suitcase with the cocaine. 'That's where I stayed before I got caught. Before I went to the airport.' It was true, but it all seemed like a dream.

'Same for me – that's where I stayed before I did my run,' Bruce said. 'Must be fate.' Some little bastard of a hotel clerk probably tipped off the cops in the airport every time a gringo stayed and had people visiting him in his room with a suitcase. I could have been angry, but I didn't care. I was out of Los Teques: not quite a free man but halfway there.

Chapter 26

STROKE OF LUCK

I WAS BACK AT THE COURTHOUSE IN VARGAS. IT WAS MY THIRD TIME here. It was where I was first charged and later sentenced. I'd always been whisked in the back entrance with an army escort. Now I was here for my parole hearing, standing at the front door. It felt weird. This time no one had hauled me here in handcuffs. That also felt strange. But I knew if I didn't come they'd track me down. I had no passport or ID. I couldn't even book a hotel room – or buy a long-distance bus ticket. I was at the mercy of the system.

I pulled at the glass door. It didn't budge. I tried again. Nothing. It was locked. Strange, I thought. A court usher in a dark navy uniform inside the building walked up and opened it. '*Tribunal, juez,*' ('Court, judge') I said. It was Friday morning and there were about 20 minutes to go for my hearing, which had been set for 10 a.m. The judge was to give me my parole conditions and rubber-stamp my release.

'Sorry, there is no judge today,' said the usher in Spanish. 'Tuesday is the next day.' What was going on here? 'What'll I do?' I said to Bruce. He stood beside me in shorts and flip-flops, holding a suitcase. He'd taken the three-hour trip by bus from Caracas with me. He was off to rent an apartment in a resort an hour away from here on the coast where he'd spend his days swinging in a hammock and drinking rum.

'No idea,' he said. 'Join me to watch hot ass in bikinis on the beach?'

'Can't,' I said, 'need to sort this stuff out.' I had to think. Where would I go? I had a few quid but didn't want to blow

313

it on 80-dollar hotel rooms. Bruce had taken care of last night. Now he was leaving.

I decided to ring Father Pat on my mobile. I told him the judge hadn't shown up. 'Come up for dinner, Paul, come up here.' He gave me directions.

'I will, Father Pat, be there later. Looking forward to it.' I turned to Bruce. 'You might as well come with me.'

'Why not?' he said.

We walked off and I looked out into the aquamarine Caribbean sea beyond the courthouse. The waves lulled back and forth on the shore just a few yards away. A brisk breeze brought the taste of salt to my lips. A flock of white birds with yellow-tipped beaks on the shore took off into the sky. My thoughts drifted off as I looked at them flapping their wings. The judge not showing up. It was a sign. I wasn't due back here till Tuesday morning. Five days away. No one would be looking for me till then.

In that moment I knew I would flee Venezuela. 'Bruce, I'm leaving.'

'Yeah, we'll go to the priest's.'

'No, I mean I'm leaving Venezuela. The judge not showing up. No hearing till Tuesday. It's a lifeline. I'm going to get to Colombia and get out of here.'

'You're mad. You'll be caught.' Bruce hesitated, looking troubled. He sighed heavily. 'But if you're set on it, I can hook you up with people who specialise in getting illegals in and out of Colombia. See how it works out.'

* * *

Father Pat's home was a giant parochial house belonging to his religious order. It was set on the outskirts of a barrio, a short walk from the tube station. He said gunfire crackled into the night from the slums just a few blocks away. Like most of the ghettos, life there was pretty much a mirror of life inside Los Teques: gangs, guns, murder and coke. The difference was that families lived in the barrios: men, women and children trying to get on with their lives.

The door opened and Father Pat's housemaid let us in. 'Paul, good to see you,' said Father Pat in his slow drawl as he walked towards me in the hallway. We shook hands and I introduced him to Bruce. It was great to see the padre outside the grimy passageways of Los Teques. 'You're out at last. Come, come.'

We walked through a courtyard in the middle of the house, dotted with white sculptures and blooming with flowers. In the middle stood a statue of Our Lady.

The housemaid went back and forth with cups of tea. Myself and Bruce were chatting away with Father Pat in the kitchen. I told him about my last few weeks and the hell in waiting for my release papers to be signed. But I kept my plans to flee Venezuela under my hat for now.

Billy arrived back from his day working in the gardens of a university.

'Billy boy, good to see you.' We shook hands. 'I made it. I'm out.'

'Great, great,' he said. 'It's a bit better here than in Los Teques,' he laughed, grinning from ear to ear.

After lunch and the chat, myself and Bruce decided to head back to the centre of Caracas. We agreed to stay in Sabana Grande, a run-down neighbourhood where you could get held up by both the robbers and the cops – but it was cheap. We'd get a room for half the price of one in upmarket Altamira. Billy wanted to come. He wanted to party with his two mates, his old buddies from Los Teques. The boys were raring for a big night out. Coke and women. I just wanted a steak dinner and a couple of beers.

We got two rooms in a hotel on a busy street. I put my bag down on the bed. Bruce and Billy walked into my room. I filled Billy in on my plans. 'Billy, I'm leaving, I'm getting the hell out of Venezuela.'

'What, with no passport or nothing – are you mad?'

'No, I'm going. Bruce is making a few calls to get me to the border.'

'Done already, Paul,' said Bruce, standing next to him. 'I got a hold of this guy. Steve, a Slovakian. Got free from Los Teques a few years ago, met a nice Colombian chica in Caracas and stuck around. Now he's hooked into a Colombian drug outfit working out of Cali. They say they can get you to the border.'

'Excellent. How much?'

'Talk to them yourself. They want to meet tonight. One hour.'

'This is madness,' said Billy, pleading. 'You'll get caught and get sent back.'

'If I can get out now, I'm going. That's that.'

'No, no, it won't work.'

'It will and I'm doing it.'

Billy sighed, leaving me to my plans.

* * *

Two men and a woman sat at the back of the bar. 'That's them,' said Bruce. We sat down. I nodded curtly at the three. A waitress in a leather skirt and tight top put three bottles of beer in front of us. Myself and Billy sipped our beers and stayed quiet while Bruce spoke for a few minutes with Steve.

'OK,' said Bruce, interpreting, 'they say yes, they can take you.'

'How much?'

'It's ten million bolos.'

I nearly spat out my beer. 'That's about two thousand euro. Bit steep, no?'

'He says another option is they take you for free. But in Colombia they give you cocaine to take back to Europe, to Madrid.' This was how I ended up in jail in the first place. No way. But I wasn't turning it down flat. I had about ten million bolos spare to pay them. But that was cash for my flight home from Colombia. I wasn't using that.

'Tell him I'll sleep on it.' They were betting I'd go for the drug-mule option, knowing I probably didn't have ten million bolos. But I was sure I could play them too.

* * *

There was a knock on the door in the morning. I got up out of bed. It was Billy. He had been sleeping in the next room with Bruce. His hair was sticking up in all directions. 'I'm going, Paul, I'm going with you. I can't stay here for another five years.'

'Good,' I said, sitting up. 'We'll get out of here together.' I knew there was a long, dangerous road ahead. But I was getting out of this country.

Later I told Bruce I was up for the trip and that I'd carry the drugs back to Europe. I knew in my head I wouldn't do it. Not after all I'd been through. But I could use these people to get to Colombia. There I could slip out of their hands. No matter how dangerous it was. I wasn't telling Bruce of my plans; there was no point.

He made a phone call to Steve that evening. 'Right, it's on for Monday.' Here we go.

An hour later the phone rang again. 'Sorry, he says no, it's Friday now.'

'That's fine.' It was a hiccup, but I could deal with it.

Myself and Billy bade farewell to Bruce at the hotel reception. A man in a string vest sat behind the counter waving a folded-up newspaper in his face in the heat. 'You sure you're not coming with us?' I said to Bruce.

'Nah, I've a hammock on the coast. Rum and cokes for a few months, with the chica coming up to visit me.'

'OK, Bruce.'

Billy made a call to Father Pat. 'He says the two of us can stay for a few nights.' Great. That was that sorted out.

317

Later we stood in Father Pat's kitchen drinking tea, chatting about how lucky myself and Billy were to get out of Los Teques alive. I kept my plans about fleeing Venezuela to myself. I didn't want the authorities knocking on Father Pat's door some day asking questions about my whereabouts. If they did, he could honestly say he didn't know.

* * *

The parole hearing. The judge stared down at me in sympathy. My cheeks bulged. I had balls of cotton wool shoved into them, stuffed up at the gums. Saliva was dribbling down my chin.

After I got my papers I was supposed to go straight to the halfway house. My mission was to postpone that. To buy a few days till Friday, when I'd skip the country. If not, I'd have to go to the halfway house tonight and sign in and out every day. Questions would be asked if I didn't return after the day release.

Billy stood up and spoke in Spanish. 'Mr Keany is very sick, your honour, in a lot of pain,' he said to the lady judge. She nodded earnestly. 'He has had heavy dental work and asks that he delays going to the detention centre for another few days till he finishes his appointments with the dentist.'

I started rolling my head back and forth. 'Uugggh, uggggggggggh,' I groaned, pointing at my cheeks. The public gallery was packed. Some were laughing. The Venos looked on as though myself and Billy were in a two-man gringo comedy act. They'd be right.

'Yes, tell Mr Keany I had some heavy dental work too recently,' she said in Spanish, 'and he can take all the time that he needs.' Another stroke of luck.

The next few days passed easily in Father Pat's house. He gave me a list of odd jobs to do to pay for my keep. I was delighted. It was the least I could do considering all he'd done for me over the past two years. I busied about fixing his washing machine and hinges on doors and doing other DIY work around the house. It helped me keep focused on the escape.

Chapter 27

ON THE RUN

WE EMERGED UP FROM THE TUBE STATION OF LA BANDERA IN A GRIMY district in Caracas. On the opposite side of the road graffiti of a hammer with a red star read '*Sigue con* Chávez' ('Follow Chávez'). That was the last thing I wanted. It was Friday lunchtime. Cars and buses had ground to a halt. No one was going anywhere in a hurry. I wondered whether Steve, his girlfriend and his father would get here on time.

'Where are they?' said Billy.

'They're coming. Steve texted me.' I saw the three of them abandon a taxi a block up the road and run towards us.

'Bit late. Traffic crazy,' said Steve, panting.

'I see that.'

'But you know the deal: you go with my girl's father to the border.' I didn't know he could speak such good English. 'Myself and my girl,' he said, 'we gotta go for a meeting. My girl's father Miguel will take care of all.' The old guy nodded. He was in his 50s, had a leathery face and wore a checked shirt. Too old for drug running, I thought. Then again, so was I. 'The bus station is just a few minutes' walk,' continued Steve. 'The bus goes all the way to the border overnight.' His girlfriend pulled at his arm. 'I gotta go,' he said, running off hand in hand with his chica. 'Miguel will take care of everything.'

Billy spoke with Miguel. 'We follow him,' he said.

The entrance to the bus station was a mass of bodies pushing and shoving. We walked up three ramps that zigzagged up into an area where the bus-company offices were. Miguel kept a close eye on us all the time. He bought three tickets to San Cristóbal. 'That's it,' said Billy, 'the city near Colombia.' Silvio had told us it was a good 18-hour bus journey from Caracas to San Cristóbal in one of his escape-route classes.

We boarded the bus. It was a proper, professional coach. I was expecting something like you'd see in the movies in places like Peru: a bus with squawking chickens and kids on the roof.

Miguel took a seat at the back. We sat in the two seats just in front. The bus pulled off and inched through traffic. I looked at my phone. It was just after 4 p.m. All going well we'd be in San Cristóbal the next day at about midday.

* * *

After a couple of hours I woke up from a deep sleep as the bus jerked to a halt. It was dark outside. All I could make out through the window was a thicket of trees on the opposite side of the road. We were deep in Venezuelan countryside. It was about midnight. Then I noticed two jeeps with Guardia Nacional written on the side. Blue lights flashed.

No. It can't be.

One of the troops boarded the bus. 'Just play it cool, Billy,' I said. My heart raced, but I didn't want Billy panicking too. The guard walked slowly down the aisle. He went from seat to seat checking IDs. We were at the back of the bus. He came closer now. My body tensed. Don't let it all be over.

'*Pasaporte,*' he said, standing in front of us. My eyes jumped out at him. Myself and Billy looked at each other, thinking the same thing: what do we do? I wanted to shout 'let us go', then I calmed myself.

'*No pasaporte,*' I said. '*Compañero,*' I added, pointing behind to Miguel. The soldier looked back at Miguel. He held out his hand with a 100-bolo note (about 20 euro) tucked in behind his ID card.

I sat there sweating, my hands clenched into fists.

The soldier pocketed the note and handed Miguel back his ID. He then turned and walked up the opposite side of the bus towards the front.

I watched the soldier descend the bus steps. The bus engine rumbled. The cop walked over to the two parked jeeps. I saw him talking to two other troops. Please don't tell them. Let us go.

The bus pulled off and about ten minutes down the road I relaxed. 'Jesus, that was a close call.'

'Too close,' said Billy, shaking his head. 'I thought we were gone.'

'That'll be the last one now,' I said. Silvio's escape classes were coming back to me. 'You will get one or maybe two army stops,' he said. I hoped it would only be one.

* * *

The next morning I watched the sun rising. It peeped over a mountain ridge in the distance, almost winking at me. Soon dark clouds were scattered across the sky and light rain sprayed the window. The bus was ascending a mountain, labouring up steep roads. I stared out at the landscape. Swollen rivers. Jagged mountains.

Soon we started descending from the mountains and doing good speed on a wide motorway with brisk traffic. I could make out a town in the distance. On the left I saw a sign for an 'Aeropuerto'. 'Be nice to get out of here, Billy, fly home,' I said.

'Yeah, hit the skies.' But without passports, no chance.

I later saw a sign for San Cristóbal. I knew from studying the map before the trip we were on the last leg to the border. 'This is it.' I looked at my phone. It was just midday. We'd been travelling for 18 hours. I was sweaty, groggy and hungry.

The bus turned off onto a dusty road where up ahead I saw what looked like a border-control building. It came to rest and a cop stepped on. Shit. This wasn't good. I hoped he could be easily paid off like the last one.

I looked back to Miguel then to Billy. Our eyes met again. Was this it? Would we be hauled off? Handcuffed? Trucked back to Los Teques? Billy spoke to Miguel. '*No problema,*' he said. He looked relaxed. In control.

The cop moved closer. Same drill: he checked IDs. A quick scan and a cursory nod. Then came the dreaded word. '*Pasaporte?*'

'We were robbed,' said Billy. That was our story.

'*Cómo?*' ('What?') he said. '*No pasaporte?*' His brow furrowed. My stomach knotted again. Billy motioned to Miguel. He held up his identity card, a note folded behind it. 'No,' the cop said, waving it off. Oh my God. This was no Deputy Dawg to be bought off with a few notes. '*Oficina,*' he said. I looked at Billy. Our hearts sank.

'The cop says we take our luggage,' said Billy. His face looked worried, like he was about to cry.

The cop waved us into a white building like an army barracks. For a moment myself and Billy looked at each other. Let's run for it. But where? There were open fields behind. How far would we get? There was a table on a footpath where two cops sat, guns in their holsters. No chance of fleeing.

We stood in a large room. Miguel's face was flushed with fear. His *tranquilidad* was gone. 'You two take your clothes off,' said the cop in Spanish, 'one by one.' I stripped off first. Thank God my cash was hidden in my rear end. But would he slip on the plastic gloves? I emptied my pockets, taking out about 100 euros' worth of bolos.

It was Billy's turn. He slipped off his T-shirt, showing a money belt strapped on his waist. 'Ah,' said the cop, 'take it off.' Billy took out the cash. There was about 1,000 euro in bolos. The guard's eyes lit up. 'Get dressed,' he said. He stepped up to the table and put the money into a pile. Miguel's eyes now nearly popped out of his head. He didn't know we had money. But he was supposed to pay any bribes. I could have strangled him. The deal was we'd smuggle the coke to Europe. They'd pay the bribes. 'Over there,' said the cop. He led us to a room at the side.

We stepped in. The door closed. 'Fuck, Billy, it looks like we're going back to Los Teques.' He stood there shaking. His hands trembled. Tears welled up in his eyes.

I wanted to kick myself. How could I be so stupid? Why did I rush it all? Why didn't I just stay in Caracas longer and organise a false passport? You stupid bastard, Paul. You've blown it. We'd be rushed back to Los Teques. I'd have to serve the full eight years. I'd be 54 when I got out. No. I sat down and put my head in my hands.

We heard the cop and Miguel speak in the next room. Raised voices. Billy put his ear to the door. 'I can't make it out.'

'Hopefully he'll take the money, Billy.' I took in a deep breath of hot, sticky air.

The door opened. The cop stood there. I saw Miguel wipe sweat off his brow. Time stood still. The cop pointed to the money. '*Todo es para mí?*' ('It's all for me?') A smile broke out on his face. I just nodded and smiled with him. This was the moment of truth. He'd take the bribe. I could feel it.

'*Todo es para tí,*' ('It's all for you') I said.

'*Sí,*' added Billy. There were about 1,200 euro in bolos on the table: about a year's salary for the cop.

'*Gracias amigos,*' he said. I breathed out a sigh of relief, like letting the air out of a bicycle tube. Yeah, happy Christmas, you bastard.

Miguel nodded at us. 'Billy, we get our things and get out of here – now.' I grabbed my bag. We walked past the police outside. I wanted to say, 'Your mate in there's after winning the lottery – and he's not sharing with you.' I was sure of that.

The three of us boarded a local bus to San Antonio. I knew this was the town right on the border; Silvio told us in the escape classes. We sat midway down the bus. Miguel sat at the front. We were the only three passengers. It revved up and pulled out.

'That prick,' said Billy. 'He's supposed to be paying the bribes.'

'Prick is right. I'll kill him. Strangle him.' The last few minutes in the cop shop rushed through my head. I felt numb. It was all like a dream.

The bus chugged along dusty roads. Miguel was chatting to the driver, glancing at us with his beady eyes. 'He's getting ready to jump,' I said. 'I don't trust the bastard.'

'I know. He'll run for it if the cops pull us in again,' said Billy. 'He knows we've no money for more bribes.' I had, but I wasn't broadcasting it just yet.

I made a split-second decision. I knew if the cops boarded again we were trapped. Nowhere to go. 'Right, we're getting out of here. Get off, now. I'm not staying on.' We picked up our bags. 'Off, now.' The brakes screeched. The bus jerked. We jumped off.

Miguel ran after us. '*Qué pasa?*' ('What's happening?') he said, waving his arms.

'*Tú no dinero,*' ('You no money') I said, getting in his face. I wanted to kill him. But it wasn't the time or place. We still might need him. 'How do we cross the border?' I said in Spanish.

'Bus,' said Miguel, looking worried. We were like two dogs in his care. He knew his master would make his head roll if he didn't get us to Colombia safe.

It was just a few minutes' walk to San Antonio. We walked along a road where traffic snaked around a dog's-leg bend. Old men with sombreros stood outside car-part shops. Up ahead I saw the frontier. A white building, a checkpoint. Drivers pulled down their windows to cops. Locals walked through. We watched for a while and realised that pedestrians weren't being stopped. We knew it was time for us to go for it.

Freedom. It was so close I could taste it.

Nearly there. Faster, Paul, walk faster. One more step. One more.

Billy was speed-walking up ahead, as if he was competing in the Olympics. I watched him pass through the checkpoint.

I walked past a hatch in the wall. It slid up. '*Pasaporte?*'

That's what I expected, but it didn't happen.

I passed through and stepped out onto a bridge, a trickle of a stream below. We were free. Venezuela was just a few feet behind, but we were on Colombian soil.

Billy kept walking. He stopped at the end of the bridge. It was about 100 yards to the other side. I knew Miguel was right behind. I didn't care. 'Billy, we're through, we're through.' We shook hands.

'We made it, I know,' he said, with a beaming smile. 'We made it.' His face then darkened. 'What about him?' he said, nodding at Miguel.

'Don't worry about him,' I said. 'I'll take care of that.' I was hard and fit. Months of gym work had prepared me for this trip. An old Colombian wasn't stopping me from getting home to my family. If it came to it, I'd have to hurt him. I knew I would do it.

'Where do we go now?' said Billy.

'Get a hotel,' I said. We walked about 500 yards. Miguel was behind me. I thought about giving him a few slaps and running. But this was Colombia – his territory. For all I knew he'd have a local drug cartel swoop on us in minutes. Best to keep him on board for now.

The sun was beating down. We passed makeshift foreign-exchange offices: a table and chairs on the side of the road where locals were buying and selling Colombian pesos and Venezuelan bolos. Others sat next to oil cans, using plastic tubes to fill up motorbikes and cars with dirt-cheap petrol from back over the bridge in Venezuela.

'*Hotel, acá,*' ('Hotel, here') said Miguel, pointing at a two-storey building set back off the main road. He said his boss owned it and we'd stay there for the night. Interesting. A hotel on the border. These boyos had it all sorted out.

Miguel showed us our room, which was up a flight of concrete steps. Two single beds and a TV. The door closed. I heard feet shuffle in the next room. Miguel was staying close by. Billy went and showered. I sat down with only one thing on my mind: how do we get away from Miguel? I had some ideas, but now it was time for a drink.

I walked past the reception and under an archway that led outside. Miguel stepped out. 'No, where you go?' He stood in front of me.

'*Amigo, cervezas,*' ('Beers') I said. He stepped aside. I bought a bag of a dozen cold beers from a woman on the side of the road.

Back in the room, Billy stepped out of the bathroom with a towel around his waist. 'This guy's keeping us prisoner here.'

'Billy, we're free – and if that cunt thinks we owe him anything, he can think again.' If it wasn't for our cash windfall to the cop in the bus station we'd be on our way back to Los Teques, handcuffed. Both of us wanted to strangle Miguel.

In the bathroom I fished out my money and showered. I sat down on the bed and started counting it. 'How'd you hide that from the cop?' asked Billy.

I pointed at my feet. 'Where'd you think? Down there for dancing, up here in the head for thinking.'

It was evening and we were starving. Miguel was still stationed in a chair at the hotel entrance. '*Amigo, restaurante,*' I said. I had money to pay for good food somewhere but didn't want him to know.

In a roadside cafeteria three plates were pushed in front of us containing food that looked like beans mixed up in dogfood. I pushed it away. Billy ate two mouthfuls and put down his fork. 'Muck.' Myself and Billy chatted. Miguel was sat beside me, eating away. He didn't say a word. I decided to prod him about his plans.

'Tomorrow, we go to Bogotá?' I said, with Billy interpreting.

'No, change of plans,' Miguel said.

'What?'

'We go to Cali.' Myself and Billy looked at each other.

'And your boss?' Miguel's jefe was due to arrive tonight.

'The weather is bad. Rains too heavy. Cars can't pass. Tomorrow he'll come.'

Another stroke of luck. My mind spun with escape ideas, which I kept to myself for now. As far as Miguel was concerned, we had no passports and no money and were dependent on him. He was wrong about the cash. The passports? Well, I had a plan.

I had been online in Caracas and scribbled down the phone number and address for the Irish consulate in Bogotá. My plan was to sneak out of the hotel in Bogotá, where we were due to go with Miguel, with Billy in the morning. We would report our passports stolen in a cop shop, get the paperwork and go to the consulate, and with that be able to organise two emergency passports. Fly out of Colombia and home.

That was now up in the air. Bogotá was a good 24-hour trip by bus. Cali was two days away. Miguel's plan was for us to stay in an apartment there belonging to his jefe. That meant we would be his prisoners. There was already a Dutch guy there who'd been holed up for months waiting for a passport. That's what Miguel said. More like they were stringing him along. I wasn't going down that road.

The next 24 hours would see me get home. Or fall into the hands of a Cali cartel.

Billy was quiet on the walk back to the hotel. 'It's going wrong, Paul.'

'Don't worry. I'm hatching something.' All we had to do was get up at the crack of dawn. Sneak out of the hotel. Get to the bus station and board a coach to Bogotá, and we'd be free from Miguel.

* * *

My eyes opened. I looked at the clock on the bedside. It was 5 a.m. My Los Teques internal alarm clock still worked. Billy's deep snores filled the room. I shook him gently.

'What? What?'

'We're going.'

'Going? Going where?'

'Ssshh.' I put my finger to my lips. 'Outta here. Get up and get your stuff.'

Minutes later we crept down the stairs with our bags. They were concrete steps, no squeaks. Miguel's room was next to ours. If he opened his door I was ready. I'd do what I had to do. I was on edge, but my thoughts were calm.

We stepped under the archway. The sun was rising. Birds chirped. There was no traffic. How would we get to the bus station? Suddenly a taxi rolled past on the opposite side as we stepped out onto a dusty embankment. The driver saw us and did a U-turn. It was the only car on the road. Another sign. The gods were on our side.

'Now, Billy, get in,' I said quickly. I slid into the back seat beside him.

About ten minutes later we pulled up at the bus station in the centre of Cúcuta town. We went upstairs to a cafeteria where I changed a bunch of bolos into pesos and bought two tickets to Bogotá from a guy behind the counter. The same guy then sold us breakfast. Enterprising, I thought. Billy did the talking.

'When does the first bus leave?' I asked.

'Eight,' he said. It was only just after 6 a.m. now.

'Jesus,' I said. 'Is there nothing earlier?'

'That's it, he says, the first one out.'

We sat at a booth by a window. We could see down to the bus bay. Perfect. We'd stay here and dash down when it arrived. We'd stay out of sight for now.

I sipped a couple of spoonfuls of the soup we'd ordered. I couldn't keep it down. My stomach was doing somersaults. We both took turns dashing in and out of the toilet in the back of the cafeteria. The term 'shitting it' out of fear was true. Our eyes darted back and forth, down to the bus bay below. I could see out into the car park. I was expecting the cartel members with greased-back hair to swoop in and start shooting at us and we'd have to run for our lives.

Two hours ticked by. It felt like two days.

'*Amigo, bus,*' said the old man behind the counter. I looked down and the coach was pulling into the bay.

'Billy, get your bags, let's go.' We ran down the stairs to the ground floor. No cartel heads with guns. So far, so good.

We joined a queue. 'Bogotá?' I said to the driver, who was checking the tickets.

'*Sí,*' he said, nodding. No one asked us for ID. Phew.

We took our seats. The bus engine rumbled and we moved off. Neither of us spoke. The bus drove through a wide avenue dotted with trees and was soon on an open road, leaving the city behind. With every kilometre put between us and Cúcuta I felt better.

About 45 minutes passed. 'Billy, I think we're in the clear,' I said.

'I know,' he said. 'If they were after us they'd have caught up by now.'

After about an hour the bus began to climb and then hit heavy traffic. It inched along for about ten minutes then stopped. The driver opened the door and we got off. The traffic stretched for a kilometre ahead. The whole mountainside to our left had collapsed. Landslides. Yellow diggers were chugging away up ahead, scooping up mud. 'There's nothing we can do here, Billy, we'll just have to wait. But I still think we're OK.' I was sure we were. But I'd prefer to be hurtling towards Bogotá. Not stuck here.

We found a restaurant: a few tables and chairs at the side of the road. A woman walked past with a plate of sliced watermelons for sale. Billy was off chatting to girls again – to a dark-haired chica sitting on her own drinking Coke through a straw. 'She's Italian,' said Billy. 'I told her we'd been in Los

Teques and did a runner.' I looked at him. 'You idiot,' I thought. 'She was there herself,' said Billy. Another bizarre twist.

'I'm Andrea,' she said. 'Three years in Los Teques, in the women's prison.'

'Did two,' I said, 'and got out on parole after 18 months. Got lucky: great lawyer.'

'How many months did you spend in Caracas after you got out?'

'Five days.'

'That's all?' she said, shifting in her chair.

'That's it. Wasn't staying there. Took my chances and left.' I said nothing about our botched drug run with the Cali boyos.

She stayed in Caracas for a year after she got out, she said, then organised a fake passport and fled. Like most do. She was on her way to Bogotá on another bus.

'Heavy rains. Landslides, *derrumbes* they call them,' she said. 'It's all over Colombia. I heard it on the news.'

'Let's hope we're not stopped again.'

She looked away at the road. 'I've to go to Bogotá and try and get home. Go to an embassy and try to get a passport.' She paused.

'I wish you the best,' I said. I wasn't getting involved. I had enough on my plate.

The traffic started to move. I finished my coffee, said goodbye and we left.

The bus moved slowly, inching past the diggers and road workers. The traffic eased off and the bus rolled on. It then started to shake violently. It was like a plane in heavy turbulence. I looked down at the road. The surface was gone, probably washed away. It was just stones. I grabbed the hand rest, my body shuddering for hours.

My eyes opened. Where was I? Where was Billy? Miguel, was he following us? I was asleep and had just woken in a panic. Billy was snoring. Dawn was breaking, a halo of sun shining over a mountain peak and a mist floating through trees on the right. I felt a bit more relaxed but was still on edge. The Cali boys could have someone waiting for us at the bus station in Bogotá. It wasn't over yet, as far as I was concerned.

A few hours later we started a slow descent into a giant valley. Below I could see a criss-cross of streets lined with skyscrapers and office blocks. 'Bogotá, look,' said a woman to her child, a little girl, in the seats in front of us. So we were nearly there.

The coach pulled into the station on the outskirts of the city. Billy woke up. 'We're here,' I said. 'Sleeping Beauty.' I looked at my watch. It was just after 8 a.m. Twenty-four hours ago we'd got on the bus. 'I'll call the consulate.' I found the number in my pocket and rang it after I stepped off the coach

'*Consulado de Irlanda*,' ('Consulate of Ireland') said a woman. Music to my ears.

'*Inglés?*' I said.

'Yes.'

'My name is Paul Keany. I'm here with another Irish national. Our passports have been robbed. Would you be able to organise two emergency ones?'

'Yes, of course,' she said. I could have jumped down the phone and kissed her. We had to bring copies of official reports saying our travel documents had been stolen. 'Go to any police station and you can do it.' The consulate was closing at 1 p.m. Time was tight.

'We'll be there,' I said, and hung up. 'It's all good,' I said to Billy. 'They can get the passports for us today.'

'Jesus,' said Billy, smiling. This was happening for real.

'Yeah, but we haven't much time. We need police reports for our passports. I said they were stolen and that our flights were leaving tonight. So she said she'd do them on the spot.'

* * *

In a police station we found after walking for a few blocks a cop at the reception told us to sit down. I looked at my watch. It was almost 10 a.m. We had to get the passports organised quickly and try to get a flight as soon as possible.

A cop with round-lensed glasses called us into his office. '*Sí*,' he said, nodding, as Billy explained to him that our documents had been robbed. '*No problema.*' After about half an hour we walked out with two forms completed. I could see that Colombia was decades ahead of Venezuela when it came to getting things done.

Outside, we piled into a taxi. '*Consulado de Irlanda*,' I said to the driver, showing him the piece of paper with the address. We drove past modern buildings and shopping malls with McDonald's and upmarket cafes. I felt safe. Caracas this wasn't.

The taxi driver got lost and started going around in circles. 'Here, here,' I said, pointing at the address. He drove around the same block again. Up ahead I saw a gold Irish harp insignia on a plaque at a building entrance. 'There, Billy. Look, look, we're here. The harp.'

'The harp,' he said. 'Heyyyyyyy.' We started cheering and hugging each other in the taxi. The driver glanced at us in the rear-view mirror. I paid the guy and we stepped out. It was 11.30 a.m. Plenty of time to do our paperwork.

We walked into the offices. A beautiful Colombian woman in a grey suit attended to us. 'Mr Keany?' she said.

'Yes,' I said.

'Please sit down.' We spun our story again: that our passports were lifted on the bus to Bogotá. We handed her the police report and passport photos we had organised in Caracas. 'Everything seems to be in order,' she said. 'Just give me a few moments.'

She stepped out.

'Nearly there, Billy, all looks good.'

* * *

We're at El Dorado airport. We check our bags in at the Lufthansa desk. A stewardess with a yellow scarf taps our travel details into a keyboard. 'Mr Keany, Mr O'Reilly. Your boarding passes,' she says, handing us our documents. I have only a light bag. Billy checks one bag in. I watch it disappear down the baggage belt and under plastic flaps. Visions of my suitcase in Caracas airport flow back to me. Relax, Paul, there's no coke this time.

'Paul, let's go,' says Billy, 'it's done.'

'Yeah,' I say, 'I was just thinking. And good work with the tickets.' Billy had contacted his father and he'd agreed to pay for both our tickets home. Another saviour. I also emailed the flight details to my nephew Mick to let my family know I was homeward bound.

We walk through security and then queue at immigration. I'm still nervous. I've no cocaine in my suitcase this time, but officials in Latin American airports still give me the jitters. The official looks at both our passports.

'Where is your stamp for Colombia?' he says.

'What stamp?' says Billy.

'Your entry stamp when you arrived?' I never thought of this one.

'We came from Venezuela.'

The official calls a woman over. Not again, I think. Let us go. She studies our passports. 'You must come this way,' she says in English. No. We step into an office with windows. I look out at passengers passing through to their boarding gates. I want to run and join them.

'You have no entry stamps. You are illegal in Colombia,' she says. An official with a gun in a holster stands next to her.

'We didn't know,' I say. 'We came from Venezuela. They never stopped us at the border and asked us to get our passports stamped.'

'You are obliged to do it yourself. You are illegals. It is a crime. You have to go to jail.' The male official steps forward, reaching for his handcuffs. I want to puke.

'No, hang on,' I plead. 'We didn't know. We're tourists. We made a mistake.'

Her face softens. She speaks to the immigration cop in fast Spanish. 'OK. You can pay a fine. That is the only way you will leave for Ireland.' Thank God. She tells me the price in Colombian pesos and I work out in my head it's about 300 euro. It's about what I have left.

She tells me I have to go to the immigration office downstairs in the departures area and pay there. 'One of you will have to remain here.'

'I'll take care of this,' I say. Billy stays put. I run off down a flight of stairs. It's 9 p.m. The flight is leaving in 40 minutes. I run up to an office that says '*inmigración*'. I see a shutter slowly being pulled down at the teller window where a woman stands. 'No, please,' I say, rapping on the glass with my knuckles. 'I have to pay a fine, a *multa*.' I show her the paper from the immigration official.

'*Sí*,' she says. I hand over 300 euros' worth of pesos. It is almost every penny I have except for a few loose coins. The gods are with me again. I grab the receipt and run. At the security checkpoint I stand in the queue, almost hopping on my feet in a panic. I pass through and run to the immigration office.

Billy stands inside, his mouth open.

'I have it. It's done.' I'm out of breath.

The woman looks over the receipt. 'OK, everything is in order. Have a good flight.'

'I will,' I say.

We're at the boarding gate now. I start to relax. We have to empty our pockets and show all our belongings to a security official. I have nothing, only a few loose peso notes and coins. 'That's it, Billy,' I say. 'That's it, there's nothing stopping us now.'

'You're right, boy, we're on our way home.' We sit down and I watch a European-looking man being led away at the security check. His face has a look of despair I know only too well. 'Look, Billy, look at him.' Two cops escort him. Good luck.

The plane takes off and soars into the sky. We made it.

EPILOGUE

WE LANDED IN DUBLIN AIRPORT. BACK ON IRISH SOIL. WE ALIGHTED FROM the plane and I felt a shiver. It was a chilly winter's afternoon in December. No tropics here. I didn't believe we were home and dry yet, though. Neither of us wanted to jump for joy. We were still edgy. To me it wasn't 100 per cent certain we were in the clear. We stood in line inside the airport at the passport checkpoint. What if our name came up on some Interpol system? 'Two Irish drug smugglers on the run from Venezuela. Detain immediately.' We'd be handcuffed and frogmarched off by security.

I stepped forward to the Garda immigration officer, a policewoman. Billy was behind me, almost rattling with worry. I handed over my temporary passport through a hatch in a window. The questions started. 'What happened to your original passport?'

'Got robbed on a bus on holiday in Colombia,' I said. The officer looked over the small four-page document for a few moments. Let me through, let me through.

'No problem,' she said. Phew.

'He's the same,' I said, pointing back to Billy. 'He was robbed with me.'

'OK,' said the official, nodding with a serious expression, 'that's fine.'

We walked on. Finally home and dry. Up ahead in a corridor I saw a large sign on the wall. '*Céad míle fáilte*' (Irish for 'A hundred thousand welcomes'). I could have cried.

Billy went to collect his case at the baggage carousel. I saw a guy running towards me. Jesus, who was this?

'Paul, isn't it?' he said.

'Yeah,' I said, baffled. He was dressed casually and didn't look like a cop.

'I know you,' he said, smiling. 'We met in Venezuela.'

It suddenly dawned on me. 'Jeff, Jeff the reporter. You came in to visit me.' How did he know I'd be here? I thought to myself.

'Jeff Farrell, yeah, good to see you.' He said he had recognised me in the immigration queue; he was on his way home from South America and had just got off the same flight from Bogotá as myself and Billy. I couldn't believe it. The chances of it were one in a million. If you had a dollar on it you'd be a rich man. 'What are you doing home so early?' he said, smiling. 'I thought you had a few years more to do in Los Teques.'

'We did a runner,' I laughed. I gave him a quick rundown of our escape across Venezuela to Colombia and home. We agreed to meet again. It was fate we were on the same flight. I had it in my head some day he could help me write down my 'adventure' in Venezuela.

I walked into the arrivals hall. Sharon, my sister, was there and started crying, her lip trembling. 'Welcome home,' she said, and gave me a big bear hug. Mick then gave me a long embrace. He'd seen me off in the airport before I left for Venezuela; now he was greeting me at home more than two years later. It was weird.

'This is Billy boy,' I said, introducing Billy to them. They all shook hands.

My mother met me at the door of my parents' house. 'It's great to see you,' she said, giving me a big hug. It was fantastic being home: the familiar smells of the house, my mother's stew cooking in the kitchen.

Inside, I said hello to my father. He was seated at the table in the kitchen where he always sat, the telly up at 100 decibels as usual. 'It's great to see you, son,' he said. It was wonderful to see the pair of them still alive. I doubt I would have, had my 'holiday' in Venezuela not been cut short.

Billy was supposed to stay the night, but he got a taste of being home and wanted to go all the way so we put him on a train for the trip. His journey wasn't quite over.

* * *

I buried myself away for a few weeks. I didn't feel up to running around and seeing everyone – even my kids. I put a portable TV up in my old bedroom in my parents' house and that's where I passed the time – up there on my own. I wasn't ready for the big world yet.

Finally I came out of my shell. The day after Christmas I went to the local pub where I usually met up with my mates every year. It was all hugs and back claps when I walked in. Dano, my son, suddenly arrived and we had a long embrace – but there was no sign of my daughter, Katie. That would have to wait. I knew there were bridges to be built.

For more than two years it had been my goal to get home and get away from Los Teques and Venezuela. It wasn't all easy being home, though. The nightmares of that world followed me. For months I couldn't sleep properly. I kept having one nightmare where dark-skinned people were holding a machete over me ready to chop my head off. When the blade fell I'd wake up in a sweat. In another recurring dream I was arrested in an airport with my suitcase. When the cops went to search it I was sure there were no drugs in it; then when they opened it it was full of white bags of coke. Again, I woke up in a sweat.

I went to a local doctor and he prescribed me sleeping tablets. He later referred me to a hospital consultant when I wanted to continue with the tablets. I told the consultant about all the killings, stabbings and shootings in Los Teques. He said I was suffering from Post-traumatic Stress Disorder, like soldiers get on the front line. He said he could see I was trying to rebuild my life and approved a repeat prescription of the tablets, which I took for months.

Not long after my visit to the consultant, I was rushed to hospital one morning, bleeding heavily from my rear end. I was immediately operated on, and five cysts, each the size of an egg, were removed. My back passage was damaged – probably both from hiding condoms stuffed with cash up there and from being gang raped by the Venezuelan anti-drugs cops. I still carry the anger with me over that. Anger and shame. But it's nice to finally tell others, and not bottle it up. This will be the first time it comes out – to my family, my son and daughter, and everyone. It'll be like therapy for me. To finally rid me of the shame – shame that I shouldn't feel. It's the animals in soldiers' uniforms who should feel like that, not me; and I want the world to know what's happening in that justice system in Venezuela. That there is no justice. No one deserves what happened to me on that horrible night. Anyone who thinks I did, I'd tell them they are mad.

When I got home I started to worry I might have caught some sexually transmitted disease from the guards. I got checked for HIV and got the all-clear, but I was told it could take up to five years for something to show up. I think I'll be OK, though, and it's not something I dwell on.

One thing I'm sure about after getting home is that I won't take coke again. I won't go near it. After two years of abuse to my system from snorting a few lines most nights so I could get to sleep (we were sure it was mixed with horse tranquilliser), I couldn't look at coke again. I'd get sick. I hardly even drink now, either. I can barely put a pint down my neck. A few beers and I'm exhausted, and it's home to bed for an early night.

I was worried for a while that officials from Venezuela would come after me for going on the run. That they'd ask the Irish authorities to send me back to finish my sentence. Not now. I'm not looking over my shoulder any more. I've served my time as far as I'm concerned. Anyway, there's no extradition treaty between Venezuela and Ireland – and even if there was, I doubt the Venezuelans would be bothered about me. They have bigger problems.

I never again heard from the gang that hired me to go to Venezuela – and I don't want to. A mate contacted them after I got banged up because they said they would pay the ten grand for the run, whether I got caught or not. That was the deal. Soon after, the gang contact changed his phone number. I don't care. I want nothing to do with them. I could be angry with them, but I'm not. I'm more angry with myself for being so stupid.

Soon after getting home I had a look around for some plumbing work. I rang all my contacts on the old construction crew I used to work with. No one called me back. There were no jobs, nixers, nothing. Ireland was in the depths of recession.

I signed up with the local job centre and they put me on a start-your-own-business course. There's not much work in plumbing, with the construction industry the way it is, so I put my thinking cap on and branched out into offering general DIY services, from painting to installing radiators and so on. I've only got a few jobs so far, but it's a start. Some day in the future I hope to have a decent income – till then I'll have to make do with little, like many. Still, Ireland in recession is a thousand times better than where I was.

My debts are still there. A few weeks after I got home, my father said, 'You'd better check the biscuit tin, son.' It was full of letters from the bank over the loan and from the finance company for the work van I had, which was repossessed after I got locked up. They were all looking for their money. The last letter was dated six months previously. I guess they'd lost interest in me. There were bigger fish to fry who owed millions and billions. I only owed about ten grand to the bank and a few thousand to the finance company – I'm only a tadpole, not a shark.

I'll try to pay it some day, but I'm not stressed out about it. Not worrying over small things: that's one thing I learned in Los Teques. I'm lucky to have my life and to be back with my family. That's the most important thing to me now.

I got a package in the post a month or so after I got home.

It was my laptop I'd smuggled into Los Teques. I'd left it with Father Pat before I fled Venezuela, telling him I was going to the coast for the weekend. Soon after I got home I emailed asking him to send it on to me. As always, he came good. Now I had my diaries back: more than 160,000 words from my daily writing while locked up. Phew, I thought, delighted I'd got my hands on them again. If I hadn't, I couldn't have written this book.

I'm still in touch with young Billy. Some time ago he heard me talking on the radio about my experience in Los Teques. He said it brought tears to his eyes. He's a sensitive lad, Billy, and I'd say it'll take him a while to get over that part of his life.

I was desperate to see Katie, my daughter. She was living with me when I left for Venezuela. I'd left her in the lurch when I got caught. Bridges had to be built. I sent her a few text messages after I got home. She replied, but she didn't ask to meet. I didn't want to invade her space and knew she probably needed more time, so I didn't want to hassle her. A year after I got home, though, I texted her just before her birthday. 'I missed your last two birthdays,' I wrote. 'It'd be nice to meet you for your 20th.'

'Yeah, sure,' she replied. It was the best feeling. We met outside a restaurant soon after and had a big hug. I finally had my baby back in my arms – nearly three years after I last saw her. We spoke over lunch and I could see she was flying in her new career as a hairdresser. I was so proud of her. Seeing her was like the final piece of the jigsaw clicking into place. After that I never needed another sleeping tablet. The nightmares ended.

I'm still writing away. Keeping a diary kept me going in Los Teques. Writing is something I enjoy and would like to keep doing. And putting pen to paper to tell you my story helps me heal. All I ask is that you don't judge me – and, like Katie, give me a second chance. Everyone deserves that.

AFTERWORD

FATHER PAT CONTINUES TO VISIT INMATES IN VENEZUELA'S PRISONS – both gringos and locals from his Caracas parish – putting himself in harm's way to make life a little better for others. He was adamant his real name should not be used in this book, fearing the authorities would not allow him to continue his welfare work in the jails.

We're still in touch and I hope we'll be friends for life.

He has put me in touch with a British prisoner in Los Teques. I'm emailing him and plan to send him a small sum of cash to make things a bit better for him.

Viviana is still representing foreign prisoners, her honesty and hard work a breath of fresh air in an otherwise blighted system.

Billy is back with his family and looking for work, like most in Ireland.

Vito has returned to Italy, where he works in a successful family business.

After about a year on parole in Caracas, Bruce fled over the border to Colombia and soon after headed home Down Under.

Silvio returned to London.

Ricardo is back in Holland.

Roberto and Terry are still serving their time on parole in Caracas, as are most of the gringos I knew in Los Teques. Ruut, however, is still believed to be behind bars in another Venezuelan jail, stuck in some legal limbo.

Eddy was released six months after I got out on parole. I last heard he was back in Manchester, working in a fish and chip shop.

Un abrazo to all of you.

APPENDIX

'It is said that no one truly knows a nation until one has been inside its jails. A nation should not be judged by how it treats its highest citizens, but its lowest ones.'

Nelson Mandela

Paul Keany spent more than two years in jail in Venezuela, held in some of the most appalling and dangerous prison conditions in the world. He maintains that he had no problem doing the time for his attempt to smuggle cocaine but that no one deserves what happened to him: he was raped by police officers, stabbed by an inmate, shot at by prisoners in cell-block gun battles and starved in forced hunger strikes over jail conditions and the painfully slow judicial process in Venezuela, where many are held for up to two years before going to trial.

In light of Nelson Mandela's quote above, here we put Los Teques jail to the test, using the United Nations' *Basic Principles for the Treatment of Prisoners* document as a benchmark.

Basic Principles for the Treatment of Prisoners
(A/RES/45/111, United Nations, 68th plenary meeting, 14 December 1990)

1. All prisoners shall be treated with the respect due to their inherent dignity and value as human beings.

Venezuela: FAILED. Paul Keany was raped by two National Guard anti-drugs officers while held in their custody for five days handcuffed to a staircase with no access to food or water.

9. Prisoners shall have access to the health services available in the country without discrimination on the grounds of their legal situation.

Venezuela: FAILED. Los Teques prison authorities repeatedly failed to provide Paul Keany with access to an ambulance to attend a hospital with severe head pains, despite having secured a court order for same.

Standard Minimum Rules for the Treatment of Prisoners
(Adopted by the First United Nations Congress on the Prevention of Crime and the Treatment of Offenders, held at Geneva in 1955, and approved by the Economic and Social Council by its resolution 663 C (XXIV) of 31 July 1957 and 2076 (LXII) of 13 May 1977)

9. (1) Where sleeping accommodation is in individual cells or rooms, each prisoner shall occupy by night a cell or room by himself . . .

Los Teques prison: FAILED. Paul Keany, along with most inmates in Los Teques, was forced to sleep on the floor in Los Teques for more than a year before buying the use of a bed from his cell-block boss.

12. The sanitary installations shall be adequate to enable every prisoner to comply with the needs of nature when necessary and in a clean and decent manner.

Los Teques prison: FAILED. Paul Keany was forced to share one toilet with up to two hundred inmates. Many had to defecate in plastic bags while held on the prison roof for up to eight hours during random cell-block searches by the National Guard.

22. (2) Sick prisoners who require specialist treatment shall be transferred to specialized institutions or to civil hospitals . . .

Venezuela: FAILED. Los Teques prison authorities repeatedly failed to provide Paul Keany with access to an ambulance to attend a hospital with severe head pains, despite having secured a court order for same.

63. (3) It is desirable that the number of prisoners in closed institutions should not be so large that the individualization of treatment is hindered. In some countries it is considered that the population of such institutions should not exceed five hundred. In open institutions the population should be as small as possible.

Los Teques prison: FAILED. Number of prisoners in Los Teques, an institution built for 350 prisoners, rose as high as 1,800, according to Paul Keany and campaign group Venezuelan Prison Observatory.

GLOSSARY

Abogado: Lawyer.

Agua: Literally means 'water', but in the context of this book it is slang for cops in navy-blue uniforms.

Asesinos: Assassins.

Bolos: Slang for Venezuelan currency, bolívares fuertes.

Bombas: Bombs.

Buggy: A bed cordoned off with curtains to allow privacy for inmates and their wives on conjugal visits.

Causa: Literally 'cause', but in the context of this book it means the sum of money the inmates paid to their wing jefe to protect them and defend the wing from attacks by other wing bosses. The money was used to buy guns, bullets and so on, but was also used for maintenance of the wing, for example, painting walls.

Colchoneta: Long, thin cushions rolled out onto the floor of the wing and used by the inmates as mattresses to sleep on.

Garita: Literally means 'sentry box': denotes an inmate on lookout duties at the wing door.

Guantes: Literally means 'gloves'; in the context of this book it usually means boxing gloves.

Highlites: The name used by gringo prisoners for underbosses or second-in-commands, of which there are usually two.

Jefe: Boss. Also referred to as *padrinos*.

Luceros: A *lucero* literally means 'bright star', but used in the plural it means 'eyes'. In the context of this book it denotes cell-block foot soldiers or henchmen, who are the 'eyes' of the wing bosses.

Luz: Literally means 'light', but it can also mean an incident coming to light, so in the context of this book it is the word cell-block bosses call out when they want inmates to assemble in the yard while they hide guns and drugs or deal with a prisoner they believe has stepped out of line.

Malandro: Literally means 'scrounger' or 'scoundrel', but it is also used by inmates to denote a 'hard man'.

Mama huevo: Derogatory slang that basically means 'cocksucker'.

Mañana seguro: 'Tomorrow for sure': a common phrase used in Venezuela meaning something will be done tomorrow if it doesn't happen today.

Maricón: Literally means 'weak', but in the context of this book it is mostly used to refer to a gay man in a derogatory way.

Masacre: Massacre.

Número: Literally means 'number', but in the context of this book it means the headcount performed by the prison cops.

Padrino: Boss.

Pato: 'Duck', as in the bird, not the verb 'to duck'. Also used as a derogatory slang word for gay people.

Perico: Literally means 'parrot', but in the context of this book it is slang for cocaine.

Pernocta: The word used for visitors' overnight stays in jail.

PWVs: Prisoners Without Visitors.

Rancho grande/cantina: The big canteen in Los Teques.

Sapo: Literally means 'toad', but in the context of this book it means 'grass' (i.e. an inmate who 'rats' on another or betrays the confidence of another).

Tobo: The word used for a 'bucket', which each inmate

used to store their belongings and to sit on.

Verde: Literally means 'green', but in the context of this book it is slang for the Venezuelan National Guard because of their olive-green uniforms.

Visita: Visit.